Advance Praise for *Christian Women on the Job*

"In this great new book, Dr. Goetsch has captured the dilemma many Christian women face in today's marketplace. *Christian Women on the Job* is a book of encouragement, outlining strategies while providing examples and resources to stay strong in your faith. This book is an inspirational roadmap that shows women how they can be strong, career-minded individuals while standing firm in God's Word. A must read for all Christian women."
  — Katie Tingle, Construction Estimating and Purchasing
    Professional

"This book speaks to one of the biggest challenges Christian women face in their lives—excelling at work without compromising their faith. Apply the strategies Dr. Goetsch recommends in this excellent book and you will meet this challenge."
  — Carolyn Ketchel, County Commissioner and Radio Talk
    Show Host

"Christian women who work in my field—healthcare—experience all of the unique challenges covered in Dr. Goetsch's excellent new book. I wish this book had been available earlier in my career. I recommend it for all Christian woman who work outside of the home. It will help you overcome the obstacles to excellence we all face."
  — Judy Schneider, RN, BS, Hospice Nurse

"*Christian Women on the Job* is a book that has been needed for a long time. As a working Christian woman and mother, I look forward to using this book myself and sharing it with my daughters when the time comes for them to enter the workforce."
  — Caroline McCoy, Economic Development Professional

"It is important for Christian women to be able to work well with people from a lot of different backgrounds and worldviews. This outstanding new book by Dr. Goetsch demonstrates how to do this as well as how setting a consistent Christian example will help women not just survive, but thrive on the job."

— Wanjiku Jackson, Director of Business and Computer Technology

"Dr. Goetsch's excellent new book clearly demonstrates that Christian women working in secular jobs do not have to separate from their spirituality, but instead can minister by building relationships. I am grateful to be able to witness every day using the strategies set recommended in this book."

— Dr. Holley Handley, University Professor

"As a Christian woman and an educator I have experienced the unique challenges Dr. Goetsch speaks to in his excellent new book, *Christian Women on the Job*. This book is an excellent resource that provides Biblical wisdom and prayerful applications. It is a must-read for Christian women in the workforce."

— Brooke Cosby, Special Education Teacher

"*Christian Women on the Job* is a must-read for all working women. Dr. Goetsch offers the best advice I have ever seen for the difficult situations working women often face. Karen Moore's prayers provide the practical focus our prayers so often lack. You will want to read this excellent new book, keep it handy, and make motivational reminder notes on every page."

— Jenny Jones, Professor of Political Science and History

C H R I S T I A N
WOMEN
O N   T H E   J O B

Excelling at Work
without Compromising
Your Faith

David Goetsch
and Karen Moore

Post Hill
PRESS

A FIDELIS BOOKS BOOK
An Imprint of Post Hill Press
ISBN: 978-1-64293-392-5
ISBN (eBook): 978-1-64293-393-2

Christian Women on the Job:
Excelling at Work without Compromising Your Faith
© 2020 by David Goetsch and Karen Moore
All Rights Reserved

Cover Design by Jomel Cequina

Post Hill Press
New York • Nashville
posthillpress.com

Published in the United States of America

Dedicated to my daughter,
Savannah Marie King, with love.
I am so proud of you for being an outstanding
daughter, wife, mother, college professor, and editor.

TABLE OF CONTENTS

Note to Readers

The text of each chapter in this book was written by David Goetsch. The prayers provided at the end of each chapter were written by Karen Moore.

Unless otherwise noted, all biblical quotations are from the English Standard Version©. Scripture quoted from the English Standard Version© is copyright© 2004 by Crossway Bibles. A publishing ministry of Good News Publishers. Used by permission. All rights reserved.

Prayer for All Who Read this Book

Lord,

Workplace environments may vary, and responsibilities may be measured differently but, no matter what the job is or where it may be, every Christian woman needs Your faithful guidance and grace. Bless each one who seeks Your direction within these pages and bring peace of mind and joy of heart through Your gracious Spirit.

CHAPTER 1

EXCELLING IN SPITE OF THE UNIQUE OBSTACLES

. . . .

"If the world hates you, know that it has hated me before it hated you." John 15:18

This book was written to help you, a Christian woman, excel in your career in spite of the unique challenges you face at work. Further, it was written to help you do this without compromising your faith. Faith requires placing your life in God's hands and entrusting the outcome to Him. The blessings of God come to those who have faith in Him. This is important to understand if you are going to excel in your career without compromising your faith. What distinguishes you from others in the workplace—more than your education, experience, or talent—is your faith in God. Faith in God is the guiding force in your life. As such, it can put you at odds with others who don't share your beliefs. In so doing, it can erect obstacles in your path—obstacles unique to Christian women.

I begin with this fact because there may be times when it will appear your faith in God is holding you back in the workplace; the raises, promotions, status, and perquisites are going to coworkers willing to do things you cannot do without violating your faith. An unpleasant reality you may face on the job is that this kind of thing might happen from time to time, at least in the short term. Building a career is a long-term proposition, not to be defined by a single experience. In the long run, your Christian principles, more than anything else, will propel you up the career ladder. Keep this thought in mind as you face the unique obstacles Christian women must overcome to excel on the job.

The origin of this book can be traced to a question I was asked by a college student. Melinda was a committed Christian majoring in business. An excellent student, Melinda had enormous potential. I arranged interviews for her with several employers, two of which were interested in hiring her. That was the good news; however, Melinda was having misgivings about a career—not just in business, but in any field. Only weeks away from graduating with her Bachelor's degree, Melinda was no longer certain she wanted to pursue a career. Her misgivings had their origins in several discussions which took place during my class.

Many of the students in Melinda's class were already well along in their careers. These older students were going to college at night to complete a degree they postponed earlier in life for various reasons. They brought their experiences in the workplace to class and shared them openly in discussions. These older students occasionally told horror stories of people in their companies who lied, cheated, and politicked their way up the career ladder. They told of people filing false or inflated performance reports, taking credit for the work of others, poaching clients from colleagues, sabotaging the work of coworkers they viewed as competitors, and all manner of other underhanded deeds. Their stories demonstrated in stark terms how the workplace can be a challenging environment for Christians.

For several class meetings, I could tell something was bothering Melinda. As the stories told by her older classmates swirled around her,

Melinda—normally an active participant in class discussions—became quiet and pensive. She wasn't herself. Finally, she approached me after class and asked a question that had been troubling her for some time: "With all of the unethical behavior that goes on in the workplace, is it possible for a Christian like me to have a successful career without compromising my faith? There seem to be so many obstacles."

She went on to explain how some of the business publications she read contained stories even worse than those we heard in class. In fact, a publication focused on business ethics was replete with stories of prominent business leaders who engaged in behavior clearly inappropriate and, in some cases, illegal. What concerned Melinda even more was the anti-Christian tone that seemed to keep cropping up in articles about the latest trends in corporate policies. As a result, after nearly four years of college, this intelligent, dynamic, Christian woman was having second thoughts about pursuing a career.

Fast forward to the present. Since that meeting with Melinda, I have counseled numerous Christian women who have expressed similar concerns; some were college students, but most were working professionals. What I told Melinda and the women I have counseled since is contained in this book. As a Christian woman, you will differ from your working peers in what you believe, how you behave, what is important to you, and how you do your job. Being different can (and probably will) put you at odds with your coworkers at times. As you work to build a career, your faith is going to be challenged in ways both subtle and overt. There will be obstacles to your success, some of them tied directly to your faith. Fortunately, there are also strategies directly from Scripture for overcoming these obstacles—strategies that will allow you to excel without compromising your faith.

In fact, not only can you survive at work, you can thrive (and do it without compromising your faith). More than anything else, your Christian values, principles, and work ethic will make you successful in the long run, provided you apply them consistently and wisely. Of course, as you might expect, this is easier said than done. Hence, this book. Be encouraged. Melinda did it. She accepted a position in banking and is doing well. In fact, she is enjoying an exceptionally successful career. This is good news, indeed. But even better news is she is excelling without compromising her faith, and so can you.

EXPECT TO BE DIFFERENT

Tuwanda didn't know it would be like this. As a committed Christian, Tuwanda knew she was different from many of the people she met in college. But she chose her friends wisely, most of them from the student Christian organization at her school. Consequently, worldview differences between Tuwanda and her college friends were minimized; however, having embarked on a career, Tuwanda didn't get to choose her coworkers (a fact that was causing problems). The differences between her values and those of her coworkers were, in some cases, stark.

Tuwanda told me that when she was with her coworkers, she often felt like a cosmic alien. Some of her coworkers openly rejected Christianity while others seemed to float along in a fog of religious ambiguity, never making a decision one way or the other. What really bothered Tuwanda about some of her coworkers was they shared a seemingly self-centered moral code. To them, right was whatever advanced their personal agendas or made them happy in the moment. Many of her coworkers seemed to be guided solely by self-gratification, self-indulgence, self-interest, and ego.

All Christians who work outside the home are soon confronted by their differentness. A fellow college professor once called me "unsophisticated" and "naïve" because of my Christian beliefs. He asked me, "How can an educated person believe in the virgin birth, a man rising from the dead, miracles, or heaven and hell?" This colleague was a brilliant man in worldly terms but, when it came to the things that really matter, he had no eyes to see and no ears to hear (Jeremiah 5:21). In the Gospel of Luke, we are told God hid His truth from worldly intellectuals but revealed it to those who came to Him like innocent children. In Luke, we read how worldly people view the truth of God as foolishness because they cannot understand it. They do not have eyes to see or ears to hear. They look but do not see,

14

listen but do not hear (Luke 8:10). This makes them different from us and vice-versa.

I have always found it ironic that my unbelieving colleagues in higher education do not reject subject matter outside their academic disciplines they can't understand. They do not believe their inability to understand the out-of-field subject matter invalidates its authenticity or veracity. Take calculus, for example. People accept the truth of the principles and theorems in this subject, even when they cannot understand them. They do not reject or even doubt the veracity of calculus simply because its principles are beyond their grasp. But these same people are quick to reject the Word of God when they don't understand it. This is foolishness of the worst kind, and you are going to see it exhibited daily in the workplace.

That intelligent but unwise individuals, like the professor referred to earlier, would presume to reject the God who created the universe is mind-boggling. Nevertheless, there are plenty of people out there who, because they have no eyes to see or ears to hear, reject God and His word. They are presumptuous enough to think, when what is set forth in Scripture makes no sense to them, it must be wrong. In their minds, the Bible must be wrong because they do not understand it, or they disagree with it. Worse yet are those who know it is true but do not want to accept it or live by its teachings.

This kind of attitude is hubris taken to an extreme. What is lacking in these misguided individuals is neither knowledge nor intelligence. It is faith. What resides in these individuals is self-worship. They are willing to set themselves up as little gods. In so doing, they feel empowered to believe that anything they do not understand or agree with must be wrong. You will probably work with people who have no eyes to see or ears to hear when it comes to faith in God. In my experience, the workplace teems with such individuals.

Expect to work with the kind of people referred to in Luke. The lives of those who reject God revolve around a self-centered worldview that does not comport with much of what you believe. You will work with people who do not see what you see, know what you know, or believe what you believe. Worse yet, in their ignorance, they will often assume an air of superiority and look down their noses with disdain on your most cherished beliefs. This has happened to me many times over the course of my career. It will probably happen to you, if it hasn't already.

BE GLAD YOU ARE DIFFERENT—IT IS A BLESSING

In the preceding section, I made it clear you will be different from many of your coworkers. The values taught in Scripture and the values of contemporary society are so divergent, you are bound to feel out of place at times. My advice to counseling clients who struggle with their differentness is this: Don't despair over differences relating to your faith. Embrace how being a Christian makes you different and be glad. Think of the words in Matthew 10:32, where Christ says anyone who acknowledges Him before others, He will acknowledge before the angels of God. He goes on to say anyone who refuses to acknowledge Him will, as a result, not be acknowledged.

In the long run, few things will do more to advance your career than your faith in Christ and your adherence to His example. On the other hand, you are almost certain, at some point in your career, to observe coworkers ruining their lives by behaving in ways at odds with the teachings of Scripture and their employer's code of professional ethics (a code, by the way, that incorporates Scriptural principles, even if its authors deny the fact). Being different in Christ will protect you from the pitfalls of greed, lust, self-centeredness, envy, jealousy, anger, thirst for power, status-seeking, ego, misguided ambition, and the other moral failings that so often wreak havoc on careers and lives.

Being different from those who reject Christ will help you excel in your career in the long run because it makes you the type of individual employers cry out for in today's hyper-competitive workplace. Your Christian work ethic, honesty, integrity, dependability, and commitment to excellence—the things that make you different from many of your unbelieving coworkers—can also make you an indispensable asset to your employer. This is the good news. The bad news is these same traits will sometimes put you at odds with unbelieving coworkers, particularly those who are willing to use unethical means to climb the career ladder or who have a slothful work ethic.

It is almost certain coworkers and superiors who don't share your values will occasionally tempt, encourage, or even pressure you to do things that would compromise your faith. Further, they may even become angry or vindictive if you refuse to go along with their disreputable schemes. We read about this kind of thing in John 15:18–19, where Christ warns of people who are going to hate His followers because they hated Him. Consequently, when you are tempted or pressured to act inappropriately, stand firm in your faith knowing it is better to suffer in the short run for doing what is right than to suffer in eternity for doing what is wrong.

WHY SOME WORKPLACE OBSTACLES ARE UNIQUE TO CHRISTIAN WOMEN

All women who work outside the home face obstacles to their success. Many of the challenges that women face on the job have been researched extensively and are well-documented. For example, there have been volumes written about such issues as comparable worth and the "glass ceiling." Consequently, I need to state at the outset these issues and the other more common issues faced by all women at work are not the focus of this book, at least not directly. I do not attempt to replicate herein what has already been written elsewhere about these subjects. Rather, this book is about how you can excel at work in spite of the unique obstacles you face, obstacles that exist not just because you are a woman, but because you are a Christian woman.

In dealing with the obstacles Christian women face at work and in overcoming them, you will find it helpful to heed the admonition of Christ in Matthew 10:16. Christ gave His Apostles some good advice before sending them out to spread the Gospel among people who were likely to reject it. He knew the Apostles would be like sheep among wolves. Consequently, He cautioned them to be both wise and innocent while carrying out the mission He gave them. The advice Christ gave His Apostles as they went out into the world is good advice for you and other Christian women as you go into the world of work.

The obstacles dealt with in this book were chosen for me by Christian women I have counseled and taught over the years. Each, in its own way, is unique to Christian women. Some of the challenges are unique because, if you were not a Christian woman, you would not face them. Others are unique because of the way Christian women are called to deal with them. For an example, consider the issue of work and family balance. All women in the workplace face the challenge of balancing work and family but, for Christian women, there is an added dimension: faith. Christian women must balance work, family, and faith.

Now consider the issue of coping with stress. All women in the workplace deal with stress, but Christian women are called to cope with it in ways that reflect the image of Christ for their coworkers. This makes the challenge different from working women who reject Christ. Consequently, the obstacles treated in this book are either unique to Christian women, in and of themselves, or they are unique due to how Christian women are called to handle them.

WHY THE WORKPLACE CAN BE SO CHALLENGING FOR CHRISTIAN WOMEN

The various challenges confronting Christian women at work are complicated by the fact the workplace can be a virtual factory for producing sinful behavior. Make no mistake, all people are sinners, even those who have given their lives to Christ. This is the message in 1 John 1:8, where we read that those who think they don't sin are just deceiving themselves. Of course, there is an important distinction between Christians and unbelievers when it comes to sin. As Christians, we enjoy the blessings of Christ's mercy, grace, and forgiveness. In any case, you can expect to be confronted by behavior you will find inappropriate and, on occasion, distasteful. The sinful nature of human beings is played out every day in the workplace.

Deadlines, competition for promotions, office politics, ambition, the desire for job security, economic uncertainty, personality clashes, and other factors associated with the workplace can bring out the worst in people. Sin can manifest itself at work in many ways, including dishonesty, greed, the desire for power, status-seeking, envy, jealousy, bullying, crude language, adultery, stealing, cheating, sexual harassment, and misguided ambition, to name just a few. As a result, there will be times when the workplace might feel like a hostile environment to you. When this is the case, just remember it has always been so for Christians.

There is no question that pursuing a career outside the home can pose challenges for Christian women. For more than thirty years, I have counseled Christians, men and women, who struggled with faith-related dilemmas in their jobs. In fact, the issue is personal to me because I grew up watching my mother, a single parent, struggle with these dilemmas. To survive and thrive in a workplace where secular humanism is the norm, you must be prepared to confront and overcome obstacles. When working with peers who reject, oppose, or are ambivalent about Christ, remaining steadfast in your faith is bound to cause bumps in the road from time to time. I realize I've repeatedly made this point. My purpose is not to scare you; it is to help you be prepared for reality with grace.

As a counselor who specializes in workplace issues experienced by Christians, I am familiar with the burden borne by Christian women who want to remain faithful to God while pursuing careers. Many have sought my counsel concerning how to deal with these obstacles. It has been my privilege for many years to suggest strategies for overcoming the faith-related problems Christian women encounter in their jobs. It has also been my privilege to recommend strategies for applying Scriptural principles in ways that help Christian women excel at work without compromising their faith. Many of these strategies, as well as others, are contained in this book.

The strategies I recommend for you and other Christian women are all solidly grounded in Scripture, but they are also workplace appropriate. One of the main goals of this book is to help you learn how to translate Scriptural guidance into Biblically-sound and workplace-appropriate practical action. My hope is this book will help you apply Biblically-sound strategies that will resonate with coworkers who reject your faith or are ambivalent about it.

WORKPLACE OSTACLES FACED BY CHRISTIAN WOMEN

In choosing the obstacles and challenges to include in this book, I searched my memory and consulted my counseling notes to determine which problems were raised most often. Through this process, I compiled a list of obstacles and challenges faced by Christian women in the workplace. Each of them represents a number of similar problems I've grouped for the sake of simplicity. The list follows:

1. *Why is the workplace often a challenging environment for Christian women?*

2. *How should I handle criticism from fellow believers who oppose Christian women working outside the home?*

   • What does the Bible say?

   • How do I respond to fellow Christians who think I should stay at home?

   • Should I work when I have young children?

3. *How can I balance faith, family, and work?*

   • Sometimes I feel frazzled. I never seem to have enough time.

   • Work always seems to interfere with family time or my faith life or both. What can I do?

20

4. *How can I shine my light for coworkers when I feel out of place among them or feel rejected by them?*

- I know how to interact with fellow Christians who share my beliefs, but how should I interact with coworkers who reject my faith?

- How do I avoid feelings of anger, frustration, and resentment when working closely with people who reject or are even contemptuous of my faith?

- How do I avoid the temptation to go along in order to fit in?

- How do I maintain a positive attitude in an environment where my beliefs seem so foreign?

5. *How can I stand firm against the temptations and adversity the workplace presents and still honor God?*

- How can I stand firm when my coworkers want me to do things at odds with my beliefs?

- How should I respond when my boss pressures me to do something unethical?

- How should I react to men who want more than a work relationship?

- How should I handle business travel?

- What should I do if I find myself feeling attracted to a man at work, assuming one or both of us are married?

6. *How can I control my emotions while still being aware of them? How can I effectively read and interpret the emotions of coworkers and use this information in positive, productive, and helpful ways?*

- Should I hide my emotions from coworkers?

- How should I respond to the emotions of coworkers?

21

- How can I use emotions—mine and those of coworkers—to enhance my performance at work?

- How can I deal with angry coworkers or customers without becoming angry myself?

7. *How can I lead men, particularly those who resent being supervised by a Christian woman?*

- Do I have to act like a man to supervise men?

- Will the kindness, caring, and forbearance mandated to be part of my Christian example be interpreted as weakness by men?

- How can I gain the respect of the men I am trying to lead?

- How can I lead men without doing things at odds with my faith?

8. *How should I deal with crude language and inappropriate behavior at work?*

- How should I handle dirty jokes, suggestive comments, sexual innuendo, and inappropriate language without seeming to be a self-righteous prude?

- How should I handle crude behavior exhibited by other women?

- How can I avoid being the victim of sexual harassment?

9. *How can I cope with stress and stay calm in high-pressure situations?*

- What can I do to relieve the stress I feel at work?

- How can I calm my fears and settle my nerves in highly stressful situations?

- How should I respond to adversity and emergencies?

- How can I help coworkers remain calm under pressure?

10. *How can I cope with work-related insecurity?*

- I have been a homemaker for ten years. I am back in the workplace, and I'm not sure I can do this. Will I fit in?

- What if I'm not good enough?

- Can I measure up against my coworkers?

These issues or versions of them have been raised repeatedly over the years by Christian women who have sought my advice and counsel. Each of them is the subject of a chapter in this book. Each chapter contains practical, Biblically-sound, workplace-appropriate strategies for overcoming the challenges in question without compromising your faith. Each chapter also contains a prayer relating specifically to the content of that chapter.

PRAYER FOR WOMEN ON THE JOB

Heavenly Father,

Thanks to You, my faith has grown through the years. You've guided me and lifted me, helped me over some rough spots, and continued to bless my efforts. You know my faith is not a part-time thing. It's not a Sunday obligation. It's something I cherish every day, and it makes a difference in how I think and react to the world.

Today, Lord, I ask Your help with those issues that challenge and sometimes even threaten my work life outside my home. You designed me, so I know You influenced my chosen career. I know Your Spirit is at work in me, and yet, I confess, I'm not always at

peace about some of the pressures I feel in my work environment.

Often, I sense people look at me as though I might not be as intelligent or as capable as they would expect, simply because I'm a woman of faith. I become someone they tease or mildly joke about. I know it doesn't really matter, but I worry I might be overlooked for career advancement if I don't act like those who are aggressively climbing the corporate ladder.

Forgive me when I hide my light simply because it feels awkward to do otherwise. Instead, Lord, strengthen my heart and mind to deal with work challenges with integrity and kindness. Help me be an example of what it means to be a woman of faith. Let me be a blessing.

I have a lot of responsibility in my job and sometimes the pressure becomes unwieldy. The men in my department don't seem to worry about getting home to their spouses or to tend to the needs of their children when overtime is required. I'm a team player, Lord, but sometimes I must set priorities for my husband and my children. I must honor my commitment to them as well as to my work. Let me not focus so much on the current crisis at work that I create a crisis in my personal life.

I ask, too, Father, that you help me be discerning about my actions and reactions to those who have no respect for women or for faith. Sexual innuendo, inappropriate language, and even anger erupt in meetings I attend, and I'm left to deal with it. I need Your help to know when to take a stand and when to let things go.

Lord, in all ways and always, I want to be Your loving daughter. I want to make You proud of me any place I happen to be. I pray You guide and direct my steps, so I can be a shining example of Your love, even at work. Amen.

GROUP DISCUSSION CASE: Workplace Challenges for Christian Women

Maureen excelled in a career that began back in the days when women in her field—law enforcement—were still a rarity. Now her daughter Polly is about to begin her career in the same field. Like her mother, Polly is a committed Christian. Maureen knows it will be difficult for Polly to excel without compromising her faith. She wants to warn her daughter about the types of challenges she might face but isn't sure where to start.

Discussion Questions:

1. Have you ever felt the need to warn another Christian woman who was just entering the workplace about the challenges she might face? What were the circumstances?

2. If you were Maureen, what kinds of challenges would you warn Polly about?

REVIEW QUESTIONS FOR INDIVIDUALS AND GROUPS

1. What does the author mean when he writes that Christian women should "expect to be different" from their unbelieving coworkers?

2. Explain how it can be a blessing to be different.

3. What makes certain workplace challenges unique to Christian women?

4. Explain why the workplace can be such a challenging environment for Christian women.

5. List several specific challenges Christian women can expect to face in the workplace.

CHAPTER 2

COPING WITH OPPOSITION TO WORKING OUTSIDE THE HOME

· ·

"She considers a field and buys it; with the fruit of her hands she plants a vineyard." Proverbs 31:16

Would it surprise you to learn there are still vestiges of opposition to Christian women working outside the home? Ironically, there are. Further, the bulk of the opposition comes from within the Christian community. Resistance to Christian women working outside the home is hardly universal or even widespread, but it does exist. I raise this issue because, even now, when women outnumber men in the workplace, Christian women still approach me for counseling on this issue. These are smart, educated, dynamic women who are building successful careers, but have been told they are violating the teachings of Scripture by working outside the home.

It is important for you to know how to respond if your decision to work outside the home is questioned, particularly if the opposition comes from within the Christian community. I have talked with successful Christian women who were beset by doubt because people whose opinions they valued questioned their decision to work outside the home. This is unfortunate. It is difficult enough for you and other Christian women to excel at work without having to deal with doubt. If you are going to enter the workforce or already have, it is important for you to feel you belong there. This chapter will help you resolve any questions raised about your decision to work outside the home, regardless the source of the questions.

A Christian woman who worked as an elementary school teacher once told me about a disturbing incident that occurred during a Bible study she attended. This teacher informed the other participants she was having problems at work. When she asked them to pray for her, the woman leading the Bible study responded, "You could avoid these problems by staying home where you belong." The teacher was shocked to learn several other women in the Bible study agreed with this statement. Their comments were discouraging. She went to her sisters in Christ for support but, instead, ran into opposition.

I will admit to being surprised by resistance to Christian women working outside the home. I hope you have not experienced this obstacle but would not be surprised to learn you have. Consequently, you need to be prepared if and when you are confronted by this kind of resistance. Your preparation begins with understanding what the Bible says and does not say about women working outside the home. When you know what Scripture says on this issue, you will see the opposition is more personal and cultural than biblical.

Olivia was confronted when her church hosted a guest pastor one Sunday. She had worked outside the home since joining the church and her career was never an issue. That changed when the guest pastor delivered his sermon that morning. His homily was a no-holds-barred condemnation of Christian women working outside

27

the home. According to this pastor, the Christian woman's job is to support her husband in his career and to raise their children. He based this contention on several Bible verses. The pastor ended his sermon with a question for working women in the church: "What is there in the workplace that is more important to you than your family?" Though taken aback by the tone of the pastor's sermon and even a little hurt, Olivia did not disagree with everything he said.

For example, she agreed that part of her job as a wife was to support her husband in his career and she worked hard at that. But Olivia also believed part of her husband's job was to support her career. Further, Olivia did not disagree with the pastor's statements on raising children, except she thought it was the responsibility of the husband *and* the wife to raise the children. She viewed childrearing as a partnership in which the husband and wife both played important roles. She also believed this to be the point of view most accurately reflected in the teachings of Scripture.

Until she heard this sermon, Olivia never doubted the decision she and her husband made to put her college training to work pursuing a career in nursing. In fact, she viewed her job as a ministry in which she took care of sick people in their time of need. But Olivia had to admit the visiting pastor planted seeds of doubt. It did not help that the stay-at-home wives and mothers in her congregation, several of them friends, seemed to agree with the guest pastor. Olivia was torn. On one hand, she felt like she did a good job of balancing faith, family, and work. But, on the other hand, she didn't want to do anything proscribed in Scripture. Olivia was at a loss for what to do.

WHAT THE BIBLE SAYS AND DOES NOT SAY ABOUT WOMEN WORKING

Let me begin with the bottom line. The Bible does not prohibit women from working outside the home. When reading the Bible, interpretive discernment is critical. We must be able to distinguish between indicatives versus imperatives and prescription versus proscription. Indicatives describe how things are (or were at the time). Imperatives are commands (thou shall and thou shall not). Although there are many indicatives in the Bible describing how things were for women many years ago, there are no imperatives saying women shall not work outside the home.

Scripture has much to say about this subject, but what it says is prescriptive, not proscriptive. In other words, the Bible provides guidance concerning what is expected of you as a wife and mother (prescription), but it does not tell you how to go about meeting those expectations. Nor does it proscriptively say working outside the home is incompatible with meeting its prescriptive expectations. In fact, there are several instances of prominent women in the Bible who clearly worked outside the home and these examples are not just indicatives. Rather, the women in question are held up as exemplars of Christian womanhood.

But, before getting into that part of the discussion, let me present the Bible verses usually quoted by people who oppose Christian women entering the workforce—people like Olivia's guest pastor. The most frequently quoted verses are Titus 2:4–5 and 1 Timothy 5:14. In Titus 2, Paul writes, among other things, young women should love their husbands and children and be pure, kind, and submissive working in the home. In 1 Timothy, Paul writes that he would have younger widows marry, have children, and manage their homes. Let's look at these verses individually and analyze what they say.

What is there in Titus 2 that a woman cannot do while also maintaining a job outside the home? Can you not love your husband and children and work outside the home? I think you can. Can you not be pure if you have a job? I think you can. Does working outside the home preclude working in the home? Definitely not. Will you cease to be a kind person if you pursue a career? I hope not. These are important questions you must answer for yourself, but I suspect most Christian women can answer them with little trouble.

Those who oppose women entering the workforce focus on the part of Titus 2 that deals with working in the home. They take it to mean women should work exclusively in the home. But that is not what Paul writes. Beyond the fact various translations of the Bible

29

state this verse differently and emphasize different aspects of it, the admonitions in Titus 2:4-5 are statements of expectations that apply whether a woman is a full-time homemaker or one who also works outside the home. I have never met a Christian woman who worked outside the home who did not also work in the home.

Whether a woman will love her husband and children or comply with the other admonitions in Titus 2 is determined not by whether she works solely in the home, but by what is in her heart. There are women who work exclusively in the home who comply with all the admonitions in Titus 2 and there are those who don't. Correspondingly, there are women who pursue careers outside the home who comply with all Paul's admonitions and there are those who don't. Whether or not a woman lives up to the expectations set forth in Titus 2 depends more on her commitment to being a God-honoring wife, mother, and individual than on whether she pursues a career in homemaking or in the workplace.

Now let's look at 1 Timothy 5:14. This verse is often used to support the claim that managing the household is the only career a woman should pursue, but that is not what the verse states. Putting aside the fact Paul is writing about young widows, as opposed to all women, this verse is hardly a proscription against women working outside the home. Rather, it is an expectation that unmarried women will marry and, having done so, manage their households efficiently and effectively. Paul seems to be more concerned that young women marry and do a good job of managing their households than whether or not they work outside the home. The question then becomes: can women maintain jobs outside the home and still do a good job of managing their household duties?

The obvious answer to this question is that some can and some can't, regardless their religious convictions or lack thereof. Because of this reality, opponents of women working outside the home sometimes claim working solely in the home gives women more time to manage their households. One could hardly argue. After all, one of the most persistent problems Christian women in the workplace face is trying to balance their faith, family, and work (see Chapter 3).

But there is a glaring weakness in this argument. Being a full-time homemaker is no guarantee a woman will efficiently and effectively manage her household. Again, some do and some don't.

The real issue, then, is not whether a woman works solely in the home or also outside the home, but whether, in either case, she manages her household well. Regardless whether you are a full-time homemaker or a homemaker who also pursues a career in the workplace, managing a household efficiently and effectively is not an easy task. But, on the other hand, it is something you and most Christian women can do or can learn to do. Later in this chapter and also in Chapter 3, you will find specific strategies for achieving good household management while also pursuing a career. But, first, we need to look at another pertinent passage from Scripture that figures prominently in the debate over women working outside the home: Proverbs 31.

PROVERBS 31 AND WORKING WOMEN IN THE BIBLE

In Proverbs 31, King Lemuel recounts what his mother taught him concerning the traits of an excellent wife. This chapter contains thirty-one verses, several of which have direct application in the debate over women working outside the home. For example, in verses 15–19, we read about how the excellent wife provides meals for her family, but also buys a field, plants a vineyard, spins and weaves, and is a profitable merchant. In these verses, Lemuel paints a picture of a woman who works in the home as well as outside the home. She appears to be both a dutiful homemaker and a wise businesswoman. These verses could be describing a modern-day Christian woman who not only manages her household well, but also pursues a career. They could be describing you.

In verse 16, the Proverbs 31 woman performs the duties of a farmer. In verse 18, she works as a businesswoman checking the books to make sure her merchandise is making a profit. That merchandise might be the fruit of her vineyard or the products of her spinning wheel or both. Verse 24 suggests her merchandise, at least in part, consists of the linen garments and sashes she makes. In any case, the Proverbs 31 woman who is held up as the ideal in this chapter of Scripture clearly works both inside and outside the home. She is a household manager, but she is also a farmer, tailor, and merchant.

In addition to the unnamed Proverbs 31 woman, there are others in the Bible held up as exemplars of Christian womanhood. Two of them are Deborah and Lydia. Deborah appears in the Book of Judges, Chapters 4 and 5. She was a wife who managed her household, but was also a prophetess, community activist, ruler, and warrior. Deborah not only worked outside the home, she was a warrior who helped lead the outnumbered forces of an army to victory against a better-equipped enemy.

Lydia was a businesswoman known for her ability, intelligence, and hospitality. She appears in Acts 16:12–15. Lydia was a well-known merchant who sold the scarlet cloth used in making fezzes. Lydia was so successful in business she could afford to own a large house with servants to attend her. She was also a Jew who eventually made a public profession and converted to Christianity. In fact, Lydia became the Apostle Paul's first European convert. Like Deborah, Lydia worked outside the home; however, she was also a gracious hostess much given to hospitality. Both these women from Scripture managed their households while also working outside the home.

By now, it should be clear the biblical concerns sometimes raised about Christian women working outside the home are unfounded. The issue is not whether a woman pursues a career outside the home, but whether she does so to the detriment of her household. Women who are able to maintain a healthy faith, family, and work balance honor God by their efforts. Those who are unable to maintain such a balance fall short. If you find yourself struggling to properly manage your household while working outside the home, don't despair. You can learn to be a good household manager while also excelling in a career outside the home. The process involves applying what I call the four pillars of good household management: planning, organizing, leading, and controlling.

FOUR PILLARS OF GOOD HOUSEHOLD MANAGEMENT

1 Timothy 5:14 admonishes Christian women to manage their households well, but what does that mean? Let me begin with the concept of management. Managing is a process whereby you harness resources, particularly people, and focus them on accomplishing specific goals. Good management means accomplishing the goals in question efficiently and effectively. Efficiency means getting the most done with the least investment of time, money, or labor. Effectiveness means accomplishing the goals you are pursuing.

With this background understood, managing your household well means efficiently and effectively accomplishing all the tasks necessary for the household to run smoothly and in an orderly manner. In practical terms, it means meals get served, dishes get washed, beds get made, the laundry gets done, the yard work is kept up-to-date, shopping gets done, the children do their homework, the house gets cleaned, and the children get off to school each day without giving you an ulcer. The key to ensuring these and other household tasks are accomplished efficiently and effectively is to apply the four pillars of good household management: planning, organizing, leading, and controlling.

Planning and Organizing for Good Household Management

The planning and organizing components of good household management go together. They involve sitting down with the family at least once a week and going through the *what-who-when-where-how* exercise. The *what* component of the exercise is planning. It involves making a list of what must be done that week as well as all events to be attended. Meals have to be made, dishes washed, the garbage taken out, beds made, and homework completed, for just a few examples. Further, meetings, extracurricular activities, and church events must be attended. All obligations of all family members for the upcoming week are written down.

With your planning list developed, the next step is to organize the team—your family—to ensure these obligations are efficiently and effectively carried out. Organizing begins by applying the *who-when-where-how* aspects of the exercise. You and your husband must decide who is going to do what, as well as when, where, and how they are going to do it. If you are a single woman or a single mother, this task falls to you. This means every item on your planning list should be assigned to a specific family member and put on the calendar on a specific date with a deadline for completing it.

Now, before going further, I have a caution for mothers. If you are going to manage your household well while maintaining a job outside the home, you must get comfortable with the concept of *delegation*. Delegation is fundamental to good management. The planning list is not a list of obligations, chores, and duties for Mom. Rather, it is a list for the entire family. More often than not, working mothers who seem to always be pressed for time are those who think they have to do everything themselves when it comes to household management. Management, by definition, involves assigning duties to others, monitoring to ensure the duties are completed properly and on time, and interceding appropriately when problems arise. In other words, it involves delegation and oversight.

As soon as your children are old enough to do household chores of any kind, get them started. Dressing themselves, making their beds, helping with the dishes, taking out the trash, cleaning up their rooms, and doing their homework without being coerced are all things children can and should learn to do early in life. Of course, in the beginning, they won't do these things as well as you can do them but, if you wait until they can do the chores perfectly, they will never learn how to do them at all.

As a working mother who is raising children as part of managing a household, you may have to get comfortable with *good* rather than *great* when it comes to the children's chores, at least for a while. Let me be clear about what I mean here. On the one hand, you do not allow the children to purposely do a sloppy or half-hearted job with their chores or do them with an attitude of reluctant compliance.

But, on the other hand, you have to be patient as they learn to do the chores and as they get better at doing them over time. Never forget: any chore your children can do is one less to fall to you and your husband.

Leading and Controlling for Household Management

Once you plan the household duties and organize the family to perform them, the final two pillars of household management come into play. They are leading and controlling. Leading involves inspiring others to do their best in helping achieve a common goal. The common goal in question here is to efficiently and effectively carry out the duties established in the planning and organizing steps. You inspire your family members to do their best by setting an example of doing your best at the duties assigned to you. Good leaders never say, "Do as I say, not as I do." If your children see Mom or Dad failing to complete their assignments or just doing them half-heartedly, they will take it as permission to slack off on theirs. On the other hand, if they see the two of you doing an excellent job, they will be more inclined to emulate your good example.

Controlling involves establishing the household rules and enforcing them. If you schedule a family devotional at a certain time each night, everyone in the family should be required to participate. If the children are supposed to do their homework at a certain time, they should do it regardless what is airing on television or the internet at that time. If the children are assigned a household chore, it should be done on the appointed day and no later than the deadline. Children learn to follow God's rules as well as the rules of society by first learning to follow your rules. For good household management, have family rules and stick to them. Never let your reluctance to enforce family rules become the reason your children don't learn to do their part in managing the household.

I am always surprised by parents who tell me they cannot get their children to obey willingly and with the proper attitude. I understand, in a fallen world, it is the nature of children to resist the expectation of obedience. I understand your children interact with others whose parents do not require them to obey. I understand teachers sometimes fall short when it comes to enforcing the rules at school. I understand these things can make it harder for you to enforce the rules at home. But here are some other things I also understand.

First, we are admonished in Ephesians 6:4 to bring our children up in God's instruction and discipline. It does not matter if teachers, coaches, or other authority figures fail to have expectations and enforce them. These other individuals are not your children's parents. Second, you are not a helpless bystander lacking authority or influence when it comes to your children. Think about it. Your children depend on you for everything. Without you, they have no home, food, or security. You are an adult, and they are children. This means you are in charge.

Consequently, when it comes to applying Ephesians 6:4 in your household, remember one of my favorite leadership maxims: *When you are in charge, take charge.* The goal of having family rules and enforcing them is to teach your children to do what they are expected to do willingly and with a positive attitude. If they learn this lesson while helping you and your husband manage the household, it will not only decrease your time-related burdens, it will serve them well in school, their careers, and all other aspects of their lives.

COPING WITH PUSH-BACK FROM FELLOW BELIEVERS

Hopefully, Christian brothers and sisters will be supportive of each other and helpful when it comes to making faith-related decisions. Unfortunately, this is does not always happen. As has been stated, much of the push-back against women in the workplace comes from within the Christian community. I have prayed often that fellow believers would be supportive of each other, regardless whether they work exclusively at home or also outside the home. After all, in today's workplace—an environment dominated by secular humanism, moral relativism, and political correctness—Christians face enough faith-related challenges without fellow believers adding to their burdens.

I have seen fellow believers who oppose Christian women working outside the home behave badly toward women who do. Some who hold strong views on this subject can be doggedly persistent, insensitive, and uncaring in expressing them. I have seen Christian women who work outside the home wounded deeply by the hurtful comments of fellow believers. Unfortunately, there are Christian brothers and sisters who can be all heat and no light when it comes to discussing this topic.

I have talked with Christian women who were victims of quasi-interrogations conducted by fellow believers. Victoria is one of them. Victoria is a committed Christian who does a good job of balancing faith, family, and work. In fact, she took time out of her career to care for her twins when they were born. Then, when the twins reached school age, she went back to work. But, this time, she took a less demanding job, requiring fewer hours, and allowed her a more predictable schedule than the one she left upon becoming a mother.

One day, Victoria received an invitation to a women's Bible study at her church. Looking forward to reconnecting with some of the mothers she befriended during the years of staying home to care for her twins, Victoria was shocked when the supposed Bible study turned out to be an intervention. Without letting her know ahead of time, Victoria's friends gathered not to study the Bible, but to convince her re-entering the workforce was wrong. Each woman chose a Bible verse to read out loud that supported the group's contention Victoria was failing as a wife, mother, and Christian woman by working outside the home. Then, seeing Victoria's shock and disappointment, the group assured her they were "doing this for her own good."

Victoria was deeply hurt. Rather than attempt to justify her decision about work, she quickly excused herself and left. Driving home, her emotions ran the gamut from anger to grief to doubt. She was angry women she considered friends would blindside her with an intervention and then claim to do it for her own good. She grieved over friendships damaged by the deception. But, worst of all, their questions and comments planted seeds of doubt. Victoria remembered thinking, "What if they are right?"

The Bible is clear concerning what it expects of you as a woman, wife, and mother. If you can satisfy these expectations while maintaining a job outside the home and if your decision to work is based on the right reasons, no one should question your decision; however, as Victoria's story shows, there may be fellow believers who think questioning your decision is not just their right, but their duty. This being the case, how should you respond to those who question your decision to work outside the home? I will answer this question shortly, but, first, some background.

The decision concerning whether to work exclusively in the home or also outside the home is not a community decision. Although you should be open to hearing the views of fellow believers and respectful of those views, it's not your friends from church or the broader Christian community whose validation you need for this and other family decisions. Work-related decisions are the sole province of you, your family, and God. If your family does not oppose a decision about work and you are convinced God is pleased with the decision, you are probably making the right choice. Once you and your family are in the right place with God concerning work-related decisions, the views of naysayers are irrelevant. You and they may just have to agree to disagree. My prayer is the naysayers will be sufficiently respectful to disagree without being disagreeable.

Once you and your family have made a decision about whether or not you will work outside the home, the response I recommend you give to those who raise questions about the decision is a tactful but firm non-response. The validation of fellow believers is not required when you have the blessing of God. Unless you just like to debate these kinds of issues, I recommend you simply listen patiently to fellow believers, thank them for their opinions, and then proceed with the decision you and your family have already made.

SOME FINAL THOUGHTS ON CHRISTIAN WOMEN WORKING OUTSIDE THE HOME

Regardless of whether you work exclusively in the home or also outside the home, work is a gift from God (Ecclesiastes 5:19). Consequently, we are supposed to show our gratitude by honoring God in how we do our work, both in the home and in the workplace. This being the case, those who oppose Christian women working outside the home may be missing the point. Instead of asking whether women should hold jobs, perhaps they should ask for whom the women in question are working. This is a question that applies to all Christians in the workforce, men and women. It also applies to homemakers. Regardless where you work or what your job happens to be, God expects you to do your work well because, ultimately, you are working for Him (Colossians 3:23).

As was stated in the previous section, if you are in the right place with God about a work-related decision, He will bless that decision. Self-serving work-related decisions are wrong. God-serving decisions are right. To illustrate what I mean by this, let's take a look at a few examples. Choosing to work outside the home because of economic necessity is a reason God understands. Some Christian women must work outside the home because they have no choice. Some are single mothers while others are married to men whose income is not sufficient to adequately provide for the family. A friend of mine is a retired pastor whose wife had to work throughout their married lives because the small churches he served over his career could not afford to pay him a sufficient salary.

Economic necessity is certainly a valid reason for women to maintain jobs outside the home. But a caution is in order here. Do not conflate economic necessity with a desire for an ever-increasing level of material wealth. Choosing to work outside the home for the love of money (1 Timothy 6:10) is not a valid reason. On the one hand, God expects us to support and care for our families. But, on the other hand, He is not likely to smile on material excess. Women or men who fall into the trap of working to acquire ever more material wealth will never acquire enough. Consequently, it is important to be honest with yourself about the concept of economic necessity.

Choosing to work outside the home to honor God by putting to good use the talents, education, and skills He gave you is a good reason. God expects you to use the intellectual assets and hands-on abilities He provides in ways that help support your family, contribute to the betterment of your community, care for His sheep, and honor Him (Ephesians 2:10). Ambition aimed at satisfying these expectations is a good thing. But be careful. Appropriate ambition can morph into misguided ambition in which our work becomes an idol. Allowing our work to become a false god through which we pursue power, status, and self-gratification will lead only to destruction (Exodus 20:3).

To conclude, let's return to the story of Olivia from the beginning of the chapter. The guest pastor who spoke at her church raised doubts in Olivia's mind about working outside the home. She struggled with pursuing a career for several weeks before she and her husband approached their permanent pastor for help. Their pastor apologized to Olivia and her husband for the tone of the guest pastor's sermon. He asked them both if they prayed about Olivia working and if they were in the right place with God on the issue. When they acknowledged being in the right place with God about their decision, the pastor assured them they made the right decision.

The pastor talked with Olivia and her husband about the Proverbs 31 woman. He also cited several other examples of women in the Bible who worked outside the home, while also managing their households. Olivia and her husband were encouraged by the pastor's comments and the references from Scripture. They already did a good job of maintaining a healthy faith, family, and work balance. Before leaving the pastor's office, Olivia and her husband recommitted to maintaining this balance.

As they studied Titus 2:4–5 and 1 Timothy 5:14, Olivia and her husband came to understand why some of their fellow church members opposed women working outside the home. But, on the other hand, they became more convinced than ever their friends were

40

misinterpreting these passages. After much prayer and Scripture study, Olivia and her husband were able to proceed with their lives with the peace of knowing they were honoring God at home and at work.

PRAYER FOR COPING WITH OPPOSITION TO WORKING OUTSIDE THE HOME

Gracious Lord,

Thank You for opening the door for me to come to You in prayer. I know, no matter what is on my mind, I can stop everything and bring my concerns and hopes and frustrations to You. In fact, Lord, I ask You to remind me to reach out to You more often. I know, when I don't, I end up feeling stressed and alone.

Father, today, I seek Your guidance about the work I do outside my home. I know you have blessed me with unique skills and talents and my job is a gift from You. Help me remember that, no matter what form of work I do, I only have one boss: You! Remind me quickly, I need to return to You when I wander off on my own and seek self-gratification through my work. Let me love my work because You called me to do it and let me serve You well.

Sometimes, I notice women who aren't employed outside their own home. I see them at lunch time chatting quietly with friends as I'm quickly getting my coffee at the drive-through window and going back to work. They seem to simply be enjoying life, without the pressure of working somewhere. I admit I envy that a little and wonder if I'm doing the right thing.

Now and then, I discover a woman from my church who gives me an unfriendly reminder that she doesn't

41

think it's right for me to work away from the house. She's even been so bold as to tell me You don't want women to do anything but care for their husbands and children. Is that so, Lord? Is it wrong for me to work?

Of course, You know I work because my family needs my income. My husband works hard, but, together, we can provide in better ways for our household. Since I went back to work, we've been able to pay off some of our bills and even take a vacation now and then. We are grateful to You for providing for us.

Lord, when I deal with doubt about whether I should work or not, grant me peace. Give me peace that You are pleased with my decision to work and You continue to bless my family in the process. Grant that I might be a minister for You in the workplace and an asset to my family, both at work and at home. Fill my heart with Your grace and Your joy, so I respond with love to Your calling on my life. Like the Proverbs 31 woman, let me commit all my ways to You.

Today, Lord, bless those women who work outside their homes and those who work for their families at home, because, from where I sit, Father, I believe every woman is working full time, wherever she may be. Amen.

GROUP DISCUSSION CASE: "Don't You Love Your Children?"

The question was a slap in the face. Mary Grace considered herself a good, attentive mother, and so did her husband and children. She did a good job of balancing her faith, family, and work. Consequently, Mary Grace was stunned when a friend from church asked her, "Don't you love your children?" The not-too-subtle insinuation was if Mary Grace loved her children, she wouldn't spend her days pursuing a career outside the home. Because she did not enter the workforce

until her children were in school, Mary Grace's career was never an issue. Further, the Christian women she knew who worked outside the home loved their children dearly. Caught off guard in this way, she didn't know how to respond.

Discussion Questions:

1. Have you ever been challenged by a fellow believer or anyone else about working outside the home? If so, what was the rationale behind the challenge?

2. If you were Mary Grace, how would you respond to the question about loving her children?

REVIEW QUESTIONS FOR INDIVIDUALS AND GROUPS

1. Does the Bible prohibit women from working outside the home?

2. What are the verses often cited by people who oppose women working outside the home? Do these verses really prohibit women from working outside the home? Why or why not?

3. Explain the implications of the Proverbs 31 woman for Christian women who work outside the home.

4. Are there examples in the Bible of upstanding women who worked outside the home? If so, give an example.

5. Explain the concepts of planning and organizing for good household management.

6. Explain the concepts of leading and controlling for good household management.

7. How should you handle pushback from fellow believers about working outside the home?

8. How should you decide about whether or not to work outside the home?

9. How can you know if a work-related decision you make is the right decision?

CHAPTER 3

BALANCING FAITH, FAMILY, AND WORK

· ·

"Do not toil to acquire wealth…." Proverbs 23:4

One of the most difficult challenges you will face in working outside the home is balancing your faith, family, and work. Each of these aspects of your life requires time and attention. Trying to keep them in balance is a problem faced by all Christian women who work outside the home—women like Amy. Amy didn't know it would be like this. Having returned to work after her youngest child was in school, she thought things couldn't be better. Life was good. Amy had the three things that mattered most to her: a loving family, her faith, and a promising career. But, lately, she was struggling to balance them. In fact, on some days, she felt pulled in three different directions at the same time.

Amy knew going back to work would cut down on her church and family activities. But her church's Wednesday evening and Sunday morning services would still be available to her. Further, she would still have her personal prayer time and Bible study. When it came to family, she would have evenings, weekends, and holidays with her two sons and husband, and there would still be family devotions. Besides, as she told a friend, "The boys and their dad are occupied all day with school and work anyway. Once they leave in the morning, I don't see them again until late afternoon or evening." Amy was convinced the new arrangement would work out well as soon as she adjusted to it. Unfortunately, things were not turning out the way she planned.

The pressures of her job were causing Amy to work late many nights. She also felt compelled to work on weekends when projects fell behind, which they often did. In recent months, Amy missed several Wednesday night church services. She even skipped Church on Sunday a couple of times to catch up on work. To make matters worse, she was neglecting her personal prayer life, family devotions became sporadic, her sons complained about missing her, and her husband began to refer to her only half-jokingly as "the stranger." Amy didn't know what to do. She wanted to make time in her life for faith, family, and work but, in reality, Amy was shortchanging all three.

There are a lot of Christian women who, like Amy, find it difficult to balance faith, family, and work. You might be one of them. That's the bad news—but there is good news, too. If finding a healthy balance in your life is a struggle: don't despair. It can be done. A lot of Christian women have faced this problem and learned how to overcome it, and you can, too. You can balance faith, family, and work without shortchanging any of them. This chapter provides practical strategies for making the most of your time in ways that will help you achieve a healthy, balanced life.

CHALLENGES TO ACHIEVING A BALANCED LIFE

Women who are not Christians often struggle to balance their work and family lives. But, for Christian women, the challenge is even more difficult because they have an added dimension to their

lives: faith. Complicating the struggle is the fact faith is more than just another ball to juggle; it is the foundation of everything else in your life. If your faith life is suffering from neglect, your family and work lives are probably suffering too. After all, your faith is the foundation of your family relationships and your career. It is ironic that, when life becomes hectic and we cannot juggle fast enough, faith is often the first ball we drop.

As Christians, most of us would claim God and family are more important than work, but our lives sometimes belie this claim. Too often, when we are forced to choose, work wins out over God and family. We don't mean to neglect our faith or family, nor do we want to. Work seems to be the one responsibility in our lives we cannot put off. Do you ever find yourself thinking, "I will devote more time to my faith and family once things settle down at work"? Most of us have had this thought, but the hard truth is the things that interfere with faith and family rarely settle down or go away.

Christian women work for different reasons, just as Christian men do. But one of the principal motivators for women who work outside the home is economic necessity. Most women who work do so, at least in part, because they need to. This is why work can be so effective at elbowing its way to the top of your priority list. As a motivator, economic necessity appeals to a deep personal need: survival. The survival instinct gives work a lot of *muscle* when you are trying to balance it with the other aspects of your life.

Yet another challenge when trying to balance faith, family, and work is technology. Advances in digital technology have made it difficult to get away from work. With just the press of a button or the click of a mouse, your work can be accessed anytime and anywhere, and so can you. The good old days of being able to walk out the door and leave work behind are over. Because of smartphones, laptop computers, notebook computers, and other electronic devices, work is never far away. Further, your boss can reach you twenty-four hours a day, seven days a week, 365 days a year. To complicate matters further, smartphones seem to have a hold on our psyche that makes continually checking them something resembling an addiction. The fact that technology makes work omnipresent can rob you of family and faith time, if you let it.

Try this experiment. The next time you are in a restaurant or any other setting where families gather, observe how much time the family members spend thumbing around on their smartphones versus interacting with each other. During a trip to Disneyworld, I observed a mother and father texting and talking on smartphones instead of enjoying time with their children. In a restaurant, I observed a mother, father, and two children interacting with smartphones without saying a word to each other during the entire meal. Technology has a grip on us that is allowing work and other obligations or interests to take even more time than usual away from our families and faith.

In addition to the survival instinct and intrusive technology, unnecessary outside activities can rob us of time we should devote to faith, families, and work. Women who are successful in their careers have a tendency to take on a lot of outside activities (the same is true of successful men). I have counseled women who, in addition to juggling faith, family, and work, took on such other obligations as serving on the board of the local chamber of commerce, coaching their children's soccer team, playing in the local symphony, chairing fund-raising activities for school bands, serving as officers in the PTA, teaching Sunday school, holding office in the local economic development council, and serving as board members for local charities. A few even held elective office. While I understand the motivation behind serving in these various capacities, if you are finding it difficult to balance faith, family, and work, outside activities just multiply your problems.

A final challenge to achieving a balanced life is the fact that work can seem more demanding and less forgiving than God or family. Work comes with high expectations, deadlines, pressure, and accountability. Further, there are tangible and immediate consequences for failing to meet the expectations of your employer. This is not so obviously the case for those who fall behind in their Bible reading and personal prayer time. There is no overbearing boss demanding you read the Bible and there are no pushy customers prodding you to pray. Consequently, these things are easier to move to the back burner.

When it comes to family time, your husband and children are probably willing to give you more latitude than your boss, coworkers, and customers. Even if they complain about missing you, your promise to make it up to them will usually suffice. Because of this, even family obligations can seem less pressing than work. Because it can be so demanding and because there can be tangible and immediate consequences for failing to meet the demands, work has a way of pushing faith and family aside.

When life gets hectic, what makes the most noise usually gets the most attention, and work has a tendency to make the most noise. If you neglect your family or faith, there will be consequences, but they may not seem as immediate to you as the consequences of neglecting your job. Plus, God is more forgiving than your boss and your customers. Your family probably is, too. Even if your family is unhappy about playing second fiddle to work, they can't dock your pay, demote you, or threaten your job security. Consequently, when it comes to juggling work, family, and faith, work can take priority unless you are willing to do what is necessary to achieve a better balance.

ACHIEVING A BALANCED LIFE BEGINS WITH GOD

There are a number of things you can do to help achieve a balanced life. But, before getting into them, it is important for you to understand the first step toward achieving a balanced life is to get your faith life in order. As I mentioned earlier, if your faith life is out of balance, your work and family lives probably are, too. Never forget this: God is the foundation of your life. You build your family relationships and career on a foundation of faith. There is no way to achieve a balanced life without God at the center of it. Unless He is your first priority, your other priorities are going to suffer.

When you put God first in your life, your other priorities will fall into place more easily. Putting God first will take away many of the distractions in life that are pulling you away from what is really important. For example, when God is first in your life, you will be less inclined to crash in front of the television after work instead of spending time with your family, reading the Bible, or praying. You will feel less compelled to spend your evenings and weekends checking for work-related messages on your smartphone while neglecting your responsibilities as a wife, mother, daughter, sister, or church member. When God is first in your life, you gain a whole new perspective. Some of the distractions that seem so important now will seem less important when you put God first.

Once you put God first in your life, time-related dilemmas can be solved by asking yourself a simple question: "What does God want me to do in this situation?" In fact, by asking yourself this question, you can do more than solve time-related dilemmas, you can prevent them. This is why I emphasize the key to achieving a healthy balance is to put God first in your life; however, a caveat is in order here. I readily acknowledge this advice is easier to give than take. Achieving a balanced life will never be easy, nor is it impossible. It can be done. More specifically, you can do it.

PUTTING GOD FIRST IN YOUR LIFE

To excel at work without compromising your faith while also achieving a balanced life requires putting God first. No problem, right? Few Christian women would argue against putting God first in their lives, at least theoretically. But many whose lives have become overbooked do wonder how to go about it. I have been asked many times, "How do I put God first in my life?" This is a good question. Christian women who ask it are typically like Sally.

Sally is a real estate agent and a committed Christian. She wanted to put God first in her life, but there were the household chores that never seemed to get done, soccer practice for her son, band practice for her daughter, a husband whose job required out-of-town

travel, meetings with her children's teachers, sellers and buyers who demanded her time seven days a week, grocery shopping for the family, errands for her aging mother, continuing education classes for renewing her real estate license, and a list of other obligations that seemed to just get longer, no matter what she did.

Frustrated, Sally approached me for help. We had barely begun when she threw up her hands in exasperation and asked, "With all of my responsibilities, how am I supposed to find time for my faith?" There are plenty of Christian women who, like Sally, feel as if they have too many obligations and too little time. Although their circumstances vary, one thing these women have in common is feeling stressed, overbooked, and stretched to their limits. For some of them, you can add guilt to the list.

When working late, they feel guilty about neglecting their families. They also feel guilty about shortchanging their faith. When taking time off for family or church activities, they feel stressed about the work piling up in their offices. Another thing they have in common is a desire to get off the treadmill and achieve some balance in their lives. If, like these women, you feel weighed down by a never-ending list of obligations: don't despair. The relief you need is available. It begins with putting God first in your life.

Mathew 6:33 speaks to putting God first in our lives. One of the lessons you can take from this verse is: if we seek the kingdom of God first, the other aspects of our lives will come more readily into balance. When God is first in your life, not only will you have the guidance needed to make wise choices about your time, but some of the obligations now weighing you down will seem less important. Some may even become irrelevant. Most self-help books that deal with achieving a balanced life recommend making a list of all your obligations and then prioritizing them. This is a good idea, but (with the approach I recommend) the first item on the list must be God. Putting God first will help you prioritize the other items on your list. If you want to put God first in your life and are not sure how to go about it, the following action steps will help.

Step 1: Make the Commitment

As Christians, we tend to believe we put God first in our lives or, at least, we want to believe we do. But, if we are honest with ourselves, putting God first is probably more of a goal than a reality. It reflects what we want to do rather than what we actually do. The difference between wanting to put God first in our lives and doing it is *commitment*. Commitment means more than just trying hard. It means being staunchly dedicated to carrying out a decision. Hannah finally had to face what being committed to putting God first in her life really meant.

It was during a women's Bible study when the reality of her situation dawned on her. The topic of the study was commitment. The Bible-study facilitator explained what a commitment to putting God first looked like in practical terms. That was when Hannah realized she had never made a commitment. When she thought about how she spent her time and what got overlooked first when life became hectic, Hannah had to admit God wasn't first in her life. Just the previous night, she skipped her personal prayer time and Bible reading to watch a favorite sitcom, a common occurrence for Hannah. When she thought about it, Hannah realized she often put other activities ahead of her faith.

Admitting God isn't first in your life can be a difficult pill to swallow. I have counseled Christian women who were offended I would even ask if they put God first in their lives. But, when I suggest they record the amount of time they spend each day in prayer, Bible reading, family devotions, and caring for God's sheep versus other activities, some come to the realization their commitment to God is more want-to than reality. Until we make a commitment, we run the risk of being like the people spoken of in Matthew 15:8 who honor God with their words, but not their hearts or actions.

The first and most important step in putting God first in your life is just deciding to do it—making the commitment. This step requires taking the words of Matthew 15:8 to heart and honoring God by your actions, not just your words. Once you have committed to putting God first in your life, every decision you make and every action you

take from that point on must pass the *honoring God test.* This test can be stated in the form of a simple question: Does this decision or this action honor God? For example, will God be honored if you forego your Bible reading to watch a television program? Will God be honored if you skip your daughter's softball game to squeeze in a little extra time at work? Will God be honored if you neglect your personal prayer time to surf the net or answer text messages and emails? Once you make the commitment to honor God in all you do, time-related decisions become less difficult to make.

Step 2: Do Everything to the Glory of God

Christian women are just as interested in achieving job security, climbing the career ladder, and excelling at work as anyone else, and they should be. These are all commendable goals, if pursued for the right reasons. For Christian women who want to put God first in their lives, one of the reasons for pursing these goals must be to glorify God (1 Corinthians 10:31). In this verse, we are told to do everything we do to the "glory of God." This means, if we are going to put God first in our lives, we should do our jobs, raise our families, and pursue our faith in ways that glorify Him.

Therefore, excelling at work is a virtue if it is done for the right reasons. Where we, as Christians, sometimes go astray is when we fall into the self-glorification trap. When our efforts at excellence are driven by ego or self-gratification rather than to honor God, we run the risk of becoming victims of our own misguided ambition. It is misguided ambition, in turn, that often results in the kinds of sinful behavior so often seen in the workplace (e.g., lying, cheating, stealing, power-seeking, taking credit for the work of others, etc.).

If doing everything to the glory of God sounds like a formidable challenge, it is. After all, even the most committed Christians are human, meaning we are sinners. This being the case, we will always be tempted to use work to glorify ourselves rather than God. Ego and self-gratification are powerful motivators. When you find your desire to glorify yourself outweighing your desire to glorify God:

don't despair. Rather, cast your mind back to the words of John 3:16, where we read God loves you so much He sent His only son to the cross, so you could have everlasting life. When you consider the kind of sacrifice God made for you, doing what is necessary to glorify Him becomes less difficult.

Step 3: Put Your Trust in God

Ironically, the more successful we become, the more self-sufficient we think we are. Beware. Thinking you can do everything by yourself will just complicate your efforts to achieve a balanced life. Part of establishing a balanced life is avoiding the *self-sufficiency trap.* Not only is self-sufficiency a practical impossibility, it is at odds with Scripture. Scripture is clear that we can do all things through Christ (Philippians 4:13). The obverse of this is also true. We can do nothing of lasting significance without Christ. Consequently, part of achieving a balanced life involves putting your trust in God and putting aside any misguided perceptions of self-sufficiency you may have. Donna had to do this.

Donna forgot the lesson of Philippians 4:13, and it almost ruined her career and health. When Donna lost her husband in a tragic accident, proving she could take care of herself and her family without asking for help became her way of coping. Donna got a job and threw herself into becoming a top-performing professional. At work, she was like a carpenter with a new hammer. Every problem looked like a nail, whether it was her problem or not. Before long, she became her employer's go-to person for solving difficult situations.

At home, she got up early and stayed up late to make sure the household chores got done and her home looked as orderly and neat as it did before she entered the workforce. Donna's friends were amazed at how self-sufficient she was. But refusing to ask for help and burning the candle at both ends eventually caught up with her. One day, she collapsed from exhaustion during a business meeting and had to be rushed to the hospital.

During her recovery, Donna was able to do something she had not done in a long time: pray and read the Bible. While reading Chapter 4 of Philippians, Donna realized she had fallen into the self-sufficiency trap. She was trying to run her life without the help of Christ or anyone else. When Donna was released, she made some profound changes in her life. She began by admitting her supposed self-sufficiency was a myth. Donna admitted further she needed help, and the help she needed most could come only from Christ. But, with Christ at her side, Donna was able to make some important adjustments in her life.

At work, she began delegating and mentoring rather than trying to do everything herself. She also showed others how to solve complex problems, so she was no longer the only person her employer could look to for help in that arena. At home, she assigned most of the household chores to her children, chores they should have been doing anyway. Donna's days started and ended with Bible reading and prayer. When the exigencies of life pressed down on her, Donna put her trust in God and never again fell into the self-sufficiency trap. With God first in her life, Donna's priorities changed and so did her physical and mental health—both for the better. Over time, Donna achieved a balance that made her an even better employee and mother.

Step 4: Pray Without Ceasing

The Bible tells us to pray continually (1 Thessalonians 5:17–18). One of the most fundamental aspects of putting God first in your life is prayer. Prayer is how you converse with God. It is how you determine what He would have you do when limited time forces you to make hard choices. It is also how you gain the wisdom and insight needed to honor God in all aspects of your life. Prayer is an essential step in obeying the admonition in Matthew 6:33 to seek first the kingdom of God. Trying to put God first in your life without prayer is like trying to build a happy marriage without communication. We communicate with God through prayer.

Step 5: Read the Bible Regularly

One of the reasons our lives become overbooked is we get caught up in the here and now and set our minds on the things of the earth. This is less likely to happen when we spend time every day reading the Bible. The Bible is the Word of God. If prayer is how we communicate with God, the Bible is one of the ways He communicates with us. The Bible contains the specific revelations of and about God. There is no situation you will face in life beyond the reach of Scripture. Only through Scripture can you come to intimately know your Creator. The Bible is where you will find the answers needed to extricate yourself from an unbalanced, counterproductive lifestyle. But, to find those answers, you have to spend time in the Word.

Nakeesha learned about seeking answers in the Bible by accident. Before she became a Christian, Nakeesha's overbooked life was akin to pedaling a stationary bicycle. No matter how hard she pedaled, she never seemed to make any progress. There was never enough time for work and family. As a result, both suffered. Because they suffered, Nakeesha suffered. Then, one day, she happened upon a Bible sitting open on a coworker's desk. Highlighted in yellow was Colossians 3:2, a verse admonishing us to focus on heavenly rather than earthly things. This verse struck Nakeesha like a bolt of lightning. It dawned on her she was focused on all the wrong things.

During lunch, Nakeesha went to a nearby bookstore and purchased a Bible. She sat down and started reading it hungrily, beginning with Proverbs. She heard somewhere Proverbs contained wisdom for daily life. Wisdom for life was exactly what Nakeesha needed. When she read in Proverbs 3:6 how God would direct her and crown her efforts with success if she put Him first in her life, Nakeesha was hooked. She tried for years to get her life in balance, but nothing seemed to change. Nakeesha needed help. She needed someone to direct her. For Nakeesha, that someone became God. The more she read, the more Nakeesha realized she was approaching her unbalanced, out-of-control life from a counterproductive perspective. She was focused on the wrong things.

Nakeesha's experience in finding the answers she needed in Scripture soon led her to accept Christ as her Lord and Savior. With the help of her new church family, she learned to pray and to place her burdens at God's feet. Her new-found faith changed Nakeesha's life in ways she hoped for but could not have imagined. When she put God first in her life, Nakeesha truly shed her old self and became a new person (Ephesians 4:22–24). It can do the same for you. The Bible coupled with prayer is a powerful combination, one that will help you put God first in your life. Once this happens, you will find it easier to achieve the balance you seek because, like all good things, a balanced life is a gift from God.

With God first in your life, you are well on the way to achieving the healthy balance that has eluded you up to now; however, there will never be a time when seeking to honor God, build a career, and nurture a family will be easy. Meeting this challenge will always require concerted effort, intentionality, and wisdom. The good news is there are a number of practical things you can do to help ensure you have time for your faith, family, and work without shortchanging any of them. Putting God first in your life gives you a solid foundation. The practical strategies in the rest of this chapter will help you build on that foundation and maintain a healthy faith-family-work balance once you achieve it.

PRACTICAL STRATEGIES FOR ACHIEVING BALANCE IN YOUR LIFE

Once God is first in your life, you are ready to start applying some practical strategies for finding more time in your day and, in turn, achieving a balanced life. But understand that putting God first is an on-going process. It won't happen overnight. There will probably be bumps in the road, and you may sometimes feel like you are moving backward instead of forward. When this happens, don't despair. Just keep applying the methods explained in the previous section in conjunction with those explained in this section and you will soon see progress. Stick with the process and you will eventually

achieve the balance you seek in your life. The following practical strategies will help put more time in your days, so faith, family, and work conflicts are minimized.

Understand: most things take longer to complete than you think they will

This subhead is an old management adage. It is also prophetic for Christian women who are trying to balance faith, family, and work. Because things often take longer to complete than you think they will, it is important to factor this into your planning and scheduling. Practically speaking, this means you should schedule loosely when making appointments and plans. When you develop a schedule for your day, count on things taking longer than you think they will, and plan accordingly.

Turn wasted time into Bible and prayer time

Proverbs 16:27 shows what God thinks about people who waste time. In this verse, He warns that idle hands and idle lips are tools that will be used against you by the devil. How much idle time do you have in your life? Most of us have more idle time in our days than we realize. For example, how long does it take you to drive or commute to and from work every day? How much time do you waste waiting for other people? These are times that can be put to good use reading the Bible or, in the case of driving, listening to the Bible. One of the benefits of technology is it allows you to turn wasted time into productive time. Of course, without any kind of technology or other assistance, you can always turn idle time into prayer time.

A good rule of thumb to follow if you are trying to achieve balance in your life is this: *Never just pass the time—use it.*

Accept that taking more time to climb the career ladder is sometimes the wise choice

Phyllis had a difficult decision to make. She was offered a promotion that would increase her salary by 15 percent and give her a company car to drive. That was the good news. The bad news was the promotion would require even longer hours than she currently worked. It would also require out-of-town travel. Phyllis was torn. On the one hand, she really wanted the promotion. On the other hand, she was already struggling to balance her faith, family, and work. In fact, in the previous several months, she missed her daughter's school play, had to back out of hosting a bridal shower for a friend from church, and missed more family meals than she could remember. As appealing as it was, Phyllis knew the promotion would cause work to intrude even further on her family and faith time.

Phyllis and her husband prayed about the decision. They also met with their pastor to discuss it. In the end, Phyllis made her decision by asking a simple question: "What does God want me to do in this situation?" Then she surprised her boss and coworkers by turning down the promotion. Phyllis explained she was honored by the offer. She wanted the promotion and worked hard to earn it, but it came at the wrong time for her. She would gladly accept such a promotion, once her kids were older and more self-sufficient but, for the time being, they needed her and she needed them. They were still in their formative years, and Phyllis wanted to be present in their lives to guide and nurture them. She wanted to apply the admonition in Proverbs 22:6 that parents should give their children a good start in the right direction. Consequently, Phyllis decided to take a little longer to climb the career ladder.

You work hard to excel in your career. Consequently, for me to suggest it is sometimes wise to turn down a promotion probably sounds strange to you. But, before dismissing this option, think about it. If you are reading this book, achieving a better balance in your life is probably a priority for you. Like many Christian women, you probably find it difficult to juggle the responsibilities of faith, family, and work. Consequently, before accepting a promotion, it

makes sense to consider how it might affect the other aspects of your life. Will the promotion result in less time with your family? Will it intrude on your faith life? Will it be detrimental to your emotional or physical health?

Career success is important and desirable, but it is only one aspect of your life. If you find yourself in the position Phyllis was in, remember this: Making the right decision might mean taking more time to get to the top. But, on the other hand, taking more time to climb the career ladder can make your eventual success more meaningful because you will have built it on a foundation of faith and family.

Phyllis made a difficult decision about a promotion she wanted and deserved. But, in making the decision, she considered how the promotion would affect her family and faith, not just her career. Phyllis is a committed Christian who puts God first in her life. Because of this, she was able to see through the fog of conflicting factors surrounding the decision. Based on her personal circumstances, Phyllis made a good decision for the right reasons. Consequently, I believe God will bless her decision. This is the message in Galatians 6:9. In this verse, we read that those who do the right thing and do not give up will reap "in due season." I believe Phyllis will reap her reward in due season.

Turn off the television, smartphones, computers, and other electronic devices

I wrote part of this chapter on my laptop in a restaurant. While waiting for my meal to be served, I witnessed a heart-breaking scene. Several families were seated at nearby tables. All members of these families were busily pecking away at their smartphones. I did not see one member of these families exchange one word with another member. Engaged in what should have been a pleasant family activity—a good meal in a nice restaurant—there was no interaction among family members, just the robotic, distracted, incessant tapping on smartphones. As I observed this depressing

sight, I thought of Proverbs 11:29, where we are warned that those who bring ruin on their families are in for some rough sledding in the future. I wonder how many of us are allowing technology to rob us of family and faith time.

As a society, we don't seem to be concerned that little of value comes from the time we spend watching television or surfing the Internet. Ask yourself this question: Does watching television or surfing the internet bring you closer to your loved ones or to God? Does your smartphone bring you closer to other people or is it really separating you from them? Has technology turned human interaction into something sterile and distant? I think you know the answer to these questions.

Learning to turn off the television and other electronic devices can be like trying to quit smoking or break some other habit. It can be hard. When talking with counseling clients who cannot bring themselves to press the "off" button, I give them some simple, surprisingly effective advice. Don't go cold turkey. Instead, wean yourself from entertainment technologies. Start by cutting out serialized programs and favorite web sites. The producers of serialized television programs are geniuses at getting you hooked into wondering what is going to happen next, leaving you hanging so you will tune in again next week, and getting you so absorbed in the make-believe lives of the program's characters they become like friends or family members. Many websites and blogs are also adept at getting you hooked so you are lured back on a regular basis.

Once you decide the only television you will watch is non-repetitive, non-serialized programming—such as movies and DVDs on topics of interest and value for the whole family—you will be able to break the television habit in about three months (this is an average—some people require less time and some more). The same holds true when you stop using your laptop, notebook, or smartphone for entertainment as opposed to work. Few things will give you more time in your day for faith and family than kicking your technology habit.

Teach your children to do household chores

Before Marjorie went to work, she was a stay-at-home mother who maintained a pristine household. Her home was a model of organization and efficiency. But, when she began spending her days in the workplace, the household fell into chaos and neglect; at least, that's how Marjorie viewed the situation. When we talked, Marjorie claimed the carpet needed to be vacuumed, the dishwasher was overloaded, laundry was stacked to the ceiling, and she couldn't remember the last time the bathrooms were scrubbed. Marjorie was so stressed over the state of her household she wanted to quit her job, but, as a single mother, that wasn't an option.

When Marjorie was a full-time homemaker, her children were young, and her husband was the sole breadwinner for the family. When her husband walked out on Marjorie and their twin sons, she was forced to get a job. Although she received child support and alimony, they weren't enough to pay the bills. Marjorie had to work. She liked her job but disliked coming home to a disorganized house and a list of chores yet to be completed. Marjorie wanted her household to be like it was before she got a job.

After hearing her out, I asked Marjorie how old her twins were. She told me they were in middle school. My next comment took Marjorie aback: "If your boys are in middle school and the household chores are going undone, shame on you. There is not a chore you have mentioned your boys can't do or shouldn't already be doing." When she protested that her boys didn't know how to vacuum, run the dishwasher, or do the laundry, I asked, "Whose fault is that?"

I made several additional points for Marjorie, all of which apply to any Christian woman who works outside the home. First, your children can do more than you think they can. Second, when it comes to your children doing household chores, don't be a perfectionist. Reverse the advice of James Collins in his groundbreaking book, *Good to Great.* For household chores, forget great and go for good, at least at first. Your children may not do the chores as well as you, but they can learn to do them well enough. Plus, with time and mentoring, they will get better and better. To this day, I can iron

better than anyone I have ever met—man or woman. This is because, from third grade on, my single mother needed me to do that chore to help her earn extra income. Further, we don't use a dishwasher in our home. I am the dishwasher because, from an early age, that was my responsibility, too. Your children are more capable than you think.

One of the most valuable learning experiences your children will ever have is to be given responsibility for some aspect of running the family household. When they come to realize other members of the family are depending on them, your children will learn about responsibility and accountability, two of life's most important lessons. As they learn these lessons, your children will come to appreciate knowing they are contributing to the family in an important way.

If your children balk at helping out around the house, don't become frustrated or angry and don't despair. Remember, you are in charge. You provide their food and shelter and you pay the bills. Do not argue with your children. Give instructions to your children in a positive and affirming manner. Do not yell or threaten. Tell them what you expect using as few words as possible. Further, do this in an attitude of quiet authority. Make it clear you expect to be obeyed, explain the consequences of disobedience, and stick to what you say. Don't expect your children to become obedient overnight. They are sinners, just like you and me, only smaller. This being the case, their natural response to helping out around the house and following rules might be to resist or even rebel. If this happens, be patient, positive, and persistent, but stick to your guns. In the end, you will prevail.

Second, learn to use the most important word in the English language when it comes to raising children: no. Too many parents I deal with are so reluctant to disappoint their children they cannot bring themselves to say, "No." This is unfortunate because the world outside your home is going to say no to your children, and often. Better they learn about the power and importance of this word while still in the home. If you struggle with saying no when "no" is called for, ask yourself if you are trying to be a parent to your children or a friend. The time to be a friend to your children comes later when they are adults and can interact with you on an equal footing. Until then, they need the guidance of a parent who knows what is best for them, not the latitude of a friend.

Third, as mentioned earlier, there must be consequences when your children do not willingly and promptly obey. You must be the enforcer of the consequences. This is the hard part for many parents. We have become a society in which children rule the roost and parents feel powerless because they want to be their children's friends or because they want to *protect* their children from disappointment. But there is a problem with this approach to parenting. Children who do not learn to obey at home are headed down a one-way street to trouble. If they don't learn to obey you, they won't obey their teachers, coaches, police officers, or other authority figures. Worse yet, they won't obey God. Children who disobey legitimate authority figures often find themselves in trouble that can plague them for the rest of their lives. Better they learn about consequences from you than from others who don't love and care about them like you do.

Finally, never forget we are admonished by Scripture to honor our parents (Deuteronomy 5:16). Just as you are expected to honor your parents, your children are expected to honor you. This is something they must learn to do at an early age. It doesn't come naturally to them. They must be taught to honor their parents. And you, the parents, must do the teaching. The best way children can honor their parents is to do what is expected of them promptly, willingly, and with a positive, respectful attitude. Every child can and should learn to do this but learning to honor one's parents is like learning to read; it takes time and effort on the part of the child and the parent. You may have to endure some long faces, tears, and tantrums before your children learn to honor you and your husband. Take it from a former child: if you stay the course and consistently demonstrate you mean business, they will eventually come around.

Other than love, faith, and security, the most important things parents can give their children are responsibility and accountability. We are told in 1 Timothy 3:4 to manage our households well. Part of doing this is making sure our children learn to be responsible. Parents who fail in this duty eventually wind up with offspring who are adults in age but children in temperament and maturity. Children who are not taught to be responsible before they leave home are not likely to be responsible in college, work, marriage, or life.

Maintain a work, family, and faith calendar

I talk with a lot of Christians who maintain work calendars up-to-date by the minute, but who cannot remember family birthdays, anniversaries, ball games, school plays, or church meetings. I know this may sound strange to you, but it is true. My experience with the clients I counsel bears it out. If you don't yet maintain a master calendar that covers not just work, but also family and faith activities, start doing so now. In the age of smartphones, this is a simple enough chore. There is an important point about maintaining a master calendar that must be made here. Once you put a family or faith-related activity on your calendar, guard it as assiduously as you would a work obligation. Don't treat the work events on your calendar as mandatory or the family and faith entries as optional.

Reserve evenings and weekends for family and faith activities

Learn to be just as zealous about guarding evenings and weekends for family and faith activities as you are about guarding Monday through Friday for work. If your job is in retail, hospitality, or some other field requiring evening and weekend work, guard whatever days you have off and use them for family and faith activities. Going into the office on weekends to catch up or get ahead is an easy trap to fall into, but a trap that can turn into a bottomless pit. Once you start using weekends for work obligations, the practice can become habitual. Before long, you will find a practice you consider an exception has become the rule.

Prepare for mornings the night before and enlist your family's help

Christian women who work outside the home often complain about hectic—even chaotic—mornings. Getting ready for work while also trying to prepare breakfast and get the kids off to school is the most stressful part of their day. As I listen to Christian women tell me about their chaotic mornings, I think back to when I was in Marine Corps boot camp. Our mornings began at 5:00 a.m., and they were never chaotic. Why? Because we quickly learned our drill instructors would not tolerate chaos. To avoid the punishment a hectic morning would bring, we learned to get everything ready the night before.

We spent the last thirty minutes or so before lights out shining our boots, laying out our uniforms, and getting our shaving kits in order. When reveille sounded in the morning, we could shower, shave, and dress in less than ten minutes. Of course, things didn't start out this way. The first week or so in boot camp, our mornings were a frenzied mess. Not surprisingly, we paid a price for our lack of preparation. Consequently, we learned quickly to prepare for mornings the night before. From that point on, our mornings were organized, methodical, and efficient. Yours will be, too, when the family learns to work together the night before to prepare for the next day.

A couple of points are important about preparing for mornings. First, don't let mornings be solely your responsibility. Teach your children to lay out their own clothes and expect them to do it. Second, engage them in helping do anything else that can be done the night before (e.g., preparing lunches, getting their school work in order, stuffing their backpacks, etc.). Children are never too young to begin learning what is meant by Proverbs 6:20, where they are told to heed their mother's teaching. Have a plan for breakfast and assign responsibilities ahead of time for cleaning up the table and doing the dishes. Further, have your children bathe the night before rather than in the morning. Not only will these things make mornings less hectic, they will make your children more responsible and less dependent.

Do not take on unnecessary outside activities

When I counsel fellow Christians who are struggling to balance faith, family, and work, it sometimes turns out the root cause of their problem is not work, but too many outside activities. It is not uncommon to find successful Christian women who struggle to achieve a healthy balance have loaded themselves down with extracurricular activities. Sometimes, when they list their outside activities, I just shake my head and think, "No wonder you struggle with balance." Often, these overloaded Christian women suffer from what I call the *nobody-can-do-this-but-me* syndrome.

One example stands out in my mind. Maggie was a busy CPA with two children. She was active in her church, teaching both a weekly Sunday school and a Bible study for teenagers. In addition, she was president of the local chamber of commerce, active in the PTA for her children's school, assistant coach for her daughter's softball team, and head of the booster club for her son's soccer team. I asked Maggie to write down her typical weekly schedule. The result was mind-boggling. What was really interesting, in her case, was Maggie did not see the connection between her outside activities and the struggle to find balance in her life.

There are a lot of women like Maggie. Maybe you are one of them. If so, the best advice I can give you is to make a list of all your outside activities and put each activity on the list to a simple test. For each activity, ask this question: Does this activity bring me closer to God or my family? Chances are this simple test will help you scratch a few activities from your list. It helped Maggie.

Before she could begin whittling down her list of outside activities, Maggie had to come to grips with the hard reality she was not the only person who could do the things on her list. If she stepped down from the PTA, there would be someone to take her place. If she had to choose between teaching Sunday school and conducting a weekly Bible study, someone else would step up and do what was needed. If she served only one term as president of the chamber of commerce, there would be a line of people waiting to take her place.

Once Maggie got over the *nobody-can-do-this-but-me* syndrome, she was able to narrow her list down to teaching a weekly Bible study for teens and completing her one term as president of the chamber of commerce. She retained the Bible study because both her children were in it. She considered the Bible study an important part of their family's faith life. She completed one term as president of the chamber of commerce because it helped her CPA firm network with potential new clients. If Maggie's struggle sounds familiar to you, go through the same process she used to get her outside activities under control, and remember this: You are not the only person who can do the things on your list of extracurricular activities.

Accept that you don't have to do everything

An unchanging rule of thumb in the workplace is this: Work gravitates to those who get it done. Those who can be depended on to complete important projects right, on time, and within budget typically excel in their careers. This is the good news. The bad news is, as a result of their proficiency, every important project or vexing problem that comes along winds up on their desk. People who can be counted on to do a good job and meet deadlines seldom suffer from a shortage of work. As a result, high-performing individuals often find themselves overloaded.

Before long, they are spending nights and weekends working while everyone else is enjoying time with their families. Because they are trying to excel, high performers don't want to say "no." They like being the *go-to person* for the boss. Does this sound familiar to you? If it does, you might be taking on too much. High performers who take on too much work seldom achieve a healthy faith, family, and work balance. If you are one of these, learn how to tactfully, selectively, and wisely say "no."

If you struggle with balancing faith, family, and work, remember this: *You don't have to do everything.* When you are already fully loaded and your boss wants to give you more work, saying "no" can be a life saver. But it can also be career poison if done improperly.

Consequently, it is important to learn how to say "no" in positive, productive, and helpful ways. You don't want to sound whiny or as if you lack commitment. Practice using the following types of responses for saying "no" when you are overloaded:

- I would love to take on this project but, if I do, the one I am working on now is going to fall behind schedule, and it is important to you.

- My teammate Linda really wants to show what she can do. This would be an ideal project to let her learn on. We need more go-to team members who can take on these emergency assignments for you. Why not give this one to Linda and let me monitor to make sure she gets it done right?

Accept that more is not always better

It is only natural for people who work to want to enjoy the benefits of their labor. There is nothing wrong with this unless you go overboard and find yourself on the *more-is-better treadmill*. Sure, it would be nice to have a bigger house, nicer car, more money, and other material amenities, but, once your focus becomes material acquisition, your appetite for more can be insatiable. It is easy to get caught up in amassing material wealth and lose sight of the message in Matthew 6:19–21. In these verses, we are cautioned against amassing material wealth because where our treasures are our hearts will be. Few things will undermine your faith, family, and work balance faster than an insatiable appetite for earthly treasures.

The strategies recommended in this section, though comprehensive, are not exhaustive. I am sure there are plenty of other things you can do to make more efficient and effective use of your time; however, I have recommended only those strategies used with good results by Christian women I have counseled or worked with. Consequently, I know these strategies will be helpful. Not all the strategies recommended in this section apply in all cases. Although Christian women in the workplace share many common challenges, you and your sisters in Christ are individuals who live and work in different circumstances. Therefore, choose the strategies that apply most directly to your life from among those I have recommended and ignore any that do not apply.

PRAYER FOR BALANCING FAITH, FAMILY, AND WORK

Father in Heaven,

I thank You and praise You. I can come to You with every concern weighing on my heart. I know You see me, and You already know the situations I face each day. I thank You for continually demonstrating Your love for me in wondrous ways. You have blessed me with a great family, a supportive faith community, and with a job I enjoy.

Father, I come before You today to ask You to help me find the balance in all the activities of my life. I pray for the peace that fills my soul and that what I do brings glory to You. I ask You to help me put You first in every circumstance. Help me always commit my heart and mind to Your guidance and to listen for Your voice throughout the day.

Lord, there are times, I confess, when I know I leave You out of the equation. I focus too much on the responsibilities I have at work. I get caught up in the moment and time runs away. I am grateful for my job, but I don't want my job to run my life. I want You to be the CEO of all I am and all I ever hope to be.

I remember reading a quote once that said, "God could not be everywhere, so He created mothers." The fact is, You can be everywhere, but I can't. Help me, Lord, be a dedicated mother and wife. Help me continually advocate for all those things that nurture the heart of

my family. Bless each member of my household and grant me grace when I don't manage to spend enough time with each of them.

Lord, there will be a lot of things heaped on my plate in the next few weeks. I ask You to remind me to keep my eyes focused on You, so I achieve a healthy balance of time for the things that truly matter: my faith in You, my love for my family, and my sense of responsibility toward my career.

I pray, Lord, You build my faith, inspire my heart, and help me honor You and all my commitments. Give me awareness of any time I am letting matters of work and home get out of the balance You have designed for me. I place each day of my life in Your merciful and tender hands. Amen.

GROUP DISCUSSION CASE: "If things don't change, I am going to have a nervous breakdown."

Wanjika could do it all, or so her friends and coworkers thought. She had a husband and three children, a good job as the branch manager of a bank, and an important volunteer position in her church. She was the church's coordinator of special projects. Wanjika kept a spotless house, served nutritious meals, attended PTA meetings, raised money for band and sports programs at her children's schools, was active in the chamber of commerce, made sure her church's various charity projects ran efficiently, attended school plays, helped coach her youngest daughter's tennis team, and made sure her branch was the most efficiently run branch in the bank's system.

Her friends and coworkers marveled at Wanjika's energy, stamina, and ability to multi-task. What they didn't know was this image was just a façade. Wanjika was paying a price for her I-can-do-it-all approach to life. Her children felt neglected, family Bible reading and devotionals were a rare occurrence, and she had become a tyrant at work. Wanjika was developing an ulcer and losing weight she didn't need to lose. Further, her frayed nerves were almost shot. When she sought counseling, the first thing she said was, "If things don't change, I am going to have a nervous breakdown."

Discussion Questions:

1. Have you ever known someone like Wanjika who appeared able to do it all, only to learn she couldn't? What were the circumstances?

2. If Wanjika was your friend and asked for help, what recommendations would you make for getting her life in balance?

REVIEW QUESTIONS FOR INDIVIDUALS AND GROUPS

1. What are some of the challenges often faced by Christian women in trying to balance their faith, families, and work? What challenges have you faced personally in trying to establish balance in your life?

2. Have you ever put off Bible reading, prayer, or time with your family to deal with work matters? If so, how often does this happen? Does ignoring your faith life really help you gain better balance in the other aspects of your life?

3. If your life is already overcrowded, how will putting God first help bring balance to it?

4. What does it mean to make a "commitment" to putting God first in your life?

5. How can you use the time you spend at work to give glory to God?

6. Contrast these two approaches to life: a) Trying to be self-sufficient in meeting all your obligations, and 2) Putting your trust in Christ in all aspects of your life. Which of these approaches is more likely to encourage a balanced lifestyle in the long run and why?

7. Why is prayer so important to Christian women who want to put God first in their lives?

8. Why is it so important for Christian women who want to put God first in their lives to read the Bible constantly?

9. List several practical strategies for making more efficient use of your time and explain how you might apply them in your life.

CHAPTER 4

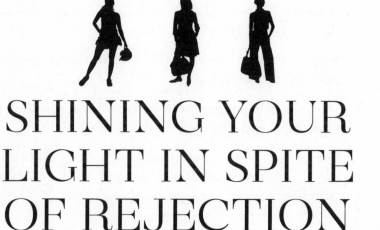

SHINING YOUR LIGHT IN SPITE OF REJECTION AND OPPOSITION

. . . .

"In the same way, let your light shine before others, so that they may see your good works and give glory to your Father who is in heaven." Matthew 5:16

The workplace can be a pressure-packed, competitive environment. Excelling in a career can be a challenge under the best circumstances, but, when working with colleagues who reject your faith, it can be especially difficult. In today's secular work environment, you will need the "Three Ps": persistence, perseverance, and prayer. Your faith can make it hard to fit in when working with colleagues who reject Christianity or are ambivalent about it. Fitting in is often a problem for Christian women who work outside the home. It is not always easy to win the trust, confidence, and cooperation of coworkers

74

whose values and corresponding assumptions about work and life are different than yours.

It is only natural to want to fit in with your coworkers. After all, humans are social beings. This is why people join clubs and other organizations where there is common ground among the members. It is also one of the benefits of being a member of a church family. There is comfort and security in the fellowship of people who share the same values. Although there are hermits in the world, they are exceptions. Most of us are not recluses. Because of this, being out of step with your coworkers can be a burden. In addition, there is a practical side to fitting in at work. Generally speaking, it is good for your career to fit in with your coworkers. In most jobs, there is an expectation of teamwork, and "fit" is important when working in a team. People who don't fit in with their teammates are sometimes viewed as poor team players. This kind of reputation can be detrimental to your career.

Because performance appraisals often include a criterion that asks whether the individual being rated is a good team player, some Christian women choose to hide their faith or, at the very least, downplay it to ensure it doesn't become an issue with teammates. Others choose this route simply because they don't want to be left out or feel like an outsider. While choosing to downplay or hide your faith is understandable from a human perspective, it is not a good idea from a Christian perspective. Hiding or downplaying your faith on the job might help you fit in better with coworkers but doing so has a downside. You cannot show your coworkers the image of Christ if you hide your faith from them. Further, it is more important you fit in with Christ than with your coworkers.

In an era when secular humanism and political correctness are the new normal in the workplace, it is more important than ever to shine the light of Christ in the example you set. Recall what is written in Matthew 5:14–16. These verses refer to believers as lights shining for others to see. Matthew 5:16 makes clear we are supposed to shine our lights before others, so they see our good works. This, of course, is an admonition to set a good example for others, a Christ-like

75

example. But shining your light for others at work can be difficult. Sometimes there is a price to pay.

In Matthew 5:11 we are cautioned that shining our lights when surrounded by the darkness of unbelief might result in rejection and opposition. You should expect this but shine your light anyway. Christ wanted us to understand that following the path He has set for us will not be easy and we shouldn't expect it to be. This is why He warned His Apostles in Matthew 10:16 that they were being sent out like sheep among wolves. Hence, they would need to be both wise and innocent. You may feel like a sheep among wolves at times. When you do, shine your light anyway.

If you encounter opposition to your faith, remember you are not the first Christian, nor will you be the last, to have this experience. The Bible is replete with stories of Christians being rejected, abused, and even persecuted because of their faith. This may happen to you from time to time and enduring it won't be easy. But, when it happens, remember you are in good company, company including Christ and His Apostles. Better to fit in with Christ than with coworkers who reject Him.

Mary Jo loved almost everything about her job teaching Humanities at the local community college. In fact, the only thing she didn't like was the attitude of her colleagues in the Humanities Department toward Christianity. It seemed her colleagues were open to every religion in the world except hers. The Humanities courses she taught covered art, music, and religion. But the only religions listed in the course syllabus she was required to use were Buddhism, Islam, Hinduism, secularism, agnosticism, and atheism. Christianity was not even mentioned. When she asked her department chairman about including Christianity, Mary Jo could tell she raised a touchy subject.

When Mary Jo asked other faculty members in the department why Christianity was excluded from the Humanities course, they hemmed, hawed, and changed the subject. But she persisted. When she asked how refusing to include the world's largest religion squared with either reality or academic integrity, they suggested she drop the

subject. Mary Jo remembered thinking the Humanities Department should post a sign at the entrance to its classroom building that read "Christianity Not Welcomed Here."

She learned her department chairman, a former minister, was the source of the antagonism toward Christianity in the department. Mary Jo did not know what soured this man on the Christian faith, nor could she find out. Instead, her fellow professors pointedly reminded Mary Jo she would need the department chairman's support when she applied for tenure. This was their not-so-subtle way of telling Mary Jo to back off and drop the subject. She found the negative attitudes toward Christianity in her department disheartening.

As time went by, Mary Jo felt more and more like a sheep among wolves. She was a committed Christian who wanted to incorporate her faith into all aspects of her life. But, like so many Christian women in the workplace, Mary Jo learned that openly professing her faith could have negative consequences when working with people who reject it. As mentioned earlier, this fact sometimes leads Christian women to hide their faith from coworkers or, at the very least, downplay it.

Both approaches—hiding or downplaying your faith—are mistakes because they are exactly what Satan wants you to do. Never forget Satan is a predator, you are his prey, and the workplace is one of his favorite hunting grounds. On the other hand, you don't have to become one of his victims. You can remain faithful to Christ when working with wolves. You can even shine your light for them. Further, you can excel at work while doing both.

WHY IT CAN BE DIFFICULT TO SHINE YOUR LIGHT IN THE WORKPLACE

Some Christian women I talk with find it difficult to shine their lights among coworkers who reject their faith. Not fitting in with coworkers is just one factor that can make it difficult. Equally problematic are the challenges of risking confrontations with unbelievers, trying to build positive relationships with coworkers

77

who don't know Christ and don't want to, and overcoming the kinds of temptations tugging at us every day on the job.

Let me begin with the issue of risking confrontations with coworkers who reject Christ. I have counseled Christian women who admit to downplaying their faith at work to avoid disagreements with unbelieving coworkers. I have been told many times by women who do this they just want to be able to do their jobs without "the hassle" of faith-related disagreements. It is easier for them to hide their faith than to deal with the slings and arrows of those who reject it.

I certainly understand the feelings of women who choose this route. I have felt like hiding my faith many times. When this happens, I quickly call to mind Christ's admonition in Matthew 5:15. In this verse, Christ reminds us to shine our lights rather than hide them under a basket. He wants us to set a Christ-like example for others, no matter how inconvenient or frustrating that might be. Let me stress here, as I do throughout this book, that obeying Christ's admonition in Matthew 5:15 does not mean pulling coworkers away from their jobs so you can verbally evangelize.

Verbally enlightening unbelievers on the lessons of Scripture is an important obligation of Christians, but there is an appropriate time for doing this. That time is not while they are supposed to be working. The best way to demonstrate the lessons of Scripture during work hours is to do just that: demonstrate them. Reflect the image of Christ in how you do your work, treat customers, interact with coworkers, make decisions, solve problems, and persevere in times of adversity. During the workday, let your example be a Scripture lesson for coworkers. Do this consistently over time and you may find yourself asked to share Scripture with coworkers during lunch or after work. This is the appropriate way to evangelize at work.

If you find yourself hoping to avoid faith-related confrontation and opposition, don't despair. It is only natural, at least for most people. Few people relish verbal combat or enjoy feeling out of place among people we spend a lot of time with, people such as coworkers. Further, trying to find common ground with coworkers whose worldviews differ from yours is not easy. This is one of the

reasons Christian women who work outside the home should spend time with fellow believers who are caring, supportive, and able to reinforce their beliefs. The time you spend with fellow believers will help you rebuild what unbelieving coworkers tear down.

Whether your support group consists of your church family, a prayer-breakfast group, a Bible-study class, or other Christian women who get together at lunch, it is important to regularly *gas up* among fellow believers. Christian women who don't have some sort of support group are more likely to give up the fight and quietly hide their faith under a basket (Matthew 5:15). The more often you fill your tank with the love, caring, and support of fellow believers, the better. Doing so will help you cope with the faith-related frustrations attending work among people whose worldviews are at odds with Scripture. It is impossible to give to others when you are running on empty yourself.

Then there is the problem of the woman in the mirror. This may be the most difficult problem you face in trying to shine your light in the workplace. Even though you are saved, the person you see in the mirror every morning is still a sinner. This means you will always be tempted to please your coworkers instead of pleasing Christ. It also means you are susceptible to other workplace temptations such as hubris, ego, envy, greed, power-seeking, the desire for status, and misguided ambition, to name just a few. These sins can manifest themselves in behaviors the opposite of shining your light for coworkers.

Temptation can lead even the most committed Christians astray, and the workplace teems with temptations of all kinds. For example, there is the ever-present temptation to give in to pressure from coworkers or superiors to do things that would compromise your faith. Standing firm in your faith against peer pressure can make you an outcast among your coworkers. Standing firm against the unethical demands of superiors can threaten your job security or career advancement. Shining your light in the midst of coworkers who reject your faith will never be easy, but it can be done, and you can do it.

You can excel at work without compromising your faith. You can shine the light of Christ when working with people who reject Him. Doing so might require sacrifices on your part. You might have to sacrifice the comfort of fitting in with your peers or the supposed benefits that come from going along to get along. You might even have to endure threats to your job security. Don't be surprised when these things happen. The Bible warns us over and over that following Christ will require sacrifice. When you find yourself in uncomfortable situations because of your faith, consider what I tell Christians who approach me for counseling: It is better to suffer in the short run for standing firm in the faith than to suffer in eternity for compromising your faith.

Romans 12:1 makes clear we are to offer ourselves as living sacrifices to God. Consequently, as Christians, we must be prepared for the sacrifices shining our lights in the workplace might demand. This can be a frightening prospect; however, it doesn't have to be. In Psalm 1:5–6, we read the wicked will be called to account. These verses allude, no doubt, to the ultimate fate of the wicked, not necessarily their worldly fate. Bad actors don't always get what they deserve on earth. But, on the other hand, they often do. Therefore, you and I need to accept that the end of the story for unethical coworkers is written by God, not us. As Christians, our challenge is to shine the light of Christ among our coworkers, even when doing so requires sacrifice, and let God sort out when the wicked will be called to account.

The strategies provided in this book for helping you excel at work without compromising your faith all come from Scripture. In keeping with Christ's admonition in Matthew 10:16, they are Biblically sound (innocent) and workplace appropriate (wise). Further, the strategies presented herein have been tested in the workplace. They have been effective in helping Christian women face the kinds of challenges you may be facing in your job; however, before getting into specific strategies for specific situations, you have a decision to make, a decision alluded to throughout this chapter. In responding to the faith-related challenges you have to cope with at work, are you going

to downplay your faith in an attempt to fit in or set an example that reflects the image of Christ in all you do? Answering this simple but profound question is half the battle for Christian women who sometimes feel like sheep working among wolves.

RESPONDING TO FAITH-RELATED CHALLENGES

The message in Matthew 5:11–16 might be summarized as follows: Be a visible Christian by setting a Christ-like example that glorifies God. But a caution is in order here. Being forthright about your faith does not mean you should spend your time at work berating or condemning coworkers for their inappropriate behavior. Embarrassing coworkers in front of their peers is not likely to lead them to Christ or help you excel at work.

I am not making light of Christians who are vocal about their beliefs. After all, in Philippians 4:9 Christ tells us we are to practice the things we have learned from Him. As Christians, we are supposed to confront and reject sin wherever it occurs, including the workplace. But how we go about confronting and rejecting sin does matter, especially on the job. In those instances when a verbal rebuke is called for, do it in private. The leadership maxim about praising in public and chastising in private is good advice when it becomes necessary to speak up against inappropriate behavior in the workplace.

Tact and consideration are important when responding to faith-related challenges, even when the challenges come from tactless, inconsiderate coworkers. Tact can be thought of as making your point without making an enemy. When we interact with unbelievers, Christ wants us to view them as opportunities, not enemies. He wants us to uphold what Scripture teaches, but He also wants us to drive in the nail without breaking the board. Unbelieving coworkers are more likely to be influenced for good by your example of a measured response that demonstrates kindness and caring than by accusatory tirades or finger-pointing condemnations. People are seldom argued or shamed into the arms of Christ, but they can be led there by a good example.

Responding to faith-related challenges in ways pleasing to Christ is more likely to bear fruit than a display of righteous anger. Granted, Christ displayed righteous anger when he threw the moneychangers out of the Temple, and there are instances in which righteous anger is appropriate. Nevertheless, I advise Christians to avoid displays of righteous anger in the workplace for two reasons. First, the workplace is not the Temple. Second, even as Christians, our tempers can get the better of us. When this happens, what we think of as righteous anger may just be an intemperate outburst by a Christian who has lost control of her temper.

Every time we respond to faith-related challenges in the workplace, we have an opportunity to show unbelieving coworkers an example of why God's way is a better way. Further, responding in ways consistent with what the Bible teaches sends a powerful message to those who have not read God's Word. A Christ-like example is an appropriate response in any setting. Like many employers, your employer may have adopted policies against open displays of Christianity on the job. Whether or not these types of policies will stand up to serious challenges in court is doubtful. But let's leave that issue aside for the moment. For now, remember this: Employers are not likely to adopt policies forbidding good examples, and there is no better example than one reflecting the image of Christ.

There is also a practical reason for setting a Christ-like example in how you respond to the unacceptable behavior of coworkers. Christian women who consistently set this kind of example are more likely to be approached by coworkers who need help dealing with their own difficulties at work. Coworkers who observe you handling problems in a Christ-like manner will want to know how you are able to do this, particularly those who become discouraged when facing adversity because they have no foundation to stand on. When you are approached for advice by coworkers who are undergoing their own on-the-job problems, your Christ-like example has opened a door. When this happens, be prepared to share your faith openly and with enthusiasm.

When you feel like a sheep among wolves, it is easy to go into survival mode. But, as Christians, we are called to do more than just hunker down and survive. We are expected to occupy. In Luke 19:13, Christ told his followers they were to claim the world as His until He comes, even if this requires not fitting in with those who reject Him. The best way to do your part in claiming the world for Christ, at least on the job, is to set an example that reflects His image for your coworkers.

As Christians, we are called to show our coworkers the way of Christ. In the workplace, this translates into consistently setting a Christ-like example in how we do our jobs, treat coworkers, interact with customers, solve problems, face adversity, bear burdens, and make decisions. This contention has been stated before and is repeated throughout this book because its importance cannot be overstated. Typically, people will follow actions more readily than words. When coworkers begin to follow your example, you have made good progress in leading them to Christ.

The next step is to share the Gospel with them. But remember my rule of thumb about timing: Don't use your employer's time to evangelize, other than by example. Instead, spend your work hours doing what you are paid to do. Christian women who spend their time on the job vocally evangelizing while neglecting their work set the wrong example for coworkers who, if shown a better example, might see the light. When a coworker expresses interest or asks questions, use words. But do this after work and during lunch breaks.

YOUR ATTITUDE IS A CHOICE AND MAKING THE RIGHT CHOICE IS IMPORTANT

Part of being a visible Christian is maintaining the kind of attitude that should come with being a child of God: a positive attitude. It is always disconcerting for me to see someone who professes Christ going through the day irritably grumbling or dejectedly moping. As Christians, our attitudes should lift others and give them hope.

Unfortunately, some Christians respond to the challenges of the workplace by developing negative attitudes.

Sybil did this. She saw the world through eyes clouded by negativity. If you gave Sybil a bag of gold, she would complain it was too heavy. Her negative attitude colored her outlook on work and rubbed off on her coworkers. Sybil was a Christian, but you wouldn't know it from observing her attitude. Her attitude not only dampened her outlook on life, it undermined her effectiveness at work. Her ineffectiveness, in turn, undercut her career potential. Never forget: A prerequisite for excelling at work and projecting a Christ-like image is maintaining a positive attitude.

HOW TO RECOGNIZE A POSITIVE ATTITUDE

Your attitude is an internal phenomenon revealing itself in external actions. People with positive attitudes can be vastly different from each other, but they share a number of things in common. Their common ground can be found in how they approach work as well as life in general. Christian women with positive attitudes approach their jobs and lives in helpful and productive ways. In all situations and circumstances, they do the following:

- Focus on the positive rather than the negative

- Expect a positive outcome even in difficult situations

- Associate with other positive people when they have a choice

- Concentrate on solutions rather than problems

- Turn mistakes into learning opportunities

- Take a *can-do* approach to new challenges

- Take the initiative in ambiguous situations rather than waiting to be told what to do

- Take a proactive approach to work and life

- Learn from the successes, mistakes, and failures of others

- Remain calm and in control when the workplace becomes hectic

Maintaining a positive attitude is like staying on a diet; you have to exercise willpower and work at it. Even with this, you will occasionally fail. Just as you will sometimes give in and have a donut you shouldn't eat, you will occasionally give in to negativity. When you feel this happening, think of the message in Philippians 2:14–15, where we are told to avoid being grouchy and negative, particularly among unbelievers who need to see us shining the light of Christ. You might also think of Proverbs 17:22, where we are told a happy heart is good medicine. In today's hectic, fast-paced, and competitive workplace, a positive attitude can be just what the doctor ordered for you and your coworkers.

PICKING YOUR ATTITUDE UP WHEN IT FALLS DOWN

Even the most committed Christians will occasionally give in to negativity. The stress of working among unbelievers coupled with the day-to-day pressures of your job can seem overwhelming. This can happen to even the most consistently positive people, so don't despair if it happens to you. Better yet, just accept this probably will happen to you from time to time. When it does, apply the following strategies. They will help you press the *reset button* and get your attitude back on track.

- *Help someone else whose attitude is slumping.* As a youngster, did you ever play softball? There is a coaching technique used to help young batters who are in a hitting slump. It works like this: Require the slumping batter to help another player who is having trouble hitting the ball. As odd as this may sound, one of the best ways to help a slumping batter improve is to have her help another batter. You can use the same technique to get your attitude back on track when you go into an attitudinal slump. As you help someone else improve her attitude, you will find yours improving at the same time. It is difficult to avoid taking the advice you give others. In addition, when you help someone else whose attitude has taken a nosedive, you often find her problems are worse than yours. At the very least, you will find you are not the only person with problems. In either case, the revelation will provide a boost to your attitude.

- *Focus on the good in others, not the bad.* The easiest thing in the world to see is the bad in others. The easiest thing to do is to focus on what they are doing wrong. When you find yourself seeing only shortcomings in your coworkers, call to mind Matthew 7:5, where we are told to take the log out of our own eye before we condemn others for the specks in theirs. In other words, before you get agitated about the behavior of your coworkers, stop and look in the mirror. Are you guilty of the same things that make you angry when coworkers do them? Are you responding in kind to their poor behavior? Are you making the mistake of expecting everyone to do things the way you do them? Even if you are not guilty of these things, it is better to try to find something good about your coworkers. This is the message in Ephesians 4:23, where we are told to allow the Holy Spirit to enter us and rejuvenate our attitudes.

- *Be thankful you have a job—some people don't.* When you find your attitude slipping because of job-related frustrations, think about the many unemployed people who would love to have your job, frustrations and all. I had this lesson driven home in stark terms years ago. An individual who worked with me at the time had the worst attitude toward her job of any individual I ever knew. She complained about everything. Her attitude was so bad it affected her coworkers. Nobody wanted to work with her. Having counseled this grumpy employee about her attitude numerous times with no discernible results, our supervisor was contemplating firing her. But, before that happened, she walked into his office one day and quit on the spot. Our supervisor cautioned her about resigning before securing another job, but she just brushed him off. Her response was direct and to the point. She said, "I would rather be unemployed than work here one more day." About a year later, our supervisor received a telephone call from her. The story she told was heartbreaking. Since leaving her job with our organization, she was unable to find another. Although she was a highly qualified drafting technician, nobody wanted to hire her because of her abrupt departure and the reluctance of others to recommend her. During that heart-wrenching telephone call, she told her former supervisor she would gladly accept a job in a fast-food restaurant if she could get one. The harsh realities of being unemployed transformed her attitude toward work and the people she worked with. Hearing this, my supervisor took a chance and re-hired her. This turned out to be a good decision. When she returned, this once obstinate grouch exhibited an attitude toward her work that was positive, productive, and helpful. An added benefit was her positive attitude bolstered the attitudes of her coworkers and teammates. If you ever find your attitude toward work or your coworkers slipping, think of this transformed employee and learn from her example. When it seems that you cannot be thankful about any aspect of your job, be thankful you have a job. Some people don't.

Doing the things recommended in this section will help you overcome the negative feelings that can slip up on you from time to time. You can also recommend these strategies to coworkers who need an attitude adjustment. If you can influence the attitudes of your coworkers for the better, it will enhance your career prospects while also helping you serve Christ.

PRAYER FOR SHINING YOUR LIGHT IN SPITE OF OPPOSITION

Dear Lord,

Some days I'm frustrated with how difficult it is to simply be myself when I'm at work. I appreciate the people I work with and I am certain most of them are just like me, trying to do a good job and do their best with life. At the day's end, they go home and hope to live meaningful lives with the people they love. I see that, but I also know I have a life view that doesn't really fit with their expectations. I know I am not just equipped to do a good job, but I've been equipped to do a good job for You as well.

I struggle to be your example, to shine a light for Your glory. I know, on occasion, I even hide my light under a bushel, as it says in Scripture. I don't want to be an invisible Christian, but I don't want to be a pushy one either. I need your help to persevere in my work and do it well and yet persist in my faith and in my belief in prayer. I need your help, Lord, to be a gracious example so I am diligent and cooperative with the members of my team, but also open to Your leading to shine Your light in a specific way.

I thank You for those friends who make it possible for me to share my faith when I'm at work and for those who give me support and wisdom. I know the people in my church and in my small group help me sustain my desire to be true to my faith. It seems funny to live in a culture where almost any belief is okay, except when our faith is in Jesus and in You. I'm saddened by the efforts made to keep people from praying together or from being able to shine the light of Your grace and mercy on others.

Today, Lord, I pray for women everywhere who may feel like they don't quite fit into their workplace environment, or who feel blatantly rejected because of their faith. Please strengthen all of us in our workplaces. Bless my spirit and my resolve to be Your humble servant when I'm at work and anywhere I may be. Help me reflect Your light in ways that may draw others to want to know more of You. I praise You for your generosity and support, for, in You, there is no opposition at all. Amen.

GROUP DISCUSSION: "Leave Your Christianity at Home..."

Marva was torn. Her supervisor was adamant that employees in her department "leave their religion at home" when they come to work. Just three months earlier, a disagreement between two employees of different religions turned into an epic feud. As a result, employees took sides and spent most of their time on the job arguing about their differing religious beliefs. Consequently, productivity in the department declined noticeably.

Neither of the employees in question subscribed to Christianity. One was Muslim and the other Hindu. In spite of this, the supervisor seemed to be aiming her leave-your-religion-at-home remarks at Marva, a Christian. Marva couldn't understand why she was being singled out when the two employees who started the feud weren't even Christians. To Marva, it appeared when the supervisor told employees to leave their religion at home, what she really meant was leave your Christianity at home.

Marva was told to stop saying "God bless you" to coworkers and to remove a Bible she normally kept on top of her desk. She felt like her supervisor, a vocal humanist, was using the religious feud between a Muslim and a Hindu as an excuse to attack her Christianity. She never made a secret of her faith; however, with the pressure being applied by her supervisor, she wondered if being less forthcoming about her beliefs might be smart. Maybe it would be better to just keep her Christianity to herself. Maybe she would be smart to comply with her supervisor's demand and leave her religion at home.

Discussion Questions:

1. Have you ever faced overt attempts to suppress your Christianity at work? If so, what were the circumstances?

2. If Marva came to you seeking wise counsel, how would you recommend she handle this situation? Should she become a covert Christian or is there a better approach?

REVIEW QUESTIONS FOR INDIVIDUALS AND GROUPS

1. What are some of the pressures in the workplace that might lead women to be covert Christians?

2. Have you ever worked with someone and been surprised to learn later he or she is a believer? How did this make you feel about the individual in question?

3. Are there any consistent Christians in your workplace? How do they *let their light shine*? How do others in the workplace respond to these Christians?

4. Have you ever been pressured by coworkers to join them in sinful endeavors? How did you respond?

5. Have you ever felt pressured by a superior to do something that violates your conscience? How did you respond?

6. Does your organization have corporate policies discouraging open displays of Christianity on the job?

7. Does your organization have a corporate ethics statement or a statement of core values? If so, what principles are covered by these statements? Can these principles be traced back to Scripture?

8.   Has your job security ever been jeopardized because of your Christian beliefs? If so, how?

9.   Have you ever had to be "wise as serpents" when responding to pressure from coworkers or superiors to act inappropriately? Explain.

10. What is the biggest challenge you have had to face in trying to be a consistent Christian in the workplace?

11. Have you ever struggled with maintaining a positive attitude when in the midst of coworkers who reject your faith?

12. If a friend asked you how to go about maintaining a positive attitude at work, what advice would you give her?

13. If you find your attitude slipping and becoming negative, what can you do to turn this situation around?

CHAPTER 5

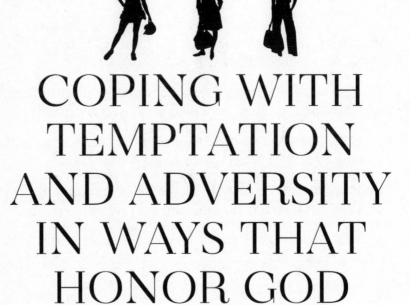

COPING WITH TEMPTATION AND ADVERSITY IN WAYS THAT HONOR GOD

· ·

"Watch and pray that you may not enter into
temptation. The spirit is indeed willing, but the flesh is
weak." Matthew 26:41

It can be difficult to cope with work-related temptation and adversity without compromising your faith. This is why Nina was struggling. When it came to temptation, it wasn't her unbelieving coworkers Nina worried about. It was the woman in the mirror. Every day, Nina faced a specific temptation luring her closer and closer to compromising her faith. She was a committed Christian, but Nina wasn't sure she could persist in standing up to the temptation she faced at work, at least not this particular temptation.

In college, Nina was a highly rated athlete. In fact, had it not been for an injury, making the Olympic team was a real possibility for her. The injury ended any hopes she had of Olympic glory. The sudden end to her athletic career was a major disappointment to Nina, but it did nothing to dampen her competitive spirit. Nina liked to compete, and she liked to win. To her delight, she found her new job to be as competitive in nature as any race she ever ran. As soon as she started working, Nina knew she found a new venue for indulging her love of competition. She also knew she could win in this new environment, provided she was willing to do what was required. But doing what was required bothered her.

Nina was recently hired by her alma mater as a recruiter for its female athletic teams. In her new position, Nina competed against recruiters from other top-flight universities nationwide. To win the competition against other recruiters, Nina needed to convince the highest-rated young athletes in the country to accept scholarships to her university. This is where the temptation she was struggling with came into play. The high school athletes Nina needed to recruit were well-schooled in how to demand the most in scholarship dollars, perquisites, and other benefits from the institutions wanting them. They knew their own value and were coached concerning how to make the most of it.

The problem was Nina and the recruiters she had to compete against were supposed to operate within strict guidelines, and there were penalties for recruiters caught in violation, some of them severe. Nevertheless, stretching the rules was common practice among her fellow recruiters. In fact, some did more than just stretch the rules, they blatantly broke them. After losing several outstanding prospects to recruiters who played fast and loose with the rules, Nina was beginning to wonder if she could compete without adopting their unethical methods.

If she didn't bend or even break the rules, her fellow recruiters would land all the best prospects and Nina would be left with nothing

but second-tier athletes. This simply would not do. Nina did not like to lose. Furthermore, doing well in her new job was important for practical reasons, too. Having gone into debt to purchase a new house in an upscale neighborhood, she had a substantial mortgage to pay every month. Consequently, the temptation to cross the line into unethical conduct was becoming almost unbearable for her.

Like Nina, many Christian women find the workplace to be a constant source of temptation. No surprise there. Temptation began in the Garden of Eden and has been one of Satan's favorite tools since. God knew His children would be tempted every day and He knew we would be susceptible to the devil's devious scheming. This is why the Bible contains so many warnings about temptation. Nobody is immune to the seductive lure of temptation. Even the most committed Christians can trip up and be led astray by temptations, at work and elsewhere.

We are all tempted to indulge in sinful behaviors such as greed, lust, and envy. We are also susceptible to the sin of worshiping false gods such as money, status, and power. Temptations such as these and others can cause even the most committed Christians to go astray. When we give in to temptation, bad choices usually follow, and these choices can lead to destructive behavior. For example, you might know of Christian women who have ruined their marriages, careers, or even lives by giving in to the seductive tug of workplace temptations. I have known several. Some of the most memorable but sad days in my career occurred when fellow believers weakened and allowed themselves to be overcome by temptation in the workplace.

A friend told me about a day she will never forget: the day two police officers walked into her office with a warrant to arrest an employee she considered one of her best and most dependable. This employee was overcome by the temptation to get out of debt by pilfering cash from the company's business office. She got away with it for a while but, when a routine audit found her out, the police were called in. The amount stolen was enough to send this misguided employee to prison for a brief time, followed by several years of probation. My friend said it broke her heart to see an employee she trusted led away in handcuffs by the police.

Temptation is and has always been a source of adversity for Christian women in the workplace. But temptation is not the only source of adversity you will face at work. In fact, the workplace can be a virtual factory for producing adversity. Think for a moment about the problems you have seen in the workplace caused by job-security concerns, competition for promotions and raises, misguided ambition, the self-centered nature of people, unforgiving deadlines, bullies, unrelenting pressure to perform, undependable suppliers, the personality quirks of coworkers, demanding customers, and the unpredictable nature of the economy, to name just a few. I have seen these and other factors introduce adversity into the lives of good people who crumbled under the weight of it.

Of course, Christian women have no monopoly on workplace adversity. Everybody at work faces problems, trials, challenges, and dilemmas. But, as a Christian woman, you face an added element of difficulty in trying to cope with adversity. Not only do you need to cope personally, you are called to do so in ways that reflect the image of Christ. Women who are unbelievers can cope with adversity in self-serving ways, but Christian women are called to respond in better ways, God-honoring ways. Often the methods self-serving people use are hurtful to others and even destructive.

Some people respond to adversity by seeking solace in a liquor bottle or through drugs. Some pull back into a shell in an attempt to hide from the world, including family and friends. Some indulge in self-pity and wonder, "Why me?" Others become angry and lash out. As a Christian woman, you are called to avoid these kinds of counterproductive responses, no matter how tempting they might seem to you in the moment. As with all other aspects of our jobs and lives, as Christians, we are called to respond in ways that reflect the image of Christ. This means you are to do more than just bear your burdens in a positive manner. You are also to set an example that gives others hope and helps others bear their burdens.

For this reason, it is important for you to be prepared to confront temptation as well as other sources of adversity in your job, and not just once in a while. At work, temptation and the various other sources of adversity, if not the rule, are certainly common. They are always present. Further, the higher you go in your profession, the more often you will face adversity and the more difficult the problems growing out of it will be.

When adversity rears its ugly head, don't despair. Rather, let it bring you closer to Christ. Lean on Him and He will help you through the tough times. Make this approach part of the example you set for others. Reach out to coworkers who are not handling adversity well and be a source of strength and hope for them. Doing this can be a powerful form of evangelism. It will allow you to share the Gospel by your example.

Christian women often have to endure adversity on the job because of their faith. I am sure there have been times when you had to. Christian women also have to face down the temptation to put aside their faith and go along with the crowd. The workplace has a way of creating situations that put Christian women between a rock and a hard place. When this happens, the temptation and pressure to compromise your faith can seem overwhelming.

Think about the times when you have had to face adversity in your job while also trying to be faithful to your Christian beliefs. There have probably been times when standing firm in your faith made getting through the workday difficult. Maintaining your faith while navigating the stormy seas of the workplace can be a daunting challenge at times. Consequently, knowing how to persevere when in the grips of adversity is critical for you and other Christian women. You need to know how to persevere in the faith when you feel like giving up.

Unfortunately, there are Christian women who tire of the daily struggle to remain faithful in an environment that doesn't support their efforts. In fact, some Christian women eventually succumb to the weariness and give up. When this happens, the most common response is to begin hiding or downplaying their faith. Before long, they find themselves compromising and going along to get along. I know of several Christian women who became so worn down by the adversity of working in a secular environment they eventually went beyond just hiding their faith to renouncing it.

I have known other women who remained true to their faith but forfeited their careers. Neither of these unfortunate outcomes need have happened. You and other Christian women can stand firm in the faith when facing temptation and adversity, and you can do so without hurting your careers. When you face difficulties at work, remember this: To enjoy a rainbow, you must first endure the storm. This chapter provides specific strategies for doing so. I begin with some specifics on how to cope with the adversity caused by temptation.

COPING WITH ADVERSITY CAUSED BY TEMPTATION

Every day in the workplace, you face temptations challenging your faith. Consequently, standing up to temptation is essential if you are going to maintain your faith while working among people who reject it. Connie struggled with temptation for six months before finally conquering it. She found herself attracted to a coworker named Barry. He was smart, attractive, a top performer in their company, and a good listener. Connie liked spending time with Barry and found herself making excuses to do so. Barry was also attracted to Connie. But there was a problem: Although Connie was single, Barry was married.

Barry made it clear he wanted their relationship to go beyond just being coworkers. When Connie raised the obvious objection, Barry brushed it aside claiming he and his wife didn't get along and would probably divorce soon anyway. Barry invited Connie to lunch several days a week. He also invited her to join him on business trips. At first, Connie resisted traveling with Barry but, over time, she began to weaken. It was during a business trip when things came to a head. After dining together at a nice restaurant, Barry suggested they go to his room, claiming they would just talk. Naively, Connie agreed to join him. Once in his hotel room, it quickly became obvious Barry was interested in more than just talking, something Connie should have known all along.

Connie made a hasty exit and returned to her own room. Then she did what she should have done six months ago: prayed for God's help. She asked for the strength to resist the temptation Barry represented. On the trip back, Connie informed Barry they would no longer see each other again outside work, and their relationship at work would be strictly professional. Connie was thankful for God's help when several months later Barry was caught in an adulterous affair with another female coworker, this one married. The affair caused such a stir both Barry and his tryst partner lost their jobs and spouses.

Temptation is an everyday phenomenon at work. Consequently, as Christians, we have to learn to deal with it. As in all things, Christ is our role model for meeting this challenge. Matthew 4:1–11 tells the well-known story of Christ being tempted by Satan. You know how this story turned out. Christ provided a memorable example of steadfastly rejecting Satan's efforts to tempt Him. His example is instructive for you and other Christian women in the workplace.

Temptation will never go away at work or in the world at large. Satan is always lurking in the shadows looking for opportunities to lure you into his web. This is the message in 1 Peter 5:8, where we are warned to be vigilant because the devil is always prowling around like a lion in search of prey. But, unlike the lion's prey, you are neither helpless nor defenseless. You have the armor of God for protection. It comes in the form of Scripture, prayer, and the wise counsel of brothers and sisters in Christ. Consequently, when you feel yourself weakening in the face of temptation, put on the armor of God and you will be able to withstand the scheming temptations of the devil. This is the message in Ephesians 6:10–18, a message that should be inscribed on the heart of every Christian woman who works outside the home.

IS TEMPTATION SIN?

Temptation is Satan's way of appealing to our fallen nature. It is the lure he uses to hook us, so he can reel us in. Satan is always lurking in the shadows trying to entice you to do things that would compromise your faith (1 Peter 5:8). Temptation in the workplace can lead to such sinful behavior as office romances among married people, fraud, abuse of power, unauthorized use of the employer's resources, lying, claiming credit for work someone else did, customer abuse, failing to give credit where it is due, bullying, stealing, selling faulty merchandise, making false claims to customers, purposely overlooking product deficiencies, wasting time on the Internet instead of working, and a host of other destructive behaviors. As a Christian woman in the workplace, you will be tested. The workplace will tempt you every day in ways both overt and subtle. When it does, remember temptation is not the problem. Giving in to temptation is the problem.

Temptation Is Not Sin, but Giving in to Temptation Is

Over the years, I have seen Christians become discouraged because they were tempted to do things they knew were wrong. A Christian colleague once told me that, on business trips, she refuses to join her coworkers for a night on the town—not because she wouldn't enjoy it but because she would enjoy it too much. My colleague is afraid, if she goes out with her friends on these trips, temptation will overpower her resolve.

We are all tempted. You are, I am, and every Christian on earth is. Satan, in the form of a serpent, used Adam and Eve to set that precedent in the Garden of Eden. This is why we were given the warning in Matthew 26:41 to watch and pray because we might be too weak to stand firm against temptation. Temptation is a deep and personal urge to do something you know is wrong. It is a manifestation of our fallen nature, but is not sin per se. Let me repeat that statement for emphasis and clarity. Temptation is not sin but giving in to temptation is. Temptation can certainly lead to sin if you give in to it, but temptation itself is not sin. Rather, it is a manifestation of human nature in a fallen world.

Let me give you an example to illustrate this contention. Assume you are walking from the parking lot to your office on a bitterly cold winter day when you find yourself passing a bakery. You are greeted by the alluring aroma of fresh donuts and hot coffee wafting out onto the street. Your mouth waters, a feeling of warmth envelops you, and a sensation of sublime comfort comes over you. A little inner voice soothingly urges you to go in. What harm could there be in having just one warm, sweet donut washed down with a steaming cup of hot coffee? This sense of enticement is what you feel when the devil is tempting you to do something you shouldn't. But, no matter how much you crave that donut, you have not sinned until you give into it and eat it.

When the Christian woman mentioned earlier was tempted by the night life on business trips, she was not sinning. She was just manifesting the fallen side of her human nature. In fact, refusing to join her coworkers in going out on the town was a commendable response on her part. Sin, in this case, would have been for her to join her friends and yield to the temptations of the night life. She was tempted, but she did not sin. The distinction is important. There is nothing wrong with going out with your colleagues. It was wrong in this case only because of what it might lead to for the individual in question.

Temptation is ever-present in your life. But, until you stop fighting it, give in, and submit to its seductive power, you have not sinned. 1 Timothy 6:9 contains a prescient warning that giving in to temptation can be self-destructive. James 1:14–15 states this warning in even stronger terms. It says temptation can lead to death. This verse, no doubt, refers primarily to spiritual death, but it can also refer to physical death when temptation leads people to make bad choices like drinking and driving.

Not everyone is tempted in the same way or by the same things, but we are all tempted. This is why, in 1 Peter 5:8, the Apostle warned that we should be alert because the devil is always prowling around

hoping to seduce God's children. As a Christian, you are not immune to the tug of temptation. But giving in to temptation is a choice. When faced with temptation, recognize it as Satan's deceitful scheming and refuse to give in. We feel temptation because of our fallen human nature, but we still have the ability to say "no" to it, just as Christ did in the wilderness. And we have the indwelling Holy Spirit who will joyfully give us stiffness in our spines when we need it.

PERSEVERING IN THE FAITH WHEN FACING TEMPTATION

Do you know any Christians who have ruined their careers by giving into work-related temptations? I certainly do. Proverbs 24:19 warns that we should not envy the wicked, but some Christians in the workplace do so anyway. I have known Christians who gave in to temptation at work because it appeared their unbelieving coworkers were having all the fun, getting all the raises, and winning all the promotions. Unfortunately, it is not uncommon for Christians to give into temptation.

In Luke 17:1, Christ warned His disciples they would encounter stumbling blocks in their paths. One of the most difficult of these stumbling blocks would be temptation. For example, His disciples would be tempted to deny Christ every time professing Him became inconvenient, costly, or dangerous. You and I face the same temptation, and plenty of others. Most of us have given in to temptation at some point and done something we later regretted. Thankfully, we have a loving Savior who forgives repentant sinners.

From time to time, coworkers are going to pressure you to do things compromising to your faith. Count on it. Peer pressure can be a powerful force, particularly when you lose sight of who you want to fit in with. As Christians, we are to be conformed to Christ, not the world (Romans 12:2); however, the human tendency is to conform ourselves to the world, which, in the current context, means to our coworkers. Peer pressure can blur your judgment. When this happens, you are susceptible to making choices you might later regret.

When you feel tempted by peer pressure, step away from the situation long enough to pray and consult Scripture. Read Romans 12:2 as a reminder of who you are supposed to be conformed to. Place your cares at God's feet and put your trust in Him. He will sustain you. This is the message in Psalm 55:22, a message that will nourish your spirit and strengthen your resolve when peer pressure is pulling you in the wrong direction.

Although giving in to temptation is not uncommon among Christians, you can stand up to temptation and overcome it. You can follow the example of Christ in the wilderness when He brushed aside Satan's efforts to tempt Him. You can also follow the advice of the great reformer, Martin Luther. Luther, who was often beset by temptation, thought the best way to stand firm against it was to pray, read Scripture, and talk with fellow believers until the temptation passed. These strategies and others are explained in more detail in the following paragraphs.

Learn by observing other people

You have probably heard the old maxim that smart people learn from their mistakes, but wise people learn from the mistakes of others. It is smart to learn from our mistakes, so we don't repeat them. But, when it comes to standing firm against temptation, an even better approach is to learn from the mistakes of others, as well as from their successes. Paul advocated this strategy in 1 Corinthians 10:6, where we read that certain things occurred to give us examples that would keep us from making the same mistakes others made. When a coworker turns her life upside down by giving in to temptation, take it as an example of behavior to avoid. The obverse is also true. When a coworker is saved from a self-destructive choice by refusing to give in to temptation, take it as an example to follow.

Read Scripture until the temptation passes

The armor of God is your best defense against temptation. Even the devil's sharpest arrows cannot penetrate it. When the devil entices you with temptation at work or anywhere else, find a quiet place and open your Bible or pull up the Bible on your smartphone. Read any of the many verses dealing with temptation. Ephesians 6:11 is a good place to start. This verse assures you the armor of God will protect you from the devil's nefarious schemes. A Christian woman I knew kept Ephesians 6:11 and several other verses bookmarked in her Bible. When she found herself struggling with temptation, this committed Christian woman opened her Bible and read the bookmarked passages. She claimed these verses rescued her on numerous occasions from the unwise choices she was tempted to make.

Bolster your resolve against temptation with prayer

Few things will stop Satan in his tracks so effectively as the prayers of a believer. If you feel pulled in the wrong direction by temptation, fortify your heart with prayer, and Satan will flee from you. This is the message in James 4:7. A Christian accountant, Victoria, began every workday with prayer. She started with the Lord's Prayer and then added specifics. Victoria told me she knew herself well enough to know she was susceptible to the lure of temptation. She also knew the workday would be full of temptations of various kinds. Consequently, she didn't wait for Satan to spring one of his devious schemes on her. Rather, she performed what she called a preemptive strike. Victoria got out in front of the temptations she would face each day by heading them off with prayer before starting work. Over time, she was joined in prayer by others in her firm, some because they suffered the consequences of giving in to temptation and others because they didn't want to.

Enlist the help of Christ and Fellow Believers in fighting temptation

Trying to fight temptation alone is unwise. Fortunately, as a Christian woman, you don't need to. Christ is always available and ready to help. All you have to do is ask. In addition to enlisting the help of Christ, it is a good idea to ask a fellow believer to serve as your accountability partner. Your accountability partner is someone you trust who is willing to meet with you or take your telephone call when temptation is tugging at you.

The concept of the accountability partner is Scriptural. It comes from Galatians 6:1–2, where we are admonished to bear each other's burdens. If you struggle with work-related temptations, don't despair. The help you need is available. Appeal to Christ and enlist the aid of an accountability partner. It is also good for you to serve as an accountability partner for other Christian women. When we help each other stand up to temptation at work, we are doing more than just providing mutual support. We are living out the Scriptural guidance in Galatians 6:1–2 to bear one another's burdens.

REMAINING FAITHFUL IN THE FACE OF OTHER TYPES OF ADVERSITY

Not all forms of adversity in the workplace relate directly to our Christian faith, but the way we respond to them does. Regardless the kind of adversity you face at work, how you handle it matters. As Christians, we are called to deal with adversity, regardless its nature, in ways that reflect the image of Christ. This applies on the job as well as in other facets of life. In other words, we are supposed to do more than just survive when times get hard; we are supposed to persevere in the faith. Doing so should be part of the example we set for our coworkers.

Terminations, layoffs, lost promotions, missed raises, difficult coworker relationships, stress, workplace bullies, setbacks, pressure to perform, competition, overbearing supervisors, plant closings, buyouts, mergers, downsizings, corporate bankruptcies, federal and state regulations, strikes, unforgiving deadlines, demanding customers, and the challenge of trying to maintain a good faith, family, and work balance are just a few of the factors that can cause work-related adversity in your life. Increasingly, you can add anti-Christian bias to the list.

Giving your life to Christ changed it for the better, but it did not free you from the trials, tribulations, challenges, frustrations, and

dilemmas of the workplace. Never forget, when the rain falls, it falls on believers and unbelievers alike. This fact should be understood by Christian women who work in an environment where adversity is common. Persevering in the faith in times of adversity is part of your unwritten job description.

You can persevere when facing adversity because God is with you (Isaiah 41:10). Christians who falter in their faith when Satan throws up obstacles risk losing their best source of strength for overcoming the obstacles. When adversity raises its ugly head at work or anywhere else, run to Christ, not away from Him. With Christ at your side, you can do more than just cope with adversity; you can overcome it in God-honoring ways and advance your career.

The fact that persevering through adversity is an integral part of the Christian walk is explained in Hebrews 12:3. In this verse, we are reminded that, when beaten down by adversity, we should remember the hostility, brutality, and abuse Christ endured on our behalf. Talk with Christian women who have built successful careers without compromising their faith. You will find they had to endure more than their share of adversity. You will also find they overcame the adversity by refusing to give up when they grew weary. They stood up to adversity and persevered. In the process, these Christian women grew stronger and closer to Christ.

As a Christian woman, you can expect adversity to be part of your work life. Only the naïve and inexperienced are surprised when bad times occur on the job. Wise Christians know adversity will come, even when there are long periods of calm between the storms. Part of being wise in the Matthew 10:16 sense of the word is avoiding the complacency trap when it comes to adversity. This is an easy trap to fall into, especially when there are extended lulls between bouts of adversity. Let me illustrate.

I have lived in Florida all of my life. Consequently, like most native Floridians, I understand hurricanes, with all their destructive power, are going to happen. In some years, we squeak by with no hurricanes and, in other years, they come one after the other, month after month. Long-time Floridians understand, no matter how much fair weather

105

we experience between storms, there will always be another storm. It's just a matter of time. Consequently, we don't become complacent about hurricanes. We use the good times between storms to prepare for the bad times sure to come.

But new Florida residents tend to view hurricanes as one-time events. Too many treat them like exceptions rather than the rule. Having survived a storm and enjoyed a period of fair weather, they become complacent. Rather than use the good times to prepare for the bad, they believe that, having survived one storm, the adversity is over and they can relax. Floridians who adopt this complacent outlook about hurricanes are almost guaranteed to suffer as a result.

People in the workplace often adopt this same outlook concerning adversity. Once a major crisis passes, they breathe a sigh of relief and carry on as if there won't be another. Don't make this mistake. Stay vigilant and be prepared for the workplace storms certain to come. When they come, use Scripture and prayer to help you remain steadfast. When the job gets difficult or relationships with coworkers become strained, use Scripture and prayer to get you through to better times. To persevere in the face of adversity while also reflecting the image of Christ for coworkers, apply the following strategies:

Expect the Unexpected and Be Prepared

A major cause of adversity at work is the unexpected event that suddenly turns your world upside down. We have all experienced this phenomenon. Things are going well at work. Customers are happy, and sales are up. Even your grumpy boss smiled this morning. Then it happens. The power goes out or the computer network crashes right in the middle of an important project. Suddenly, the day that was going so well turns into a nightmare, as coworkers wring their hands over looming deadlines. As the downtime stretches into hours, tempers begin to flare.

When the unexpected intrudes, you can either fume in frustration or go to Plan B. If you expect the unexpected, as we Floridians have learned to do throughout hurricane season, there is always a Plan B.

I advise my counseling clients to keep a copy of James 1:2–4 on their desks, at their workstations, or bookmarked on their smartphones. In this verse, we are admonished to welcome the trials and tribulations of life because they produce perseverance. I also advise clients to make sure they always have a Plan B for dealing with the trials and tribulations of life.

The example of the power failing and the network crashing is real. My team was working on a major federal grant with an unforgiving deadline. As you might suspect, we were cutting it close on completing the mountain of paperwork required. The power failure and computer outage might have wrecked our chances of submitting the grant on time, but—thanks be to God—we had a Plan B. Everything we were doing on our organization's local area network was being backup up on external storage devices for use on battery-powered laptops in the event of just the kind of problem we experienced. We not only submitted the grant on time, we won the competition and received the grant. If you expect the unexpected and prepare for it, the adversity you face at work will be more manageable.

Remember God Has a Purpose for Your Suffering

Our tendency when facing adversity is to wonder, "Why me?" While this is certainly an understandable reaction, it is important to remember God uses adversity to strengthen His children, as is shown in Romans 5:3–5. These well-known verses explain how trials give us opportunities to persevere. Perseverance, in turn, develops character, and character provides hope. Christians can be hopeful because of the message in Romans 5:3–5. We can stand up to adversity, knowing it is part of God's plan to strengthen us for even bigger challenges in the future.

Consequently, the answer to the "Why me?" question might be as simple as this: God wants to strengthen you to face future adversity. God sometimes allows trials to come our way, but He doesn't allow more than you can endure. Further, He knows even better than you how much you can endure. You are stronger than you might think.

More importantly, with Christ by your side, you can be as strong as you need to be. When adversity wears you down, remember the message in Romans 5:3–5.

Use Adversity to Bring You Closer to God

As Christians, we sometimes make the mistake of letting adversity drive a wedge between us and God. This kind of response is the opposite of what is needed in times of adversity. Let the adversity you face in the workplace bring you closer to God. As humans, we are frail but, with God, we can persevere. This is why we are told in Psalm 55:22 how the Lord will uphold us if we bring our troubles to Him. Sunny-day Christians are not likely to persevere when facing adversity, and there will be adversity. The workplace is like life: Rain is going to fall, sometimes unexpectedly. When the rain comes, it falls on believers and unbelievers alike; however, unlike those who reject God, you can seek shelter and comfort in the protective arms of Christ.

Marjorie had never known such adversity. Within just a few days, she lost her younger brother, grandfather, and husband. When the call came about her beloved younger brother being killed in a water-skiing accident, Marjorie was devastated. She and her brother were close growing up, and Marjorie struggled to grasp he was actually gone. Then, during the funeral, Marjorie's grandfather—the good man who raised Marjorie and her brother—suffered a heart attack. He was rushed to the hospital but did not survive.

Marjorie was devastated. Two of the people she loved most in the world were gone, and at the same time. Grief overwhelmed her. She could hardly move, much less function. She went through the motions at both funerals, but it was clear to those who knew her best Marjorie was in trouble. After staying with relatives for a few days after the funerals, Marjorie returned home. When she arrived, there was a note from her husband of two years which said, "Dear Marjorie, our marriage was a mistake. I'm sorry about your brother

and grandfather, but I have to leave. I have filed for divorce. My attorney will contact you in the next several days."

Marjorie stayed home in bed most of the time for the next two weeks. She might have stayed there longer but, one morning, she heard a knock on her door. It was her pastor. Pastor Mike commiserated with Marjorie and listened while she poured out her heart in racking sobs of grief. After Marjorie vented her sorrow, Pastor Mike told her, "You can let the grief you feel drive you into the ground or you can be relieved of it and move forward. To move forward, run to God and place your sorrow at his feet. He will comfort and sustain you."

It took a few days for what Pastor Mike told her to sink in but, when she finally hit rock bottom, Marjorie decided to come back to the surface. She did it by getting down on her knees and praying for God's help. She also asked friends at church for help, which they gladly provided. What she could not do alone, Marjorie was able to do with God's help. By running to God, she was able to not just recover, but become an even stronger person able to help others cope with tragedy and sorrow.

Remember That You Are Not Alone in Your Adversity

2 Timothy 3:12 warns that all who live Godly lives will be persecuted. Persecution is just one more form of adversity you might face as a Christian in the workplace. When you suffer adversity at work, remember you are not the first Christian to do so. Seek out fellow Christians who have suffered but persevered, learn from their experience, and grow from their wisdom. If you don't know any fellow Christians who have suffered because of their faith, go to Scripture and find some role models there. Begin with Job.

In the previous example about Marjorie, one of the things that sustained her was the help of friends from church. Several fellow believers made sure Marjorie was always surrounded by love and she got the help needed to cope. Having faced adversity in their lives, Marjorie's friends understood what she was going through. They made sure Marjorie knew she wasn't alone; God was right there

109

with her and always would be. Marjorie, in turn, reached out to her friends regularly. They listened when she needed to talk, gave her a shoulder to cry on, helped with her children and parents, and prayed with her. Marjorie knew she was never alone, and God was with her because He sent angels in the form of church friends to support, comfort, and sustain her.

As a Christian woman, you have a church family, too. Reach out to your fellow believers and give them a chance to love their neighbor by helping care for you during times of adversity. You might be surprised to find how willing fellow believers are to help when you will let them know you need it. Your Christian brothers and sisters are probably just waiting to help, but some might be reluctant to step forward and offer assistance unless you ask for it. Don't be afraid to ask.

Understand Perseverance Is Rewarded in God's Time

In a fallen world, life can be unfair. For example, Christians who honor God are always rewarded, but the reward may not come on your terms or in your time. Although this may seem unfair to you, it isn't. Life may not be fair, but God is. Why God sometimes seems unfair is that He gives us what we need, not what we want. When the reward you seek does not come on your terms or in your time, take comfort in knowing it will come and, when it does, nothing on earth will compare to it.

This is the promise contained in Matthew 5:11–12. The message in these verses is that we are to be thankful when our faith is challenged because our reward will come in heaven. This is not to say you won't be rewarded on earth. Earthly rewards can and do happen. But how and when you are rewarded for your faith is in God's hands. The hard part for Christians is to be content knowing God controls the outcome.

Refuse to Let Adversity Overwhelm You

When facing adversity, don't quit and never give up. Use the Bible, prayer, and wise counsel of fellow Christians to bolster your determination when you feel like quitting. God is bigger than your problems. He knows you are suffering, and He knows exactly how much you can endure. God is like the coach who knows how far she can push athletes without pushing them too far, only much better. This is why Paul gave us the assurance in Romans 8:28 that God will work things out for those who love Him. Run to God, not away from Him during times of adversity. He knows what you are enduring, and He knows your limits. As He did with Melissa, God will see you through the adversity you face.

Look Beyond the Present Darkness to a Brighter Future

In times of adversity, it is easy to get caught up in the difficulty of the moment and focus exclusively on the here and now. This is why it is important to learn to take the long view. You cannot see the light at the end of the tunnel unless you look ahead through the darkness. When you think the hard times will never end, remember what is said in James 1:2–4. These verses encourage us to be joyful, even when suffering through adversity, because trials strengthen us. In other words, focus not on the darkness but on the light at the end of the tunnel. For Christians, there is always a light at the end of the tunnel. It is Christ. Cling to God in times of trouble, and you will eventually emerge from the darkness stronger and better.

Study the Examples of Christian Women Who Were Martyred for Their Faith

When confronted with faith-related adversity in the workplace, it is easy to feel isolated and alone. If you ever find yourself feeling this way, try studying the examples of other Christian women who suffered because of their faith, particularly those who have

111

been martyred. Doing this can help put your situation in a better perspective, making it less difficult to endure.

Christian women who have been martyred are sisters in Christ who sacrificed their lives rather than deny their faith. In most cases, these women were given the chance to renounce their faith to avoid a brutal death. We tend to view Christian martyrs in abstract terms as unreal figures from the past. But the martyrdom of Christians is not just a historic phenomenon, it continues to this day. Every day, throughout the world, more than 300 Christians are martyred for their faith. Increasingly, these martyrs are women. In fact, the jihadist militant organization known as Boko Haram, based in northeastern Nigeria, targets Christian women specifically.

There are many examples of Christian women who have been martyred. One that comes to mind from the past was Felicitas. Known for her tireless efforts to convert people to Christianity, Felicitas and her seven sons were arrested by order of the Roman emperor. Roman authorities demanded she renounce Christianity. If she refused, they would kill her sons, one by one, until she gave in. All she had to do to save the lives of her sons was renounce Christ. She refused. As a result, Felicitas was forced to watch as her sons were put to death, one after the other, right before her eyes. Once all seven sons were killed by the Roman authorities, Felicitas was given one more chance to recant. Knowing it would mean her certain death, Felicitas once again refused. As a result, she became one more in a long line of Christian martyrs that continues to this day.

In more recent times, Mary Sameh George was martyred for her faith. It happened when she traveled to Cairo, Egypt, to care for a poor family. Noticing the cross hanging from the rearview mirror of her car, an anti-Christian mob attacked her. She was brutally beaten, kicked, stabbed, and finally shot. Then her car was burned. Mary knew of the danger awaiting her in Cairo, but she was committed to serving others and living a life that reflected the image of Christ. For her commitment to the Christian faith, Mary Sameh George paid the ultimate price. She died a brutal death on earth but is, no doubt, enjoying a glorious life in Heaven.

These are just two examples of Christian women who were martyred for their faith. There are many others including Blandina, Perpetua, Catherine of Alexandria, Narcissa Prentiss Whitman, Edith Stein, and Esther John, to name just a few. I provide these names so you can go online and research their stories. Studying their examples can put the adversity you face on the job in a better perspective. The lives and deaths of these martyred Christian women and others like them will show you are not alone in your suffering. Right now, as you read this book, somewhere in the world, one of your Christian sisters is giving her life *for* Christ because she gave her life *to* Christ and refused to deny Him.

As you face temptation and adversity at work, take comfort in the words of Lamentations 3:19–24. When suffering, we can have hope in the Lord because His mercy endures forever and His compassion for us is unlimited. No matter how difficult your problems may be, the Lord is bigger than the adversity you face, and his compassion will not fail you. Cling to Christ during times of adversity. He will walk you through the darkness and into the light.

Reach Out to Someone Else Who Is Suffering

One of the best ways to relieve or, at least, lessen your own suffering is to help someone else who is hurting. This is what is meant in Galatians 6:2 where we are told to bear one another's burdens. Invariably, when we reach out to others who are suffering, we gain a more positive, thankful perspective on our own problems. No matter how badly we are hurting, there is always someone else who is hurting worse. In times of adversity, help yourself by helping others. When you help others who are suffering, you take the focus off yourself and your troubles.

Pray for the Person Who Is Struggling

When you want to help a coworker who is struggling, begin with prayer. Pray God will comfort and strengthen your colleague. Pray

113

God will use the adversity or sorrow your colleague is enduring to turn that individual's heart to Christ. Pray God will help you be an angel of mercy for the person who is hurting. Finally, be prepared to share your faith if the individual you are helping asks how you manage to cope with adversity.

Be There for Coworkers Who Are Struggling

Ironically, when people in the workplace are struggling, they are sometimes treated like lepers. When they really need help, people who are hurting sometimes find themselves avoided, as if their problems are contagious. People will avoid suffering coworkers, believing they have enough problems of their own to deal with. Even those who want to help sometimes shy away from those who are hurting simply because they don't know what to say or do. Their coworker's pain makes them uncomfortable. Others will treat the hurting individual's problem like the proverbial elephant in the living room. It's there, but nobody talks about it. They ignore the obvious.

Because of these kinds of reactions, those enduring adversity can feel abandoned at the time they need help most. Consequently, when you observe a coworker struggling with sorrow, fear, anxiety, remorse, uncertainty, or any other form of adversity, be there for that individual. Don't ignore the obvious. Give hurting coworkers a shoulder to lean on. Guide them through the darkness so they don't get lost and give up.

Listen to Coworkers Who Are Hurting

People often feel tongue-tied around someone who is struggling with grief, anxiety, fear, uncertainty, or other forms of adversity. They want to say something helpful, but don't know what to say. Fortunately, you don't have to say anything. Instead, just ask if the individual in question needs to talk. Then listen. People who are hurting need to unburden themselves, to give voice to their sorrow, fears, and anxiety. Just listening without interrupting or trying

114

to solve their problems can be surprisingly helpful to people who are undergoing trials. Often, the best medicine for the emotions generated by adversity is someone who will just listen. Be that person for coworkers who are mired in despair.

Avoid Empty Platitudes and False Optimism

Some people respond to those who are struggling by voicing empty platitudes or being falsely optimistic. "Cheer up. Everything's going to be alright." "Don't worry, these things usually work out." "It's never as bad as you think it is." Overly optimistic platitudes such as these are not helpful to people who are suffering. Even if the message they convey is well-intended and true, the words can sound shallow and dismissive. This is because the timing of the message is bad. Although they may not say it, hurting individuals often respond to platitudes by thinking, "That's easy for you to say. You're not the one with the problem." There is a time for optimistic messages when trying to help people who are struggling with adversity, but it is later, after the initial shock of the situation has worn off and the hurting individual is no longer caught in the grip of emotional turmoil.

Be Proactive—Do Specific Things that Help in Practical Ways

When people are struggling with adversity, even the simplest everyday responsibilities can seem like major burdens or even insurmountable obstacles. This is an area where you can be especially helpful. Don't just tell a hurting coworker, "If you need help with anything, call me." People who need help are often reluctant to ask for it. Instead, be proactive. Run errands for hurting coworkers, temporarily take on some of their workload, prepare meals, clean their house, or help with their kids. Doing these kinds of practical things for those who are hurting is an effective way to help them. Just as Christ made a powerful statement by washing the feet of his Apostles, you can make a powerful statement by doing little things for coworkers who are hurting.

Be Patient with Coworkers Who Are Struggling

Sadly, some people quickly grow weary of the grief, fears, anxiety, or uncertainty of hurting coworkers. They become impatient and want the individual to get over it. How many times have you heard someone make these kinds of comments? "How long is this going to continue? It's been two weeks. When is she going to get over it?" A Christian woman who lost her mother to cancer told me that, after she was back at work just two days, her boss pulled her aside and said, "You need to snap out of it. I'm not paying you to mope around feeling sorry for yourself."

Putting aside the fact this manager will never be named Boss of the Year, his attitude toward my friend's grief just made matters worse. People heal in their own time, so give them time. Be patient and keep doing the things explained in this section. Healing in the aftermath of adversity is like healing after a face lift. You have to go through an ugly period before things look better, and that period cannot be rushed; however, if you are patient, things will eventually look better.

PRAYER FOR COPING WITH TEMPTATION AND ADVERSITY

Dear Father God,

Perhaps when Eve was in the Garden of Eden, she didn't recognize the Tempter for what He was and what He still is. She gave in to temptation and it changed her relationship with You. As I ponder that idea, I come to You facing temptations of my own I must deal with. I bring them before You because I need Your strength and Your wisdom, Your Holy armor to keep me safe. I want to listen for Your voice, so nothing entices me or causes me to succumb to those things that could dishonor You or bring lifelong regret.

The place where I work seems to invite temptation to come in any time it pleases. Sometimes, I'm subtly asked to look the other way when something is done that I know is not quite above board. Sometimes temptation asks me to share the gossip of the day. Other times, it suggests I could get further ahead if I simply don't wear my faith so obviously on my sleeve.

Lord, the fact is I don't park my faith at the door when I walk into work. Therefore, I need to honor You by being a person of integrity, no matter what anyone else might choose to do. Today, I humbly put all my cares at Your feet so I am nourished and strengthened to do Your will and to do what's right.

When adversity strikes me or temptation knocks on my door, I pray You will guide me to do the right thing, causing me to resist anything not of You. Help me to live in the world where I work, but to not be of the world that remains blind to Your call. Help me be a daughter who makes choices that make You proud.

Thank You for fortifying my spirit and strengthening me with Your mercy and grace. Forgive me when I don't recognize that snake in the grass who hopes only to destroy our relationship and dim my light. I pray for women I work with, that they will run from those temptations that only distract them, wound them, and cause them deep regret. Bless every woman who works for You, wherever she may be, and guard each of us from workplace temptations. Amen.

DISCUSSION CASE: "I Don't Know If I'm Strong Enough...."

Sadie thought of herself as a strong person. She was always able to exercise sufficient willpower to do the right thing in difficult situations. But the temptation tugging at her now was stronger than anything she ever faced. She recently told a friend from church, "I don't know if I'm strong enough to withstand this kind of temptation." Sadie was tempted to promote an individual in her company ahead of another employee who was clearly better qualified and truly deserved the promotion. Sadie knew the right thing to do, but her judgment was being clouded by one of the most powerful forces on earth: a mother's love. Two employees applied for the job in question; one of them was Sadie's daughter.

Sadie owned a successful small business she ran according to Christian principles. Her daughter, Linda, worked in the company's sales department. Because of a retirement, the company needed a new sales manager. Two of Sadie's employees applied for the job; one of them was Linda. Linda really wanted the promotion and made sure her mother knew it. Linda was an excellent sales representative for Sadie's company and, in time, she would make a good sales manager. But the undeniable truth was Linda was not yet ready for a managerial position, something everyone in the company understood, except (it seemed) Linda.

The other sales rep who applied for the job had been with the company since Linda was a baby. She was also a member of Sadie's church and a committed Christian. She had stayed with Sadie's company in spite of better offers over the years because of the company's faith-based corporate culture. Sadie knew she should promote this more qualified employee. But, on the other hand, Linda worked so hard, did such a good job, and really wanted the promotion. Sadie knew how much the promotion would mean to Linda, and she hated disappointing her. Because of a divorce, Sadie raised Linda by herself. They were as close as a mother and daughter can be. Further, Sadie owned the company. She could do what she wanted, couldn't she? The temptation to promote Linda, even though she wasn't yet ready, was overwhelming. Sadie didn't know what to do.

Discussion Questions:

1. Do you know someone who was tempted to do the wrong thing out of misplaced love for a family member or friend? If so, what were the circumstances?

2. If Sadie came to you for help, what advice would you give her concerning how to stand up to the temptation she was facing? How can Sadie honor God in how she responds in this situation?

DISCUSSION CASE: "I don't know how much more of this I can take."

Connie is no stranger to adversity. She lost both of her parents in an airplane accident the day before her college graduation ceremony. They were flying to the graduation to see her honored as a Magna Cum Laude graduate. Later, she lost a baby in childbirth. Both losses were devastating but, with the help of a caring church family and a lot of prayer, Connie eventually came through both of these tragedies even more committed to her faith than before. She knows how to weather the storms of adversity. But a situation at work is testing her ability to cope.

Connie's boss is an overbearing micromanager who treats all of his direct reports the same: badly. He pushes them hard, takes credit for their work, is unforgiving of mistakes, punishes initiative, refuses to back them in confrontations with higher management, focuses on their weaknesses while ignoring their strengths, and is prone to hire and promote the wrong people. He makes work a miserable experience for Connie and her coworkers, one of whom summed up how all of them feel when he said: "Working for this tyrant is like going to a funeral every day."

Like her coworkers, Connie needs her job. She cannot leave it for a better job without relocating to a different community, something she does not want to do. Her children go to an excellent school in the community where they have plenty of friends and are doing well. Her husband's job is tied to the community. He is executive director of the

local chamber of commerce. Hence, moving is not an option. Connie needs to persevere in her current situation but doing so is a trial.

Discussion Questions:

1. Have you ever been trapped in a difficult work situation that made just going to work drudgery? If so, what were the circumstances? Do you know of anyone who is trapped in such a situation?

2. If Connie came to you for wise counsel about persevering through the adversity she faces, what advice would you give her?

REVIEW QUESTIONS FOR INDIVIDUALS AND GROUPS

1. Is feeling tempted a sin? Why or why not?

2. How would you define the concept of "temptation"?

3. Is everyone tempted? Explain your response.

4. How can Christians use the mistakes and success of others to help them stand up to temptation in the workplace?

5. How can Christians use the Word of God as their armor against temptation?

6. How can Christians use prayer to fortify their hearts against temptation?

7. Why should Christians avoid trying to fight temptation alone?

8. Does being a Christian exempt you from adversity? Explain your response.

9. How can reaching out to someone else who is suffering through adversity help you stand up to the adversity you face? What specific steps can you take to help coworkers who are struggling through tough times?

CHAPTER 6

APPLYING GOD'S GIFT OF EMOTIONAL INTELLIGENCE

"Whoever is slow to anger is better than the mighty, and he who rules his spirit than he who takes a city." Proverbs 16:32

You will face many situations at work that can press your buttons if you let them. The buttons I refer to are your anger, impatience, and frustration. We all have these buttons. It can be difficult to cope with the frustrations, pressures, and stress of your job without allowing these buttons to be pressed and responding in ways that compromise your faith. This is where God's gift of emotional intelligence comes into play; however, to gain the benefits of your emotional intelligence, you have to make a conscious effort to use it and use it wisely. Charlotte found this out the hard way.

Charlotte had no idea Mark would react the way he did. All she wanted was a simple answer to a simple question. She never dreamed he would erupt in anger. But he did and now, instead of sympathizing, Charlotte's coworkers blamed her for the incident. Yes, she knew Mark was just turned down for a promotion. In retrospect, she could understand why Mark might have been in a foul mood as a result. And yes, she responded to Mark's anger by bursting into tears and running from the room. Who wouldn't have?

In the aftermath of the incident, an exasperated Charlotte asked their supervisor to explain why Mark could not have answered just one little question. Charlotte was shocked when he claimed she was missing the point. But what really upset Charlotte was when the supervisor said she could have prevented the unfortunate incident by applying her emotional intelligence. Emotional intelligence? Charlotte had never heard the term. She didn't know what he was talking about.

WHAT IS EMOTIONAL INTELLIGENCE AND WHY IS IT IMPORTANT?

Emotional intelligence has several different components. For the purpose of this book, I will focus on the two most applicable in your job. The first is your ability to perceive, interpret, and manage your own emotions. Mark failed to do this when he blew up at Charlotte. Correspondingly, Charlotte failed to do this when she burst into tears and ran from the room after Mark yelled at her. The second is your ability to perceive, interpret, and wisely respond to the emotions of others. Charlotte failed to do this when she approached Mark in spite of his obvious distress rather than waiting for a better time. Hence, emotional intelligence involves both self-awareness and awareness of others. It also involves using your awareness to decide what actions you should take or avoid, depending on your current emotions and those of others.

Applying emotional intelligence involves paying attention to your emotions as well as those of others, and then responding in positive,

productive, and helpful ways. In the case of Charlotte, sensing Mark's emotional state, she could have chosen to wait for a better time to approach him. This would have been a more intelligent decision than the one that led to the blow up with him. Her supervisor was right. Had Charlotte applied the emotional intelligence God gave her instead of being too self-absorbed to consider Mark's emotional state, there would have been no incident. Of course, Mark is also complicit. Had he managed his emotions rather than blowing up, he could have suggested they talk at another time.

To understand how important emotional intelligence is, ask yourself two questions: 1) Do you want to control your emotions or let them control you? And 2) Do you want to positively influence your coworkers or contribute to their causing problems by failing to control their emotions? As to the first question, people who are controlled by their emotions often act on impulse and, as a result, act rashly. They do whatever their feelings suggest at the moment without considering the consequences of their actions or words.

As to the second question, people who are unaware of the emotions of others are unable to make wise decisions about how and when to engage them. They are also unable to help their coworkers avoid behaving in counter-productive and even self-destructive ways. When people who are oblivious to the emotions of others get involved in a situation, they often make it worse. At the very least, their lack of awareness does nothing to alleviate bad situations. Failing to observe and properly interpret the emotions of coworkers can make you an accomplice to their inappropriate behavior as it did with Charlotte and Mark.

As a Christian, it is important you understand emotional intelligence is a gift from God. It is a Scriptural concept, as is shown in Proverbs 16:32. This verse makes clear God expects us to rule our spirits or, said another way, manage our emotions. This is important because God always blesses us with the ability to do what He expects us to do. He would not expect us to manage our emotions unless he has given us the ability. This is the message in 1 Corinthians

10:13, where we are told God will not let us be challenged beyond our ability.

Emotional intelligence tests (EQ tests) notwithstanding, we are all blessed with this asset to some extent and in varying degrees. As an aside, there is research suggesting women are more abundantly blessed with emotional intelligence than men. As a woman reading this, you are probably thinking, "Those researchers certainly have a firm grasp of the obvious." Political correctness and secular thinking aside, this may be one of those areas in which men and women are truly different; however, comparing the emotional intelligence of men and women is a debate for another forum. For the purpose of this book, just understand emotional intelligence is a gift from God and we all have enough of it to make a positive difference in the workplace, if we are willing to intentionally apply it. Also understand your emotional intelligence is like a muscle. Regardless of its size right now, it can be developed and improved, if you are willing to put forth the effort.

What is missing in people like Charlotte is not ability but intentionality. People like Charlotte have sufficient emotional intelligence to manage their anger, sadness, anxiety, and other emotions. They also have the ability to sense these emotions in others; however, people like Charlotte are not intentional in applying this gift from God. They make no effort at self-awareness or the awareness of others. Hence, they allow emotions, theirs and those of coworkers, to control their lives on the job and elsewhere.

People who fail to apply their emotional intelligence are like people who fail to exert the willpower God has given them. You have probably heard people claim the reason they don't eat properly, exercise regularly, or get out of bed on time is they have no willpower. This claim is not a legitimate reason. Rather, it's an excuse and a lame one at that. We all have willpower. The difference is some of us exercise it and some don't. It is no easier for one person to say no to a donut than it is for another. The difference is found in conscious choice and intentionality. It's the same with emotional intelligence. With very few exceptions, we are all gifted with a workable level of

124

emotional intelligence. We just have to make the commitment to be intentional in applying and continually improving it.

WHAT ABOUT EMOTIONAL INTELLIGENCE TESTS?

Like IQ tests once were, EQ tests or tests of emotional intelligence are all the rage these days. These tests purport to measure your innate emotional ability, just as IQ tests measure your innate cognitive ability. But there are serious concerns about EQ tests. For example, one could argue EQ testing has not been around long enough for the results to be considered sufficiently trustworthy.; however, that is a debate for another forum. For the purpose of this book, there are other more pressing concerns about EQ testing.

First, tests of this nature have an unfortunate tendency to be misinterpreted. People often attach too much significance to the test results. Those who score low on them sometimes view the results as unchangeable and respond by adopting a negative self-image that, in turn, becomes a self-fulfilling prophecy. Those who score high on them sometimes view themselves as gifted and respond by resting on their test score instead of putting forth the effort to effectively apply their gift. Both of these approaches to interpreting the results of EQ tests are misguided and harmful. Another problem with EQ tests is they emphasize nature over nurture when, in fact, emotional intelligence is a product of both.

In addition to counseling Christians on workplace issues, I have been a college professor for almost forty-five years. I do the two things simultaneously. The latter is my profession, the former my ministry. My experience wearing a college professor's hat has shown, over and over, that the correlation between IQ and success is limited, at best. The same could be said for EQ. Students with high IQs who do not apply themselves often do poorly in spite of their innate intelligence. In the same manner, people with high EQ scores who do not apply their innate ability will be ineffective at managing emotions.

For example, I have worked with plenty of college students over the years whose IQs were off the charts, but who never lived up to

125

their potential because they failed to apply themselves. On the other hand, I have also worked with college students with average IQs who, by dint of hard work, a positive attitude, and a commitment to self-improvement, succeeded beyond what anyone would have predicted. Some of the most successful people you know would score only average on an IQ test. This same kind of relationship between innate ability and actual performance applies to emotional intelligence.

It is unfortunate EQ tests have come to be viewed as similar to IQ tests because the two differ in an important way. Although some still debate the issue, it is widely accepted your IQ is a fairly static asset. It is not improved much by hard work or long hours of study. What improves from hard work and study is your level of knowledge, not your level of intelligence; however, emotional intelligence is different. It can be developed. The level you start at is just that: a starting point. It can be improved. This is an important distinction. Emotional intelligence would be better compared with physical fitness, since both can be improved if you are willing to put forth the effort.

BENEFITS OF APPLYING YOUR EMOTIONAL INTELLIGENCE

Part of managing your emotions is using them in positive, productive, and helpful ways for you and your coworkers. If you manage your emotions well and help coworkers manage theirs, the result can be a better level of performance for you, them, and, your employer. In other words, properly applying the emotional intelligence God has given you can lead to that much desired but rarely achieved result: the win-win-win situation. In addition to being a catalyst for better performance, the effective application of emotional intelligence can lead to the following specific benefits, all of which, in turn, contribute to better performance.

Better Decision-Making

Applying your emotional intelligence can prevent rash decisions, yours and those of coworkers. Being self-aware allows you to recognize when you are too distracted by emotional turmoil to make important decisions. Being tuned in to the emotions of coworkers helps you know when it would be better to put off engaging them in discussion or debate for the purpose of decision-making. For example, Neena created an unfortunate situation for herself by deciding to conduct a performance appraisal for one of her direct reports, Jonathan, at a time when she was angry. Jonathan was not the cause of her anger, but he became the victim of it.

Neena rated Jonathan, a high-performing and dependable employee, lower than she should have on all criteria. She even added a few caustic remarks to the appraisal. It was as if she were evaluating a different employee. When Jonathan saw the appraisal, he was taken aback. He challenged Neena on the low ratings, but this just made her even angrier. Jonathan responded by resigning on the spot. Later, when her anger cooled, Neena knew she made a terrible mistake. She contacted Jonathan, apologized, and asked him to rescind his resignation. But, by the time she called him, Jonathan had already approached a competing company and received a job offer that came with a higher salary and better benefits.

Losing Jonathan, a valuable employee, to the competition cost Neena in more ways than one. Not only did she have to cope with getting her department's work done without one of her best team members, she had to deal with the sagging morale his sudden departure caused in the department. Ironically, on her next performance appraisal, Neena's supervisor gave her the lowest rating she had ever received and added a warning about making decisions or taking action when angry. The poor performance appraisal, in turn, meant Neena would not receive a salary increase that fiscal year. This unfortunate situation could have been prevented, had Neena applied her emotional intelligence and waited until her anger passed before deciding to conduct a performance appraisal.

Better Conflict Management

Conflicts on the job cost employers millions of dollars every year in lost productivity. Invariably, conflict absorbs the mental energy of those involved and distracts them from their work. Consequently, those who can prevent or manage conflict are invaluable assets to employers. Few things will prevent human conflict in the workplace better than the effective application of emotional intelligence. Human conflict often grows out of inconsiderate or ill-conceived actions, decisions, or behaviors that might not have happened had the parties involved applied their emotional intelligence.

Being self-aware lets you know your emotions are in turmoil at the moment. Knowing this allows you to take a few deep breaths and compose yourself before responding to or engaging with coworkers. Being aware of the emotions of others lets you know when it is better to step back from a brewing confrontation and give them time to regain their composure. Regardless of whether the emotional turmoil is yours or a coworker's, emotional intelligence—if properly heeded—can prevent it from causing conflict.

Better Communication

The essence of good communication is effective listening. Listening intentionally to verbal and nonverbal messages is, in turn, an essential tool of the emotionally intelligent. Few things will promote good communication better than good listening. When you listen to the words and non-verbal cues in a conversation, you are more likely to know if you are receiving an accurate, complete, and truthful message. You are also more likely to pick up on the speaker's emotional state. Learning to listen empathetically will enhance your career prospects. Listening empathetically requires applying your emotional intelligence.

Better Crisis Management

Crises are common in the workplace. Important deadlines loom, and the work is behind schedule. Negotiations for a major contract fall through. An important client or customer migrates to a competing firm. An ethics-related incident turns into a scandal. What is needed in the midst of a crisis is calm, clear-headed thinking that focuses on solutions rather than problems. There is probably no situation in the workplace that calls for the effective application of emotional intelligence more than a crisis.

In a crisis, applying the emotional intelligence God gave you makes it possible to recognize your own anxiety and do what is necessary to get it under control before making decisions or taking action. For example, your emotional intelligence might cue you to take several deep breaths, block out the negative, and focus on what needs to be done rather than becoming transfixed by the problem. Your calmness in the midst of a storm will have a positive effect on coworkers. It will allow you to help them stay calm, clear-headed, and focused rather than panicking. Further, because you are tuned into the emotions of coworkers, you can recognize those who need help getting their anxiety under control.

Finally, your emotional intelligence allows you to recognize when certain coworkers are going to be unable to get their emotions under control in a crisis. When this happens, it is best to separate these individuals from those who are responding more appropriately to the crisis. Remember, anxiety is contagious. Tune in to the emotions of your coworkers and sense the level of their anxiety. If it looks like a coworker won't be able to get her emotions under control, remove that individual from the scene so her anxiety does not spread. If all else fails, send her on an errand.

Better Stress Reduction

Professional literature is replete with strategies for reducing stress. This is important because, as you know, the workplace can be a virtual factory for producing stress. A stress-reduction strategy often overlooked is the wise application of emotional intelligence. Because much of the stress felt in the workplace is generated by human conflict, applying the emotional intelligence God gave you can reduce the amount of stress you have to deal with. Being self-aware and aware of the emotions of others can prevent much of the stress associated with human conflict in the workplace.

What is even more important is that emotional intelligence is a stress preventer rather than an after-the-fact coping mechanism. Most of the strategies found in the professional literature for reducing stress (e.g., exercise, fresh air, massage therapy, yoga, meditation, etc.) provide stress relief after the fact. But wisely applying your emotional intelligence can prevent stress from occurring in the first place. Needless to say, the less stress you have to deal with, the better your physical and emotional health will be. This is important because the better your physical and emotional health, the better your performance on the job.

Better Relationships at Work

People who wisely apply their emotional intelligence tend to have better relationships with coworkers. Being in touch with your own emotions as well as those of coworkers can prevent misunderstandings, inconsiderate actions, and insensitive timing. It can let you know when the other individual needs an ear to listen or a shoulder to cry on. Further, it can help you make better decisions. This is important because your decisions almost always affect your coworkers, sometimes positively and sometimes negatively. It is important to know which will be the case. An added benefit is your coworkers will appreciate your ability to help them manage their emotions.

Better Feedback to Subordinates and Coworkers

Providing constructive criticism is an important part of what we all do in the workplace. Honest, constructive criticism tactfully provided can help subordinates and coworkers improve. Given properly, constructive criticism is a gift to the recipient. However, people are typically sensitive to criticism. Thus, constructive criticism can be viewed by the recipient as a negative, if not delivered well.

Applying your emotional intelligence will help you provide constructive criticism without insulting, disparaging, or angering the recipient. First, it will allow you to know if the timing is right for providing constructive criticism. Second, it will allow you to sense the emotions of the recipient as you are delivering the constructive criticism and adjust your message or timing accordingly. For example, if the constructive criticism you are providing seems to be disconcerting the recipient, your emotional intelligence will inform you of the fact and allow you to make the necessary adjustments. You might commend the recipient for things she does well and assure her the constructive criticism is intended to help her do equally well on the issue in question.

Better Meeting Management

Meetings are used to convey information to a group of people and to discuss and debate issues of common concern, among other things. For those who chair meetings, effectively applying emotional intelligence is essential. The chair needs to be able to observe and interpret the emotions of participants in meetings. Is their reaction to the information you are conveying positive or negative? Are they going to support or oppose the idea under consideration? Do they understand the significance of what is being proposed? Are they focused on the topic of the meeting or other more pressing issues? Is the debate getting out of control and turning ugly?

Questions of this nature can be answered and acted on in positive, productive, and helpful ways by tuning into the emotions of participants in the meeting. As a college vice president, I once conducted a meeting of my staff in the aftermath of a shooting on one of our campuses. The meeting agenda topics were not particularly pressing, nor did they have anything to do with the shooting. It soon became obvious my staff members were still focused on the shooting. Sensing the timing of the meeting was bad, I did what I should have done in the first place: put aside the meeting agenda and let my staffers share their feelings about the shooting.

IMPROVING YOUR EMOTIONAL INTELLIGENCE

At the beginning of this chapter, Charlotte failed at the two most important aspects of emotional intelligence. She was insensitive to the emotional state of a coworker. Then, when her coworker lost control of his emotions, she responded by losing control of hers. These failures contributed to making an already unpleasant situation worse. This is what the supervisor meant when he told Charlotte she could have prevented the incident. Had she applied the emotional intelligence God gave her, she would have noticed Mark's mood and waited for a better time to approach him. Of course, Mark was also guilty of failing to apply his emotional intelligence. Both Charlotte and Mark need to improve their emotional intelligence and learn to apply it effectively.

Improving your emotional intelligence begins with the message in Galatians 5:22–23. In these verses, we are told the fruit of the spirit manifests itself in forbearance and self-control. When you decide to be intentional about exerting self-control over your own emotions, while being kind and patient with the emotions of others, you have taken an important step toward improving your emotional intelligence. This is because the characteristics recommended in Galatians 5:22–23 are all elements of humility, and humility is a fundamental element of emotional intelligence.

You will never realize the full benefit of your emotional intelligence until you develop the humility to accept this statement: *It's not all about me.* I am not saying you should avoid improving your self-awareness. To apply your emotional intelligence, you must become more self-aware. On the surface, this might seem like a self-centered undertaking, but it isn't. Self-awareness and self-centeredness are two different things. The former can help you interact with coworkers without losing control and acting rashly, while the latter can blind you to the emotions of others. You cannot tune in to the emotions of others when you are completely self-focused. In addition to heeding the admonition in Galatians 5:22–23, there are other things you can do to improve your emotional intelligence while also applying it more effectively. The following strategies will help.

Put Aside Technology and Connect with People Face-to-Face

Few things will undermine the effective application of emotional intelligence more thoroughly than electronic communication (i.e., texting, tweeting, email, social media, etc.). Emoticons and emojis notwithstanding, computers and smartphones cannot begin to match the emotional power of face-to-face interaction. Although manufacturers of electronic communication devices claim they will keep you connected, evidence is mounting that our reliance on these devices is actually disconnecting us. Being disconnected, in turn, robs us of our ability to apply emotional intelligence. This should come as no surprise. How many times have you observed people sitting together in a restaurant or some other setting absorbed in using their smartphones while ignoring each other? The phenomenon is hardly rare. In fact, it has become commonplace.

It is not my intention here to disparage electronic communication. It offers many benefits. At the very least, computers and smartphones offer convenience and immediacy. I am old enough to remember having to frantically dash about looking for a pay phone so I could call home or the office when traveling. It certainly would have been more convenient to have a smartphone. But what I am saying is electronic communication, like any technology, has a downside. One of the problems with electronic communication is it takes the humanity out of human interaction. Consequently, my advice to you is simple: If you want to improve your emotional intelligence, put down your smartphone and connect with people face-to-face.

Judith knew it was time to put away the smartphones and reconnect with her family when her son began sending her text

messages while sitting right across the room from her. She wanted to be in touch with her son's feelings, moods, and everyday emotional ups and downs, but found their smartphones had become an impediment. Instead of open, face-to-face communication in which she could observe non-verbal cues and sense his emotions, Judith's son began to communicate almost exclusively via electronic devices. Acting decisively, Judith established a new family rule: No using smartphones to communicate unless either of them was away from home. When home, all communication would be face-to-face.

Reflect and Analyze in the Aftermath of Emotionally Charged Events

Milly was adept at applying her emotional intelligence. On an EQ test, she scored 55 on a 100-point scale, which is just slightly above average. Consequently, she worked hard to improve her emotional intelligence and to apply it effectively. One of her best improvement strategies involved after-the-fact analysis and reflection. Any time Milly became involved in an emotionally charged situation, she did her best to manage her own emotions while sensing those of others and responding helpfully to them.

Then, in the aftermath of the event, she took time to analyze her behavior, responses, and attitude. Did she handle the situation in a positive, productive, and helpful way? Is there anything she could have done better? Is there anything she should have done differently? Are there any lessons to be learned from the event? By undergoing this kind of after-the-fact analysis, Milly was able to continually improve her emotional intelligence and become more adept at applying it. But Milly didn't stop there.

In addition to analyzing her own behavior and responses, she observed how others behaved in highly emotional situations. Milly looked for positive, productive, and helpful behavior in others, as well as counterproductive and hurtful behavior. Then she analyzed the behavior she observed in the same way she analyzed her own. By doing this, Milly not only learned from her mistakes and successes, she also learned from those of others. Like Milly, you can improve your emotional intelligence as well as your effectiveness at applying it by taking the time to engage in after-the-fact reflection and analysis.

Practice Exercising Self-Restraint

A common mistake made by people who fail to apply their emotional intelligence is speaking or acting rashly. They do not think before they speak or act. Just because you have certain feelings at a given time—anger, frustration, bitterness, or even joy—does not mean you should act on or express them. This is what is meant in Proverbs 16:32, where we read a patient person with self-control is better than a warrior who takes a city. In emotional situations, it is better to exercise self-restraint and wait until the emotions of the moment pass. Appearing to lack self-restraint is not the kind of impression you want to make in the workplace.

Practice Responding Impersonally to Rude or Inconsiderate Comments

When coworkers act out their anger, frustration, worries, or fears by making rude or inconsiderate comments, it can be tempting to take their behavior personally. In fact, it is hard not to when you are on the receiving end of sarcastic or mean-spirited barbs; however, emotionally intelligent people learn to avoid falling into this trap. They do not allow rude or inconsiderate coworkers to take control of their emotions. This is important because, when people learn they can press your emotional buttons to their benefit, they will press them often.

1 Peter 3:9 offers some excellent advice on how to deal with rude and inconsiderate comments. This verse cautions against repaying rudeness with rudeness. Applying self-restraint when someone is rude or inconsiderate is the emotionally intelligent response and the Scripturally appropriate response. Luke 6:27–9 is also instructive for dealing with these situations. These verses remind us to do good to

those who mistreat us and to turn the other cheek to them. Turning the other cheek in the context of the workplace does not mean just passively absorbing the insensitive comments or behavior of others. Rather, it means not responding in kind. By taking the high road and responding to rudeness with grace (Colossians 4:6), you can show your coworkers a better way: the way of Christ.

In addition to these Biblical admonitions, there are three practical reasons for exercising restraint in the face of rudeness. First, your coworker's rude comments are not necessarily meant to hurt you specifically. People are sometimes rude because they have been hurt or feel threatened. In response, they lash out. Rude or inconsiderate comments are often a clumsy defense offered by people who are hurt, threatened, or angry. Your kindness might be the thing that turns away their wrath (Proverbs 15:1) and gives them an opportunity to respond differently. Further, in the aftermath of the situation, they may come to regret their behavior because you responded with grace. By refusing to take their rudeness personally and responding in kind, you make it easier for them to apologize, once they have gotten a grip on their emotions. Said another way, by refusing to allow them to control your emotions, you avoid becoming a stumbling block to them controlling their own emotions (Romans 14:13).

Second, the individual in question might be purposefully trying to bait you into losing control. This is a common enough tactic. Once someone controls your emotions, she controls you. If someone can cause you to lose control of your emotions, you will be less able to logically and convincingly argue your point of view. I worked with an individual for years who used this tactic. If you opposed an idea or recommendation he tossed out during a meeting, this individual would immediately go on the attack. He would make ridiculous accusations against you and question your motives for opposing him. He was a master at putting people on the defensive who had no reason to be defensive. But he knew you could not effectively oppose his ideas while trying to defend yourself against his accusations. You might work with someone who uses similar tactics. Consequently, taking inconsiderate or rude comments personally can mean you have fallen into their devious trap. Better to manage your emotions and let the individual in question see his perverse strategy isn't going to work with you.

Finally, even if the individual in question means to hurt you with his rude or inconsiderate comments, losing control and responding in kind is not a positive, productive, or helpful response. You would not argue with an ill-mannered six-year-old child, so why argue with an adult who acts like one? I understand it can be difficult to bite your tongue and restrain yourself from lashing out when you know the other person is intentionally trying to hurt you. But you can do it, and you will feel better about having done so, once the dust-up is over. The same cannot be said for the other individual.

If you find yourself on the receiving end of intentionally rude or inconsiderate comments, remember the admonition in Ephesians 6:11. In this verse, we are told to put on the whole armor of God, so we can stand up to the evil schemes of the devil. You might also think about the encouraging words contained in Philippians 4:13, where we are assured we can do all things through Christ who strengthens us. Use prayer to don the armor of God. You do this when you enlist the help of Christ.

Practice Listening and Thinking before Making Decisions

Those who fail to apply their emotional intelligence often act impulsively because they don't listen carefully and, as a result, act rashly. This is why we are warned in Proverbs 1:5 that it is wise to listen and in James 1:19 that we should be quick to listen and slow to speak. When dealing with a coworker or subordinate, have you ever had the experience of your emotions getting stirred up to the point you stopped listening even before she finished saying what she had to say? Once your emotions go into high gear, your ability to listen attentively shuts down. In other words, you stop listening carefully. When this happens, you risk making decisions or acting on the basis of erroneous or incomplete information.

137

Those who apply their emotional intelligence most effectively practice listening carefully and allowing the other party to state her case completely. Then, before responding, they take time to think the issue through completely. A common response from an emotionally intelligent person in these situations is this: "Thanks for your recommendation. Let me give it some thought and get back to you. I will have an answer for you no later than _____." In this way, emotionally intelligent people are able to avoid making rash decisions based on emotional impulses rather than complete and accurate information.

Practice "Listening" to Non-Verbal Cues

In Matthew 11:15 we are told that, if we have ears, we should hear and listen. This verse also applies to the type of *hearing* required in non-verbal communication. *Listening* to non-verbal cues is included here as a reminder that doing so takes practice. Picking up on non-verbal cues requires you tuning in to the other person's emotions as expressed through gestures, facial expressions, voice, tone, and proximity. Some non-verbal cues—especially those associated with anger—are hard to miss, but others can be subtle. You don't want to miss the subtle cues. Sometimes they can be even more important than the more obvious cues. Further, you want to be able to compare non-verbal cues with verbal messages to determine if there is agreement or disagreement between them. Doing these things requires intentional effort and practice.

Practice Controlling Your Temper

Proverbs 15:18 goes right to the heart of the matter when it comes to the subject of the human temper. This verse makes clear that those who lose their tempers cause problems while those who control their tempers solve problems. Psalms 37:8 is just as edifying on the subject. This verse warns that anger, wrath, and fretting push us toward evil. Typically, you are hurt worse by a display of anger

than is the recipient of your anger. Losing your temper is not only bad for your career, it also undermines the Christ-like example you want to set for coworkers.

There are a number of things you can do to control your temper but, before getting into specific strategies, I want to share what (to me) is the most important principle of anger management. That principle is this: People, circumstances, and things do *not* make you angry. Rather, when you become angry, you are allowing people, circumstances, or things to press your anger button. The cause of your anger is not the outside factors you might want to blame it on. Rather, it is your own lack of self-control. Your temper is not controlled by outside factors. It is controlled by you. You control or fail to control your temper. No one and nothing can make you angry without your permission. Therefore, blaming your anger on outside factors is just a way to avoid blaming the person who is really responsible. That person is you. To maintain control over your temper, try the following strategies:

Stop, breathe, freeze, and think

When you feel anger bubbling up inside you, apply what I call the *stop-breathe-freeze-think* strategy. Stop means do not act on the anger impulse. Breathe means take a few deep calming breaths. Freeze means hold your tongue until the anger subsides. Think means consider carefully what you plan to say once you have regained control of your emotions. There is nothing wrong with expressing frustration, but you want to do this only after your temper is under control. In this way, you will avoid making the situation worse and possibly saying things you will later regret. In most cases, all four of these steps can be accomplished in a matter of seconds. Further, the more you practice applying this strategy, the faster you will be able to move through each step.

Vent your anger in private

Most people are like tea pots. If they don't vent, they will explode. When you find your temper getting the better of you, separate yourself from coworkers, find a private place where you can be alone, and vent your anger forcefully. Pretend you are talking to the individual who pressed your anger button. Tell that person in no uncertain terms what you think of her. Don't hold back. Speak as if she were right there in the room with you. In addition to venting your anger, this exercise may prove cathartic. Once you have vented sufficiently to gain control of your temper, seek out the individual in question and express your concerns and frustration in a calm, positive, and helpful manner.

Exercise away your anger

One of the worst things you can do with your anger is hold it in and let it simmer. Not only is this unhealthy—emotionally and physically—it can lead to intemperate eruptions when you eventually encounter the proverbial last straw. What makes these deferred explosions especially unfortunate is when they occur, your anger is often directed at someone who has nothing to do with what you are really angry about. It happens like this. You are harboring anger toward a coworker but, when it finally explodes, the person on the receiving end of your anger is a friend, family member, or another coworker who has nothing to do with the situation in question. Don't let this happen. To get rid of pent up anger, exercise it off. Walk, run, or go to the gym. Physical exertion is one of the fastest and most effective ways to work off simmering anger.

Look for responses that are positive, helpful, and productive

Even when the words or actions of a coworker are rude or inconsiderate, your response should be positive, helpful, and productive. Part of reflecting the image of Christ in the workplace is

140

responding to situations—no matter how distasteful they may be—in positive, helpful, and productive ways. In fact, when coworkers are behaving like children, it is even more important for you to respond like an adult. By refusing to respond in kind to someone who is being negative, you might be able to turn the situation into something positive.

Practice Defusing the Anger of Coworkers, Customers, and Others

Being confronted by angry people is an all-too-common occurrence in today's workplace. The angry person might be a coworker who is out of sorts, an unhappy customer, a supplier who didn't get paid on time, or a stressed-out supervisor. The angry person might even be someone who is offended by your Christian views. The scenarios will differ, but one thing won't: Regardless your career field, you are going to have to deal with angry people.

Anger has become a common reaction when people don't get what they want, when they want it, and how they want it. There are a lot of angry people in the world, as evidenced by the increasing number of road rage and workplace violence incidents. This is the bad news. The good news is, if you are able to control your own temper, you might be able to help others control theirs. When you become adept at dealing effectively with angry people, you can be a peacemaker. Employers appreciate peacemakers who can defuse tense situations before they get out of control and become ugly.

Being known as a peacemaker among your coworkers is good for your career—but, even more importantly, it is also Scriptural. Matthew 5:9 tells us peacemakers are the blessed children of God. Consequently, there is every reason for you to practice dealing with angry people and using what you learn to defuse tense situations at work. The following strategies are used by emotionally intelligent women who are adept at dealing with angry people:

- *Get some company before proceeding.* When confronted by an angry person, whether a coworker or an outsider, the first thing to do is get some company. In this era of workplace violence, it is a good idea to have company when trying to deal with an angry person. Just having someone else present is often enough to bring an angry person back from the edge; however, in the event the angry person becomes threatening or even dangerous, having help could prevent a tragedy.

- *Suppress the urge to fight fire with fire.* Never respond to anger with anger. Anger is like a fire in that it must be fed, or it will go out. Responding to anger with anger just fuels the flames and makes a bigger fire. You can suppress the urge to fight fire with fire by applying the *stop-breathe-freeze-think* strategy. Once your temper is under control, you can do what is necessary to help the angry person get his under control.

- *Avoid taking the other person's anger personally.* People will say things in anger they don't really mean. In fact, in fits of anger, people often say things they regret later. You have probably done this yourself or, at least, seen it happen. Then there are the perverse schemers who will intentionally say rude or inconsiderate things to put you on the defensive or to cloud the issue in question. Either way, it is important for you to avoid falling into the trap of taking rude or inconsiderate comments personally. Do not react or respond to the anger. Keep your emotions and your non-verbal cues in neutral. Put some emotional distance between yourself and the other person. Once you fall into the trap of taking another individual's anger personally, the situation becomes doubly explosive because now both of you are angry.

- *Look past the anger to what might be causing it.* When someone angrily confronts you, their rude and inconsiderate behavior is a symptom, not a cause. To effectively defuse an angry situation, look past the symptoms and try to identify the cause. An effective way to defuse anger is to identify what is causing it and, then, work with the angry individual to eliminate or mitigate the cause. You will not solve the problem behind the anger by getting bogged down in the

symptoms. An effective method for getting to the cause of a person's anger is to acknowledge it and then ask why she feels the way she does. For example, assume a coworker is acting out her anger and you are on the receiving end of it. You might say, "I can see you are really angry about this. Tell me why you feel this way." Then listen in a concerned, caring, non-argumentative manner. You might have to repeat the why question several times before getting to what is really causing the anger. Repeating the why question is the verbal equivalent of peeling the onion until you get to the core of the problem.

- *Apologize, if appropriate.* Few things will defuse anger faster than a sincere apology. If it turns out something you said, did, or didn't do is the cause of the anger, apologize. It is difficult to stay angry at someone who is willing to take responsibility and say *mea culpa.* Even if you are not at fault, you can use a neutral form of apology as a tool for defusing anger. You can always tell the angry person you are sorry the situation occurred. Saying things like, "I am sorry this happened," or, "I am sorry things did not turn out the way you hoped," can be balm to an angry person.

- *Work with the angry person to find a solution.* Once you have identified the problem behind the individual's anger, the next step is obvious. Work with her to find a solution. If something you said or did is the cause, your sincere apology might be all that is necessary. It might be the solution. If the anger is attributed to something you didn't do, getting it done as soon as possible is the likely solution. If the cause of the anger has nothing to do with you, helping the individual talk through potential solutions can itself be the solution.

PRAYER FOR APPLYING EMOTIONAL INTELLIGENCE

Heavenly Father,

Even as a child, I recognized the wisdom of learning from others. As I've matured, I've understood more clearly the gift You've given me to be compassionate and considerate of the feelings and moods of those around me. You've taught me it is good to observe and listen with my heart before I offer opinions or ideas, and I've found that to be a good strategy.

I confess today that, even though these things are true, I sometimes forget what You've taught me. I don't always stop my impatience or my frustration from giving vent to anyone near enough to listen. Of course, when the venting is over, I regret the lack of control I've exhibited and know I need to return to You for strength and guidance. More than likely, I must go about repairing any damage I may have caused as well. When it's all said and done, I most always regret any emotional outburst at work.

I pray I will develop strength of character and the emotional intelligence You've given me, so I am more aware of the feelings and the needs of others. I pray my mind would be other-directed, and not self-serving. Lord, I long to be a peacemaker because the world is too chaotic and boisterous. It cannot hear Your loving voice, and so anger and selfishness have become the order of the day.

I ask You to continue to train me, teach me, and guide me in Your ways so I offer clarity and solace to those I work with. Open my eyes to see how I can serve others and honor You in the work I do. Give me a heart that looks at each situation and each person I encounter with Your eyes.

Grant that, at work and at home and wherever I am in the world, I would remember this life is not simply about me and what I need or want, but the story is much bigger, and it's about Your children everywhere. Bless each of my coworkers today with wisdom and divinely inspired emotional intelligence. Amen.

GROUP DISCUSSION CASE: "I need to improve my emotional intelligence"

Cassie had been reading about emotional intelligence in various business publications for months. Finally, she decided to take an EQ test. The result was 58 points out of 100, an above-average score; however, Cassie was not satisfied. She told a friend at work, "I need to improve my emotional intelligence." Cassie's friend wanted to help her, but had no idea how someone might go about improving her emotional intelligence.

Discussion Questions:

1. Have you ever worked with someone who needed to improve her or his emotional intelligence? In what ways did this individual's lack of emotional intelligence manifest itself at work?

2. If this individual came to you for advice concerning how to improve her or his level of emotional intelligence, what steps would you recommend?

GROUP DISCUSSION CASE: "I don't handle anger well"

Bianca was the best sales representative in her company. She worked for her current employer for six years and for five of them, she was "Sales Professional of the Year." In spite of her consistently high sales volume, Bianca was stuck in her current position. Anyone else with her performance record would have been promoted to sales

145

manager by now, but Bianca had a problem: her temper. She couldn't seem to control it. When things did not go her way, Bianca was prone to fits of temper—a fact that created problems with her coworkers.

Bianca knew she had to learn to control her temper if she hoped to become a sales manager. Consequently, she scheduled an appointment with her pastor for counseling. During the meeting, Bianca got right to the point. She told her pastor, "I don't handle anger well." Her pastor wasn't surprised by this admission. On several occasions, he witnessed Bianca losing her temper during church functions. Consequently, he welcomed the opportunity to discuss the problem with her. Unfortunately, he wasn't sure how to go about helping her.

Discussion Questions:

1. Have you ever worked with someone whose temper was a detriment to her career? If so, what were the circumstances?

2. If Bianca came to you instead of her pastor, what advice would you give her concerning how to control her temper?

REVIEW QUESTIONS FOR INDIVIDUALS AND GROUPS

1. What is emotional intelligence and why is it important?

2. Explain the author's concerns about the use of emotional intelligence tests.

3. Describe the connection between emotional intelligence and non-verbal communication.

4. List and explain the benefits of applying emotional intelligence.

5. Describe how you can improve your emotional intelligence.

6. What effect might electronic communication devices have on the emotional intelligence of people?

7. Explain the key to effectively interpreting non-verbal cues.

8. List and explain several strategies for controlling your temper.

9. List and explain several strategies for defusing the anger of others.

10. Explain how to use an apology to help others gain control of their temper.

CHAPTER 7

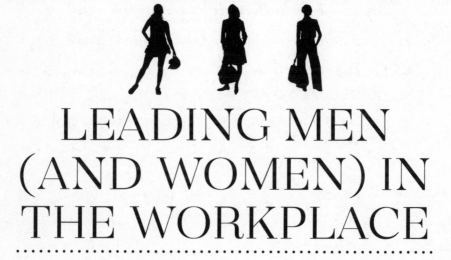

LEADING MEN (AND WOMEN) IN THE WORKPLACE

"Not domineering over those in your charge, but being examples to the flock." 1 Peter 5:3

Women who excel in the workplace eventually find themselves in charge of teams, departments, divisions, branch operations, and, ultimately, organizations. Managing a work unit of any size is likely to involve leading men. No problem, right? After all, this is the 21st century. There is no question: attitudes governing the workplace have changed over time. Women serving in leadership positions are no longer the rare phenomenon they once were. That's the good news. The bad news is acceptance of this socio-cultural phenomenon is not yet universal. Some men—and even some women—still resist it. Further, there is a lot of bad advice promulgated in business publications about what it takes for a woman to succeed as a leader in today's workplace.

When it comes to leading men (or women, for that matter) on the job, you are going to be encouraged and possibly even pressured to act in ways at odds with your faith and could undermine your efforts to excel. Consequently, it is important to understand from the outset that, whether leading men or women on the job, the best way to excel is to be the person God made you and apply the Biblical principles presented in this chapter.

SHOULD WOMEN LEAD MEN ON THE JOB?

The issue of women leading men is no longer as controversial as it once was. In fact, I admit to being surprised it still comes up as an issue at all; however, women I counsel claim they still encounter sporadic resistance on this question, much of it from fellow believers. Further, not all of the naysayers are men. Christians who believe women are prohibited from leading men tend to quote such verses as 1 Corinthians 11:3 and 1 Timothy 2:11–15, among others.

1 Corinthians 11:3 states the husband is the head of his wife. The verses from 1 Timothy state women are not allowed to teach men or to have authority over them. Taken out of context, these verses seem to prohibit Christian women from aspiring to management positions. This is why interpretive discernment and a systematic approach to reading the Bible are so important. Verses taken out of context can lead to questionable interpretations and even misinterpretations. When placed in context, it becomes clear the verses in question as well as others frequently quoted on this subject refer to women leading men in the church and home, not on the job.

This book is about women on the job. Consequently, debates over women leading in the church and home will have to be left for other authors and other books. Rather than getting sidetracked by these debates, let's stay focused on women leading men in the workplace. In this book, as well as in my counseling sessions, I take the view there are no Biblical prohibitions against women leading men at work. This is the view that enjoys the broadest (if not universal) acceptance in the Christian community and society, in general.

CHALLENGES FACED BY CHRISTIAN WOMEN WHO ASPIRE TO LEADERSHIP POSITIONS

In 1988, I established The Leadership Institute at the college where I teach. The Institute offers intensive leadership instruction and hands-on learning activities for rising stars in the private, public, and non-profit sectors. Employers look to the Institute to help them develop carefully-selected personnel who will, they hope, lead their organizations in the future. Every year, more than half of the participants are women. Many of them, as it turns out, are Christians.

Interacting with these dynamic young Christian professionals for so many years has given me insight into the types of challenges they face or will face as managers in their organizations. The more common of these challenges are explained in the remainder of this section. Many women who aspire to management positions face these same obstacles, but what makes these challenges unique to you as a Christian woman is not only do you have to cope with them as most women do, you are called to do so without compromising your faith.

Act-Like-a-Man Syndrome

One of the problems all new supervisors and managers face— women and men—is the ubiquitous but false perception of what constitutes leadership in today's society. Some view leaders as gruff, cigar-chomping, macho men who spend their days making cliff-hanger decisions based on nothing more than gut instinct. The chief assets of these so-called leaders are aggressiveness and volume. Others view leaders as goal-driven, Type A workaholics who push themselves and everyone else to the limit every day. The philosophy of these so-called leaders can be summed up in just a few words: "Don't give me excuses. Show me results."

I exaggerate here to make a point, but only slightly. In reality, the pictures I have painted of how leaders are viewed seem to dominate in American society. But how are women in leadership positions

150

viewed? Ironically, the picture doesn't change much. The prevailing image is one of women who act like men. This is why women sometimes struggle with moving into management positions. They feel as if they have to act like a man in order to lead, and not just any man, but the kind described in the previous paragraph. Let me be clear from the outset that adopting the *act-like-a-man* approach is a mistake for you and other Christian women who aspire to be leaders on the job.

The false images of leaders I just described make for good drama on television and in the movies, but I would remind you that the entertainment industry is about fantasy, not reality. The truth is nobody likes to be led by intimidation, coercion, yelling, or threats. Bossing is not leading. Further, nobody likes to be led by a domineering micromanager who spends the day shouting orders and demanding the impossible. People in the workplace might obey such individuals up to a point, if only to escape their wrath. But people who are intimidated, coerced, yelled at, and threatened do not put their whole hearts into their work. Instead, they give their loud, pushy bosses what I call *reluctant compliance*. This means they go along to get along, doing just enough to stay out of trouble, but not enough to be truly productive. Worse yet, they can become adept at finding subtle ways to retaliate to make their overbearing boss look bad.

The kind of leadership men and women in the workplace respond to best is called *servant leadership*. It is an approach to leading people based on Christ's example as well as selected Biblical principles, and it works. Better yet, it works regardless whether your subordinates are men or women. Servant leadership is explained in detail later in this chapter. For now, just understand that trying to act like a man when you become a manager is a mistake for Christian women. In fact, trying to act like anyone but the faithful child of God you are is a mistake.

God made you who you are and how you are. He gave you certain strengths, assets, and weaknesses. He wants you to use your God-given strengths and assets for the betterment of His kingdom, while

simultaneously working to improve your weaknesses. This is an obvious extension of the message in Ephesians 2:10. This verse states we were created by God to do good works. To do good works, we must apply the strengths God gave us while working to improve our weaknesses. Consequently, when you find yourself in a leadership position, be the person God made you. Don't try to be anyone else. Apply your God-given strengths to maximum effect and minimize your weaknesses. The concept of servant leadership will help you do this.

Resentment from Male Subordinates

An obvious but often ignored fact is you cannot lead people unless they are willing to follow. Consequently, to lead people, you must first earn their trust and respect. Doing this can be a difficult challenge for Christian women who hope to lead men. Women who participate in my leadership classes as well as those I counsel tell me some of their strongest supporters in the workplace are men. But they also tell me there are a lot of men who have learned to say the right things about women as leaders who, in reality, are better at talking the talk than walking the walk.

Such individuals are all for women getting ahead at work until it actually happens. When a woman becomes their supervisor or manager, resentment that, up to now, has been hidden begins to reveal itself. Luke predicted this kind of phenomenon in his Gospel. In Luke 12:2, we are assured there is nothing concealed that will not eventually be revealed. Hence, don't be disheartened if you find some of the men who claim to support your efforts to excel at work are more committed in theory than reality.

As a committed Christian, Macy was familiar with the message in Luke 12:2. Consequently, she had no reason to be surprised when once-supportive men in her department suddenly became resentful. Macy worked in a department of two women and twelve men. She interacted well with her coworkers and seemed to have their respect.

But, when she was promoted to manager of the department, her relationships with the men in it quickly went from warm to chilly.

Several of the men in her department seemed to resent Macy's promotion. One of them was always Macy's biggest supporter, or so she thought. Once Macy became his supervisor, this supposed ally began a campaign to undermine her authority and effectiveness. Macy didn't know if he resented her winning the promotion instead of someone else or if he just resented working for a woman. One thing she did know was that his resentment was counterproductive, and she was going to have to deal with it.

As a Christian woman, be prepared to face resentment when you become a supervisor or manager. Not all, but some men will chafe at working for a woman. Their negativity might grow out of professional jealousy or feeling threatened by women in positions of authority or even previously disguised misogyny. In some cases, there might even be the kinds of misguided Scriptural concerns dealt with earlier in this chapter. Some men who resent you might not even understand why. Dealing with rejection from those who report to you—men or women—is part of being a servant leader. The concept is covered later in this chapter. For now, just understand some men will view women in leadership positions as threats and some women will be jealous of the success of other women.

Jealousy of Other Women in Your Organization

One would hope a woman being promoted to a management position in an organization would be viewed as a victory by all women in the organization, but this is not always the case. At least, this is what I am told by women who participate in my leadership classes and counseling sessions. Here is a story I was told by a Christian woman named Madelyn. Madelyn was recently promoted to lead a department of eight paralegals.

Madelyn's law firm employed a complement of twenty-four attorneys—all men—and eight paralegals, seven of them women. The seven women paralegals were historically supervised by the firm's one male paralegal. That individual decided to take an early retirement after receiving a substantial inheritance. Madelyn was the only insider who applied for the position, and she won the promotion easily. Hence, one would expect the firm's paralegals to be pleased. After all, they long considered themselves better qualified than the man who was their supervisor. The women paralegals attributed their former male supervisor's status to gender bias, a belief long a bone of contention among them. Consequently, Madelyn expected her promotion to be viewed as a victory by all the female paralegals. Unfortunately, it wasn't.

After years of working well with Madelyn as a member of the team, several of the paralegals engaged in efforts to undermine her effectiveness. The Bible warns of just this kind of reaction. In 1 Corinthians 3:1-3, we are warned when people react out of jealousy, they are being human. These verses do not excuse jealousy. Rather, they warn us to expect it. Envy and jealousy are powerful forces of human nature. The sinful nature of human beings exists in all of us and Satan is always lurking in the shadows waiting for an opportunity to exploit it. The potential for jealousy among coworkers—female and male—is just the kind of opportunity Satan craves, so don't be surprised when the green monster rears its ugly head on the job and you become its target.

Bad Advice from Well-Intended People

When Vanessa was just weeks away from assuming the role of department supervisor, she began to get a lot of advice from people who cared about her and wanted to see her succeed. Their intentions were good, but their advice wasn't. One colleague told her she needed to stop thinking like a woman and start thinking like a man. Another told her she should try to deepen her voice. According to this friend: the deeper the voice, the more authoritative it sounded. Yet another colleague advised her to stop wearing dresses and skirts. From this point forward, she should wear only dark pantsuits so she would look like a leader. One colleague even told her to select a sacrificial lamb in the department and fire him on her first day as supervisor to demonstrate her authority.

Women who aspire to leadership positions get a lot of advice—some good and some not-so-good. One piece of advice many Christian women I have taught, counseled, and worked with claim they received is this: *Don't get close to those you lead.* People who offer this advice are trying to spare women who are newly minted managers the heartache of having to correct, discipline, lay off, or even fire people they know and care about. The theory behind this advice is that it will be easier to make the hard decisions managers often have to make if the affected employees are viewed with cold objectivity rather than as people you care about.

This is bad advice, no matter how well-intended. It is the opposite of what is expected of servant leaders and of Christians who are trying to reflect the image of Christ in how they do their jobs. Managers who do not care about their employees cannot lead them, no matter how good they might be at the other aspects of management (i.e., planning, organizing, and controlling). This is the origin of the leadership maxim that says *your employees don't care how much you know until they know how much you care.* Granted, it is difficult to take unwelcome action against people you care about. This is the rationale for the bad advice some give on this subject. But the willingness to take unwelcome action when necessary is one of the differences between those who can lead and those who cannot. If you are a parent, just think about how often you have had to correct your own children. But, because you love them, you do what must be done.

Think of Christ and how He led His Apostles and other followers. He loved them and cared about them, but He never hesitated to correct them when necessary. For example, in Luke 9:37–41, we see Jesus rebuking His disciples for failing to drive an evil spirit out of a child. In Luke 9:46–48, Christ read the thoughts of His disciples concerning which of them was the greatest. Disappointed, Christ rebuked them and explained, using the example of a little child, the least among them would be first.

Perhaps the most telling example of Christ rebuking someone He loved is found in Matthew 16:23. In this verse, Christ is unhappy with His Apostle Peter for dwelling on the things of man rather than the things of God. In rebuke, He gives Peter a first-class chewing out. Christ's words to Peter would be eye-opening coming from anyone but, coming from the Son of God, they must have been devastating. Nevertheless, with His rebuke of Peter, Christ demonstrated leaders must be prepared to say and do the right thing, no matter how much they care about the people involved. You don't really become a leader until you can make hard but necessary decisions about people you care for.

Others Viewing Your Christianity as Weakness

As Christians, we are supposed to be kind, caring, forgiving, long-suffering, forbearing, and patient in our dealings with people (Ephesians 4:31–32). Unfortunately, in the workplace, these characteristics can be misinterpreted, particularly by those who subscribe to society's stereotype of the leader. Those who accept the common stereotype might view Christian characteristics, such as kindness and caring, as signs of weakness, particularly when they are exhibited by women. As a result, some Christian women make the mistake of suppressing these characteristics at work. This is what Myra did until she learned a hard lesson about ignoring what the Bible teaches.

When Myra was promoted to supervisor of a staff of twelve accountants, her predecessor took her aside and gave her what he thought was good advice. He said, "Myra, you are one of the kindest, most caring people I know. But those traits will get you into trouble as a supervisor. If you are too kind to the people you supervise, they will take advantage of you." Myra admired her former supervisor, so she took his words to heart. Soon, the kind and caring Myra became a formal, by-the-book, all-business supervisor. She seemed to care only about the work to be done. Overnight, Myra no longer cared about the people who did the work. This is what got her into trouble.

When the performance of Dave, one of her best accountants, dropped off markedly, Myra called him on the carpet. She told Dave, in no uncertain terms, he needed to improve his performance or she would take disciplinary action against him. The new all-business Myra assumed Dave was taking advantage of their relationship and slacking off. When, after a month, Dave's performance did not improve, Myra upped the ante and gave him a written warning that went into his personnel file. When Dave asked for a meeting to explain why his performance was suffering, Myra brushed him off, saying she didn't want to hear any excuses. Within the hour, Dave submitted his resignation. Soon thereafter, Myra learned Dave's marriage was falling apart. On the day Dave tried to explain things to Myra, his wife left him and took their only child with her. His lagging performance was the result of family difficulties, not insubordination.

It didn't take long for the news of Dave's departure and the circumstances surrounding it to make the rounds. When this occurred, two things happened. First, Myra was suddenly viewed as an uncaring ogre by Dave's fellow accountants. One of them talked to Dave and was given the details of how Myra handled the situation. Not surprisingly, resentment toward her was palpable. Predictably, morale in Myra's department declined noticeably. The department's work suffered in quantity and quality as resentment toward Myra grew. Myra's team members were spending more time discussing her treatment of Dave than doing their jobs. Several requested transfers to other departments.

The second thing that happened was even more ominous: Myra was summoned to the office of the firm's CEO. He wanted to know how she managed to lose one of the company's best accountants. When the CEO told Myra a little kindness and understanding on her part could have prevented the unfortunate incident, she was taken aback. Myra explained about the advice she received from her predecessor. The CEO's response was brief and to the point: "Myra, that was bad advice. I hope you see that now." Then he explained that kindness and caring could be signs of strength in a leader, rather than weakness, if applied properly. He told her being confident enough in oneself to be kind and caring is a sign of strength.

The CEO, like Myra, was a Christian. He asked her: "Do you think Christ was weak?" When Myra responded she thought Christ was the strongest leader who ever lived, the CEO smiled and posed another question: "I agree, but He was also kind and caring, was He not?" Then he handed Myra a folder containing the PowerPoint slides from a seminar he recently attended on servant leadership. He asked her to look through the slides and then make an appointment with him to discuss what she learned.

He also told her to call Dave immediately and get him back on board before another accounting firm snapped him up. Then he told Myra something that put the whole episode into perspective for her. He said, "Myra, if I treated you in this situation the way you treated Dave, you would be looking for another job right now. But I am going to forgive your mishandling of this situation and give you a chance to make things right. I know you are a kind and caring person. From now on, put those traits to good use as a supervisor, as you always did as a staff accountant. The slides I gave you on servant leadership will help."

SERVANT LEADERSHIP DEFINED

Perhaps the best way to explain the concept of servant leadership is that it is Christ-like leadership. Christ led his followers by serving them and setting an example of service to others. In Matthew 20:28, we read Christ came to serve, not to be served. Christ wasn't a pushy boss or a Type A workaholic who spent His days shouting orders and making demands. Rather, He led his followers by showing them His vision of the Gospel, providing for their basic needs, and then guiding, teaching, counseling, and correcting them. Christ set the bar high for those who wanted to follow Him in that His disciples were expected to leave behind their families, professions, creature comforts, and worldly possessions. Only if they were willing to do these things could they follow Him.

Recall the episode in the Gospel of Mark where the rich young man wanted to follow Christ and be assured of going to heaven. This young man claimed to have obeyed the law of God all of his life, but Jesus, knowing his heart, told him there was one more thing he needed to do: Sell all he had and give the proceeds to the poor. Having done this, the young man could then follow Christ. That is setting the bar high and, as you know, the rich young man balked (Mark 10:21). Christ knew all along this rich young man was not suited to be one of His followers and He knew exactly how to make this point.

The foundation of servant leadership can be found in Philippians 2:3, where it is written we are to avoid selfishness and conceit in all we do. Rather, we are to be humble and regard serving others as more important than serving ourselves. Not surprisingly, servant leadership involves leading by serving because it is based on Christ's example. Servant leadership is about upholding and uplifting others rather than self, a concept antithetical to contemporary cultural norms, norms advocating looking out for number one.

Because they strive to be Christ-like, servant leaders don't threaten, coerce, or manage by tirade. Rather, they interact with their followers in ways that influence them for good. By setting an example of applying Scriptural principles in how they do their work, interact with others, solve problems, and face adversity, servant leaders influence their followers in ways that make them both better employees and better people. This is why I tell my leadership students and counseling clients that servant leaders inspire people to *do* better and *be* better.

Like Christ, servant leaders in the workplace set the bar high for their followers. Also, like Christ, they set an example of consistently exceeding these expectations themselves. Christ was willing to set an example of enduring abasement, abuse, torture, and finally an agonizing death on the cross to ensure His vision would be realized. Christ's commitment as their leader had a powerful effect on His followers, just as your commitment as a servant leader will have a powerful effect on yours. To have this kind of influence with those

159

you supervise, it will be necessary to adopt and apply the defining traits of the servant leader.

DEFINING TRAITS OF SERVANT LEADERS

There can be a canyon-sized gap between what are viewed as leadership traits and the traits that actually make people good leaders. Ask almost any audience to develop a list of the personal traits they associate with leadership and their responses are likely to include such things as drive, single-mindedness, toughness, decisiveness, and dogmatic persistence. There is certainly nothing wrong with these traits in a leader. In fact, as long as they are properly tempered and applied, they can help an individual be a more effective leader. But there is an inescapable problem with these traits: They do little to engender followership, and a leader without followers is no leader at all.

For more than thirty years, I have polled my leadership classes and counseling clients concerning the kinds of traits that would make them want to follow a person who aspired to lead them. Year after year, without fail, the traits identified have two things in common: 1) they are the same or very similar, and 2) they differ notably from the traits commonly associated with leaders. The traits for generating enthusiastic, committed followers most often identified in these surveys are as follows:

- Trustworthiness (honesty and integrity)

- Vision/sense of purpose

- Listening

- Compassion/caring/consideration/empathy

- Credibility/influence

- Commitment

- Fairness

- Courage

- Perseverance

- Positive attitude (ability to give others a sense of hope)

- Patience

- Stewardship

- Initiative

These are the traits personified by servant leaders. Each of them is based on one or more Scriptural principles and is fundamental to servant leadership. As you move into a management position, these traits will make you an effective leader of men and women, not those often portrayed by actors in movies and on television.

Trustworthiness/Honesty/Integrity

If people don't trust you, they won't follow you. This is one of the most basic principles of leadership. Untrustworthy leaders rarely, if ever, have loyal, committed followers. Rather, they have resentful employees who reluctantly comply with their demands rather than putting their hearts into doing the best job they can. Honesty, integrity, and trustworthiness are Scriptural principles. The Bible is replete with guidance on these subjects, beginning with the Ninth Commandment's proscription against lying (Exodus 20:16). Ephesians 4:25 is another example of the many Scriptural verses extolling honesty, integrity, and trustworthiness. In this verse, we are told to avoid falsehoods and speak the truth.

Malita framed Ephesians 4:25 and hung it on the wall of her office. More importantly, she was faithful in following its admonition. Malita's honesty and integrity made her a trusted manager and supervisor. The personnel in her department knew they could count on her to tell the truth, even when the truth hurt or was inconvenient. As a result, they trusted and respected her. They demonstrated their trust and respect for Malita by working

161

hard to achieve peak performance. Their efforts gave Malita a high-performing department.

As a top manager, Malita was one of the few people who knew the company was going to be sold. Her boss did not want employees to know about the impending sale for fear they might panic and seek employment with a competitor. He did not want the company's sales figures to drop just before the sale went through. Poor sales figures could reduce the final selling price of the company. For this reason, the CEO placed a gag order on all his managers.

Malita complied with the gag order until word of the sale was revealed by another source. When this happened, her team members began to ask about the sale. Asked directly about the sale, Malita chose to tell the truth. She let her team members know when the sale would take place and how it might affect them. Not surprisingly, Malita's honesty got her into hot water with the company's CEO. But the CEO was way off base in chastising Malita. She was not disloyal to the company or the CEO. In addition to telling her team members the truth about the sale, she encouraged them to stay on and told them she would do everything in her power to protect their jobs.

Other managers continued to be closemouthed about the sale, in spite of the rumors occupying every employee's time and attention. As a result, by the time the sale was finalized, all departments except Malita's were reduced significantly because panicked employees migrated to other firms. Only Malita was able to present the new owners with a fully staffed, fully functioning department. For this, she and her department were rewarded with bonuses by the new owner. It turned out he wanted to keep the company's workforce intact and appreciated Malita's contribution to doing that.

Two other benefits of trustworthiness are important. First, it can go a long way toward diminishing the resentment some men might feel about being led by a woman. Second, it can also help assuage the jealousy some women might feel about your success. It is difficult for men or women to remain resentful or jealous of a leader who proves worthy of their trust. When there is resentment and jealousy, these things don't go away overnight. But, with time and persistence, you can overcome them by being a trustworthy leader.

Vision

If you want people to follow you, establish a worthy vision and share it with them. People are reluctant to follow until they know where the leader is going. Christ's vision was to have the Gospel spread throughout the world (Mark 16:15–16). This, of course, was a worthy vision, the most worthy in history. Once His Apostles finally understood the vision, they committed to achieving it. They did this because it was worthy of their time and effort and, as things turned out, their lives. John, of course, was the exception. He didn't lose his life spreading the Gospel, but he did commit the rest of it to the pursuit of Christ's vision. People will follow you more readily when they know the destination.

Listening

Servant leaders learn to be good listeners. Listening is a Scriptural concept set forth in Proverbs 1:5 as well as numerous other places in the Bible. In Proverbs 1:5, we are told it is wise to listen because, by listening, we increase our knowledge. One way to increase your knowledge at work is to listen to your followers. Servant leaders understand the people who do the day-to-day work of their organization have eyes, ears, brains, knowledge, and experience. Consequently, they are worth listening to as a way to increase knowledge. Servant leaders also understand they have no monopoly on knowledge and experience. They do not and cannot know everything. But, by listening, they can learn more than they would have otherwise.

Your team members might know things you have not thought of or have overlooked. Consequently, servant leaders listen carefully to their followers with the intention of gaining information that might help them make better decisions, generate better ideas, and arrive at better solutions. They also listen as a way to get out in front of small problems before they become big problems. Servant leaders understand they learn more by listening than talking.

Lindsey got off to a bad start as a manager because she failed to listen to her team members. She was a top performer for many years before becoming department manager. Unfortunately, Lindsey saw no need to listen to her team members. She thought she had all the answers. Otherwise, why would she have been promoted to lead the department? Lindsey thought managers had all the answers and were supposed to impart them to less-experienced team members, and she approached her job accordingly. This perception of the leader's job, not surprisingly, turned out to be a mistake.

Lindsey had a worthy vision she shared with her team members. She wanted her department's books to be the leading product line in their publishing company. Had she listened to her team members, particularly some of the younger ones, she might have achieved this vision. Lindsey was an old-school editor when she was tapped to lead the teen-fiction department of her publishing company. Consequently, she had little use for the new technologies coming on line at the time. She summarized her attitude toward electronic and audio books in these words: "Who would want to read or listen to a book on an electronic device?" As it turned out, a lot of people would, particularly teenagers who quickly adopted electronic technologies as their medium of choice. In fact, teenagers not only prefer electronic devices, they have developed a dependency on them that resembles an addiction, something Lindsey's younger employees tried to tell her.

Because she refused to listen to the input of her team members about electronic technology, Lindsey's department saw its sales figures decline instead of grow, as sales of teen-fiction sunk to an all-time low. Stopping the bleeding required a major attitude adjustment on her part as well as a willingness to listen, but Lindsey eventually caught on and turned things around. Even so, the rebuilding process was painful. During her department's slump in sales, Lindsey lost several excellent sales representatives, a couple of good editors, and a long-time author. Further, because the other department managers in her company were quicker to jump on the technology bandwagon, she was never able to make up sufficient ground to pass them in sales, even after finally putting aside her bias against technology. As she reflected on the situation, Lindsey thought, "If only I had listened."

Compassion/Caring/Kindness/Empathy

Servant leaders practice putting themselves in the shoes of those they lead. They are empathetic and considerate of their followers. Compassion, caring, kindness, and empathy are all Scriptural principles (Colossians 3:12). They are how we reflect the love of Christ for our coworkers. God is compassionate, caring, kind, and empathetic toward us, and He expects us to follow His example as we interact with others. Team members who are treated this way are more likely to put their whole hearts into achieving peak performance than those who feel they are being exploited, coerced, or threatened. But, beware: there may be some who will interpret these Christian traits as weakness and try to exploit them.

If you ever sense followers view these Christian traits in you as weakness, don't despair. This does happen. Christian women who approach me for counseling often complain about this misguided perspective. If you handle this kind of situation properly, your team members will soon learn not to confuse kindness with weakness. One servant leader I know, Valashia, told me how she had to make the point that kindness is not weakness.

Valashia told me about an employee she inherited in her first management position. This employee had an underwhelming performance record and was a borderline malingerer. When she was kind in how she explained the need for him to improve, he mistook her caring attitude for weakness, and tried to take advantage of her. When she helped him develop a plan for improvement that included specific performance goals as well as deadlines, he just scoffed and told coworkers Valashia "didn't have the guts to discipline him." That's when she fired him.

In showing this lackluster employee the door, Valashia was as kind to him as she had always been, but she was firm in her resolve that his poor performance, bad attitude, and sophomoric schemes for avoiding work merited no further patience on her part. This now-former employee realized too late he misread his new supervisor. Valashia was kind, but she was not weak. The abrupt termination of a chronic malingerer who got away with his idleness had a powerful effect on Valashia's other team members.

This is not to say you must fire someone to demonstrate Christian love is not weakness. Rather, you communicate this message by making hard decisions when they have to be made and making them on the basis of what is best for the team and the larger organization, all the while staying within the bounds of your Christian beliefs. When your team members realize you can be compassionate, caring, kind, and empathetic while maintaining high standards and strict accountability, they will no longer associate these Christian traits with weakness.

Credibility/Influence

1 Timothy 4:12 describes how servant leaders can gain influence with their followers. According to this verse, the key is to set an example for them of how a Christian interacts with people. Part of setting the right kind of example for followers is establishing high expectations and then exceeding those expectations yourself. Christ set the bar high for His followers. Emulating His example, servant leaders set the bar high for theirs. By establishing high expectations for their followers and then exceeding the expectations themselves, servant leaders earn credibility with their team members. Credibility, in turn, gives them influence.

Rather than just giving orders and making demands, servant leaders use their influence to persuade followers that giving their best in pursuit of the vision is more than just good for the team; it is good for them, too. Because they use their influence to persuade rather than using their positions to coerce, servant leaders tend to

get the best from their followers. Employees who are persuaded by their leaders instead of coerced are more likely to put their hearts into getting the job done right, on time, and within budget.

Commitment

Few things of significance are achieved without commitment. Being committed to achieving the vision is fundamental to leadership. Like the other traits of servant leaders, commitment is a Scriptural principle. Jesus was committed to His vision of sharing the Gospel throughout the world. To achieve this vision, Christ needed His followers to be equally committed. This is why He told them anyone who wanted to follow Him had to be willing to deny himself (Matthew 16:24). Jesus knew the price His Apostles would pay for committing to His vision. This is why He wanted followers who were willing to lose their lives for His sake (Matthew 16:25).

Servant leaders must demonstrate, at every opportunity, they are committed to achieving their visions. This is important because your followers will not commit to the vision if they sense you are not committed to it. Commitment means more than just trying hard. It means, within the boundaries prescribed by laws, ethics, and your Christian principles, you will to do whatever is necessary to get the job done. In other words, it means you are willing to sacrifice to achieve the vision.

Self-Sacrifice

What makes Christ's example of servant leadership so powerful is His self-sacrifice. He was willing to go voluntarily to the cross to carry out His vision. Christ not only sacrificed for the cause, He made the ultimate sacrifice. Like Christ, servant leaders must be willing to sacrifice for the vision. Christ put the importance of self-sacrifice into perspective in Luke 14:26–27. In these verses, He demonstrated that those who want to follow Him must be willing to sacrifice not just their most important relationships, but their lives.

You are not likely to have to sacrifice your life in pursuit of a vision at work, but you might have to sacrifice pieces of it. For example, you might have to sacrifice time you would like to spend doing something else, personal recognition in favor of team recognition, and even personal rewards in favor of team rewards. Your team members must know you are willing to sacrifice for the vision if you expect them to sacrifice for it.

Rosita personified the concept of self-sacrifice. Foreign competition steadily eroded the customer base of Rosita's company to the point layoffs were planned. On the upside, the company was in the process of introducing a new product line that would allow it to expand into new markets and hopefully make up for the business it lost to foreign competition. Rosita's department was responsible for the company's new product line. That was the good news. The bad news was there would be a down period of at least two months between introducing the new product line and realizing an increase in sales volume because of it. Consequently, Rosita was instructed to submit a plan for cutting her staff by 50 percent for a period of two months.

Rosita knew being without jobs in their small town, even for two months, would devastate her team members. Consequently, she proposed a different solution to higher management: keep her entire team on the payroll half-time for the next two months rather than laying them off. This would save the required 50 percent in personnel costs, pay the employees in question more than they could collect in unemployment compensation, and ensure the work of introducing the new product line would proceed on schedule. Higher management accepted her plan, as did her grateful team members.

But there was still one issue Rosita had to work out with the company's executives. As a manager, she was not included in the layoff plan. Rosita was to be kept on full-time, even after her team members were transitioned to half-time. Fearful of the effect this could have on team morale, Rosita told her boss she intended to reduce her pay by 50 percent during the period her team members were on a half-time/half-pay schedule. Higher management balked at this recommendation because they wanted Rosita in place full-time to oversee the details of getting the new product line introduced and distributed to customers.

Rosita countered she would continue to work full-time but would accept only half of her pay. When the company's human resources director expressed concerns about legal issues that could arise out of this arrangement, Rosita solved the problem by accepting her full salary, but donating half of it each payday to her team members for the two-month reduction period. Her example of self-sacrifice made a deep and lasting impression on the employees in her department. From that day forward, she had the most loyal, committed team members in the company.

There is an interesting postscript to this story. The new product line Rosita's company introduced did catch on in the marketplace, and its sales volume exceeded even the rosiest predictions of the marketing department. As a result, the company offered to reimburse Rosita for the pay she gave her team members during the reduction period and to tack on a substantial bonus. Instead of accepting the money outright, Rosita asked her boss to divide all of it including the bonus equally among her team members. She took a share of the cash for herself, but only the same amount given to each of her team members.

Rosita forfeited a substantial amount of money during the down period, but her example of self-sacrifice did not go unrewarded. In subsequent years, it was repaid many times over by the loyalty and commitment of grateful team members. An added benefit was realized when her willingness to sacrifice for the team won over a male team member who always chafed at being led by a woman. This individual just purchased a new house for his family when the layoff rumors started. Had it not been for Rosita's plan to avoid layoffs and her willingness to share half of her own earnings, this man would have been unable to meet his mortgage payments. He later told Rosita, every time he walked into his house, he remembered the sacrifice she made for him and the team.

Fairness

Life in a fallen world can be unfair at times, something most people eventually learn. In spite of this, people expect their leaders to be fair and resent any perception of unfairness. This is a reasonable expectation. After all, fairness is a Scriptural principle. The message in Psalm 9:8 is that God will judge the world and the people in it with fairness. In fact, political correctness notwithstanding, when America's founders stated all people are created equal, they did not mean equal in ability, motivation, ambition, intelligence, or even societal privilege. Rather, they meant equal in the eyes of God. Consequently, fairness is not about achieving equal results. Rather, it is about treating people equally well. As stated in Acts 10:34–35, God does not play favorites. Therefore, servant leaders should not play favorites.

Refusing to play favorites does not mean servant leaders cannot have favorites. Those employees who can be relied on to get the job done right, on time, and within budget, maintain a positive attitude, and make the team function better are bound to be your favorites. There is nothing wrong with this. Having favorites is not the same thing as playing favorites. When you play favorites, you give privileges, recognition, rewards, and special consideration to a select few on the basis of personal relationships rather than performance. In other words, you treat some followers better than others and you do it on the basis of personal feelings rather than merit.

Even Christ is thought to have had a favorite among His Apostles (John 13:23 and 19:26–27). The consensus among Biblical scholars is the favorite Apostle referred to in these verses was John. Christ may have had a favorite Apostle, but he did not play favorites among His Apostles. Rather, He treated them all with fairness, complimenting and rebuking them as appropriate. Since Christ is the ultimate servant leader, following His example is the wise course for you. Treat your followers fairly. Whether or not they are your favorites, recognize, reward, and correct them on the basis of how they do their jobs rather than your personal feelings about them.

Courage

Servant leaders must have the courage to stand up for what is right, do the right thing even when it hurts, support their team members in difficult situations, and, when necessary, give bad news to good people. The concept is known as moral courage, and you cannot lead people on the job without it. As a Christian woman, the courage you need to be an effective servant leader comes from God. The Scriptural principle is that, in difficult situations, you can do what needs to be done because God is with you. This principle is set forth numerous times throughout the Bible.

In Deuteronomy 31:8, we are reassured God will not forsake us. Therefore, we should not be afraid or discouraged when confronted by difficult situations or hard choices. Psalm 23 reminds us that, no matter how dark things seem to be at any given point in our lives, we need not fear because God is with us. Courage is a gift given to those who understand that, with God, all things are possible (Matthew 19:26). Regina understood this. As a Christian and a servant leader, she leaned on God for the courage to do the right thing, regardless of how unpopular or uncomfortable doing so might be.

She did not fit the stereotype when it came to courage. Regina was small in stature and an introvert. By nature, she was shy, humble, and unassuming. But, when it came to moral courage, Regina had plenty, and, in her job, she needed it. She was the safety manager for a large manufacturing firm, a position that often brought her into conflict with shop supervisors over the enforcement of safety regulations and procedures. To make matters worse, she supervised a staff of five male safety specialists, all of whom resented working for a woman, scoffed at her Christianity, and wanted her job.

The shop supervisors in her company viewed safety regulations as government-imposed nuisances that slowed down production. They resisted complying with the regulations and resented the fact the individual responsible for enforcing them was a woman. Consequently, for years, Regina had to swim against the current in dealing with shop supervisors who took every opportunity to ignore safety regulations and who were aided in their perfidy by Regina's

171

own staff. Regina's Christianity just made matters worse in the eyes of her detractors. They complained constantly about her "goody-goody" attitude.

The bubbling cauldron that was Regina's life at work finally boiled over when a major contract fell behind schedule. Delivery on this contract had to be on time or substantial late fees would be assessed. In response, the shop supervisors approached the vice-president for manufacturing and asked him to order Regina to back off on enforcing safety regulations. When she refused, the vice-president shouted, "They are OSHA regulations Regina, not the Ten Commandments. Cut us some slack." When she still refused, he claimed she was being insubordinate and had her suspended for two weeks. Regina, who was humble and respectful throughout the vice-president's tirade, suspected the meeting was nothing more than a ruse to get her out of the way. With Regina suspended, the shop supervisors would have two weeks to catch up on their work without the inconvenience of safety regulations they viewed as impediments to their work.

Then, on the third day of her suspension, it happened. Regina was relaxing at home and contemplating her future when the telephone rang. There was a major accident at work. Three employees were injured, one critically. The company's CEO wanted her back at work immediately to help him with damage control. While she was out, the safety specialists on her staff acquiesced in allowing shop supervisors to ignore safety regulations. Not one of them was willing to stand up to the supervisors to ensure safe working conditions. The accident and subsequent injuries quickly evolved into a major controversy for the company. Word soon spread among employees that heads were going to roll.

The Occupational Safety and Health Administration (OSHA) cited the company for numerous willful safety violations and recommended the maximum fines when its investigator learned Regina was suspended to get her out of the way. The company eventually delivered on the contract, but much later than it would have, had there been no accident. As a result, late fees were assessed.

Together, the OSHA fines and late fees were substantial, but they were only the tip of the iceberg when it came to the company's problems. The accident was picked up by the local newspaper and became an on-going front-page story. The story caught on and generated a rash of negative publicity. Like hungry sharks, competitors smelled blood in the water and went after the company's customers. Established customers turned their backs on the company, as did potential new customers. The situation became so dire bankruptcy was a possibility.

Regina was asked to meet with the company's CEO the minute she arrived at work. He wasted no time in letting her know where things stood and there were going to be changes. In fact, the CEO frankly admitted the only reason he wasn't going to be fired himself was he owned the company. Now his challenge was to save it, and he needed Regina's help. The CEO explained, from that day forward, he wanted the two of them to work together to establish a safety-first culture in the company. He explained he already fired the vice-president who suspended Regina and that his replacement would support her in maintaining a safe work environment or be fired, too. He encouraged Regina to fire all five of the safety specialists on her staff in response to their complicity.

Regina agreed to help the CEO rebuild his company, but she offered a counter proposal concerning her staff. Rather than fire them, why not use the incident to adjust their attitudes toward both safety and being supervised by a woman. If handled properly, she could turn the accident into an edifying experience for her safety specialists, all of whom probably expected to be fired. Regina asked the CEO to instruct the Human Resources Director to inform the safety specialists he wanted them fired, but she had interceded on their behalf and asked that they be given a chance to redeem themselves. Regina explained that, with their complicity in the accident, she suspected her safety specialists would welcome an opportunity for redemption. As things turned out, she was right.

Not only did the male safety specialists on her staff appreciate being given a second chance, they came away from the incident with a new respect for how difficult it was to be a safety manager and for

how well Regina performed the job. From that day until she retired, Regina had the respect of her safety staff and the cooperation of the company's shop-floor supervisors. It took years for the company to regain its market share, but it eventually did. Not only that, the company developed a reputation for providing a safe and healthy work environment. This, in turn, helped attract the best and brightest manufacturing professionals and technicians in the business. People who work in potentially dangerous occupations appreciate employers who stress safety. These good things happened, in this case, because one servant leader had the courage to do the right thing in the face of opposition.

Perseverance

Sometimes getting the job done is a matter of just staying the course when others want to give up and quit. The concept is known as perseverance. When the roadblocks to success seem insurmountable, your example of perseverance can be the difference between success and failure. If you falter, your followers will sense defeat and give up. But, if you persevere, they will gain hope from your example. This is the message found in Romans 5:3–4, where we read enduring in the face of suffering builds character, and character provides hope. James 1:2–4 admonishes us to welcome trials because our faith is strengthened when we are tested. James 1:12 states we will be blessed for remaining steadfast when life becomes difficult. Clearly, there is a Scriptural expectation that Christians will set an example of perseverance.

Your example of calm, but determined perseverance when deadlines loom, work falls behind schedule, customers demand the impossible, and other problems crop up may give your followers the hope they need to stay the course and get the job done, in spite of the challenges. When the job becomes difficult, remember the message in Roman 5:3–4 about endurance producing character and character providing hope. Your followers will look to you as their example in the midst of difficulty. Make sure you give them hope.

Positive attitude

It is said in leadership circles your attitude is the only thing in life you really control. It is also said no factor has a greater effect on success than attitude. Positive attitudes motivate, reassure, promote better relationships, enhance wellbeing, and encourage peak performance. An interesting fact about attitudes, positive or negative, is they are contagious. Your followers will *catch* your attitude by simply being exposed to it on a regular basis. Consequently, it is important you develop, maintain, and consistently exhibit a positive attitude. If your followers are going to catch what you have, make sure what you have is a positive attitude.

A positive attitude is not to be confused with false optimism. A false optimist will tell followers everything is fine, even when it isn't. In difficult situations, false optimists adopt an artificially happy tone and ignore the problems, hoping they will just go away. Leaders with positive attitudes are different. They acknowledge the problem in question but reassure followers they are up to the challenge of overcoming it. There is no artifice in a positive attitude.

If a false optimist and a leader with a positive attitude were standing at the rail of the sinking Titanic, the false optimist would put on a happy face and tell everyone there is nothing to worry about. The leader with a positive attitude, on the other hand, would acknowledge the danger they faced, reassure followers they were up to meeting the challenge, and keep them focused on getting into the lifeboats. In fact, the leader with a positive attitude would guide followers to the lifeboats and help them get aboard. In short, a positive attitude is not about maintaining an upbeat countenance while denying obvious problems. Rather, it is about squarely facing up to problems while remaining calm, reassuring, and focused on solutions rather than problems.

The Bible is clear and unequivocal about the value of a positive attitude. Proverbs 17:22 refers to a positive attitude as a happy heart. It goes on to state a crushed spirit—the kind negative attitudes produce—will dry up the bones. It should come as no surprise team members with crushed spirits will not perform at peak levels.

175

Crushed spirits resulting from negative attitudes focus the attention of people on themselves rather than what needs to be done to solve problems or mitigate crises. A positive attitude prevents "poor me" thinking and allows people to stay focused on finding solutions rather than wringing their hands over problems.

Philippians 4:8 provides an excellent description of what adopting a positive attitude looks like. This verse tells us to fix our thoughts on good things, positive, and praiseworthy. In the context of your job, this verse means, if you aspire to be a servant leader, you should focus on solutions rather than problems, strategies rather than roadblocks, success rather than failure, reassurance rather than fear, perseverance rather than quitting, and hope rather than despair.

One of the most positive, optimistic people who ever lived was the great inventor Thomas Alva Edison. It required thousands of attempts before he was able to invent a dependable light bulb filament. When asked about how frustrating it must have been to endure so many failed attempts, Edison surprised his questioner. The industrious inventor claimed he did not view the unsuccessful attempts as failures. To the contrary, each failed attempt had value because it brought him one step closer to success. When he finally found the way to make a functioning light bulb filament, Edison was pleased (of course). But he made it clear to anyone who asked he was also pleased because he now knew thousands of ways not to make a light bulb filament. That is a positive attitude.

I once had a consulting contract with an engineering firm making the transition from traditional methods to computer-aided design and drafting or CADD. This meant engineers and drafting technicians who spent years using manual tools and techniques would have to learn a whole new way of doing their jobs. The impending transition to computers was not popular with the more experienced engineers and technicians. It was a case of old dogs not wanting to learn new tricks.

My contact with the company was the chief engineer, a Christian woman named Emily. This alone was a rarity. At the time (1980s), there were few female engineers and even fewer who rose to

positions in management. Emily was an extraordinary individual in many ways. Not only was she a double anomaly as a female engineer and an engineering manager, she had the most positive, uplifting attitude of any person I have ever known. Emily simply refused to allow the challenges of the workplace to get her down or to alter her focus. Thankfully, her positive attitude was contagious, because we faced an uphill struggle trying to convince her staff of older engineers to accept the new technology. There was a lot of huffing, puffing, and grouching from the more experienced engineers as I demonstrated how they could use CADD to aid them in performing design calculations and developing drawings.

But Emily was everywhere: encouraging, keeping the engineers focused on learning, and painting a mental picture of how good things were going to be when they could make full use of the new technology. One particular example demonstrates how Emily's positive attitude ensured a successful transition. Emily found out her most senior engineer, Jim, was contemplating retirement to avoid having to learn to use the new CADD technology. He was afraid the new technology would rob him of his status as the *go-to engineer* in the department and turn him into a rookie. Jim's status as the department's most experienced and knowledgeable engineer was important to him. Emily knew intuitively what the problem was.

Emily called a meeting with Jim and asked me to be present when they met. She began the conversation by telling me Jim was an outstanding engineer who she depended on and could not do without. Then she told me I was going to work with Jim one-on-one in advance of the transition because he was going to be her go-to guy on CADD. She reminded Jim how he made the transition from slide rules to electronic calculators and he could do the same with CADD. She had confidence in him and knew what he could do when he set his mind to it. She appealed to his loyalty by telling him the department would be unable to make the transition unless he led the way.

Emily surprised both of us when she said, "In fact, let's do this. Dr. Goetsch will help you become an expert on CADD and then

177

you will teach the rest of us, beginning with me." As I watched in amazement, Emily helped Jim put his fears of becoming a rookie aside and get focused on solutions. She let him know he would still be the department's expert. Once he knew this, the crisis was over. By the time the meeting concluded, Jim went from feeling disconsolate to feeling elated. His status as the go-to engineer would be safe and his usefulness to the department assured. In this situation and many others, as I came to learn, Emily's positive attitude turned a lemon into lemonade.

Patience

I was reluctant to write this section because patience comes hard for me. In fact, my giving advice on patience is like Hagar the Horrible giving advice on table manners. I still find myself getting antsy when forced to sit through a green light because the person in front of me is texting instead of paying attention; however, through prayer and intentional effort, I do manage to maintain a modicum of patience. But I have to work at it. This is why I know you can develop patience. If I can, anyone can. To be a servant leader, you must. Being impatient with followers—particularly those who are sincerely trying to do a good job—can undermine their morale and, in turn, their performance.

Because of what occurred in the Garden of Eden (Genesis 3), we live in a fallen world and work with imperfect people, ourselves included. Christians who are servant leaders understand this. Because they understand their followers are flawed people trying to function in a fallen world, servant leaders make a point of being patient with them. Instead of fretting and fuming when team members function like people instead of machines, servant leaders mentor, teach, guide, and correct them. The best leaders help their followers improve continually, all the while understanding some will take longer than others to become peak performers.

This is not to say you should indulge those who waste time or fail to put forth an acceptable level of effort. You shouldn't. Your patience and forbearance should be fully extended to those who are sincerely trying to contribute, not to those who have no intention of even trying to contribute. But, when a follower truly wants to do a good job, servant leaders invest in that individual. They patiently devote the time and energy necessary to help her develop into a peak performer.

Patience, of course, is a Scriptural principle, something I have to remind myself of constantly. Ephesians 4:2 summarizes God's views on patience clearly and succinctly. This verse tells us, among other things, to be patient with one another. I have selfishly searched the Bible high and low for an out concerning patience. There isn't one. God is patient with us and He expects us to be patient with each other. This means I have no excuses for my impatience, nor do you or anyone who wants to be a servant leader.

I once worked with a Christian servant leader named Allison, who was the personification of patience. She was a department chair at the college where I was serving as a dean at the time. Only too aware of my shortcomings when it came to patience, I marveled at how she interacted with those she supervised. I once asked Allison how she came to be so patient. She explained that, for her, patience was a hard-won virtue because there was a time in her life when she had little or no patience. This revelation was an eye-opener for me. Here was a respected colleague, a paragon of patience, who once struggled with impatience. Perhaps there was hope for me, after all.

Allison told me her career as a college professor got off to a rocky start because of her impatience, particularly with the bureaucratic aspects of the job. Allison simply had no patience with all of the forms and reports she had to complete every semester, viewing them as a distraction from the real work of teaching students and conducting research. But there was a problem. Her first twelve months of employment at the college were a probationary period. She could not be placed on the permanent-employment track without first satisfactorily completing this probationary period, a doubtful outcome because of her impatience with mandatory paperwork.

One day near the end of her probationary year, Allison's supervisor dropped by her office for an informal, off-the-record chat. She told Allison feedback from her students was excellent, a fact boding well for a new faculty member about to complete her probationary period. Then she told Allison feedback from the administration was less encouraging, owing to her perpetual lateness in completing reports and other kinds of paperwork. Allison's impatience with the bureaucratic aspects of the job became a bone of contention.

The supervisor told Allison the only way she could recommend her for another contract—one that would put her on the tenure track—was to go out on a limb with the administration and guarantee Allison would commit to completing all required reports accurately, completely, and on time. Her final words to Allison were: "If I recommend you for another contract and you don't follow through on completing your paperwork, we will both be looking for jobs."

Allison told me she learned some months later just how much of a risk her supervisor took on her behalf. Had Allison not followed through on her promise to complete all reports and other paperwork on time, her supervisor would have been removed as department chair and relegated to a faculty position at a remote branch campus. Allison never forgot how much she owed a supervisor who was patient with her when it could have cost the supervisor so much. From that point on, she made an intentional effort to be patient with her colleagues, students, and the bureaucratic aspects of the job. Years later, when she became a department chair herself, Allison showed her faculty members the kind of patience she benefitted from years earlier. But for the patience of a servant leader, Allison's career in higher education might have ended before she had a chance to get it started.

Stewardship

Servant leaders are good stewards. This means they take care of the resources entrusted to them: human, financial, and capital. By doing this, servant leaders contribute to enhancing the performance

of their followers and, in turn, the performance of the organization. They take care of human resources—their followers—by mentoring, coaching, teaching, correcting, assisting, and listening to them as well as supporting them and advocating on their behalf. They take care of the financial resources entrusted to them by carefully managing their budgets. They take care of the capital resources (machines, equipment, and facilities) they are responsible for by being attentive to keeping them up to date and properly maintained.

A good steward will leave the resources entrusted to her better off than they were when she first became responsible for them. This is part of the message in Christ's Parable of the Ten Minas (Luke 19:11–27), in which the future king expected his servants to put the money he gave them to good use and increase its value while he was away. For example, if you manage a department for a period of time and then move up the career ladder, the department should be in better shape than when you inherited it. This means the personnel should perform at a higher level than when you first became their supervisor and the budget and capital resources should be in better condition.

Perhaps the verses that best demonstrate God's expectations concerning stewardship are Matthew 25:20–21. In these verses, the overseer who received five talents from his master invested them in ways that increased the master's principal by an additional five talents. For this, the overseer was commended and rewarded. Like the overseer, leaders at work who are good stewards will be valued by those they lead as well as by their employers.

Initiative

Initiative is willingness to make decisions and take action without being told. It is the opposite of hand-wringing indecisiveness. Servant leaders must be willing to take the initiative in their areas of responsibility. Initiative becomes especially important when facing unfamiliar situations. It is when confronted with new, different, or ambiguous situations initiative is needed most. This is because some managers in these situations become engulfed in a fog of indecision and respond by doing nothing.

Many people, when faced with unfamiliar situations, dither, fret, or freeze instead of making decisions and taking action. Some people would rather do nothing than risk making a mistake. But servant leaders understand problems cannot be solved, crises averted, or progress made until somebody takes the initiative to act. In fact, nothing good happens until someone is willing to say, "I will take responsibility, make the decision, and take the appropriate action."

Servant leaders take the initiative, even before they are in leadership positions. Doing so is important because demonstrating this or any other characteristic of servant leadership is not the sole province of people in management positions. Anyone who sets an inspiring example for others to do better and be better can be a servant leader, regardless of rank or position. Consequently, do not wait until you are in charge to demonstrate initiative when the situation calls for it.

The author of the Book of James—Bible scholars are not sure who that is—demonstrated the importance of initiative. In James 4:17, we read that anyone who knows the right thing to do but does not do it is committing a sin. Consequently, if you know a decision has to be made and no one else is willing to make it, it is a sin to refuse to take the initiative. On the other hand, taking the initiative does not mean unnecessarily pushing aside the responsible individual and taking over. It is not about usurping authority. But it can mean being willing to decide and act when these things are clearly called for and the individual who is responsible is not present or is unwilling to act.

Early in my career in higher education, I witnessed a situation that demonstrated how important taking the initiative can be. I was a department chair at the time. One of my fellow department chairs—I will call her Glenda—found herself in a bind. She a received a grant to purchase new equipment and technology for her department. The amount of the grant was substantial, but still did not provide sufficient funds to purchase all that was needed to bring her department up to date.

When I encountered Glenda in the hall of the administration building, she was clearly distraught. She had just received a telephone call from the vendor saying if she could *fax* the approved purchase order to him by the end of the day, a substantial discount would apply. In fact, the discount would save enough money to allow for the purchase of additional items her department needed. But there was a problem. This was a Friday afternoon, and college campuses on Friday afternoons are like ghost towns. She needed a signature from her dean, the vice-president, and the president. All three of these individuals had already left campus to begin their weekends. What to do?

Glenda did not have the authority to approve the purchase order herself. Unfortunately, Glenda was unable to reach the responsible administrators by telephone. This was in those inconvenient days before cell phones. To complicate matters, the president of our college was a stickler for process. Employees ignored procedures at their own peril. I sympathized with my colleague but could see no way to resolve the situation. I remember feeling helpless and useless. Fortunately, she was neither. Glenda saw what needed to be done and did it. She took the initiative.

Glenda initialed the purchase order on behalf of the dean, vice-president, and president. This done, she took the purchase order to the college's comptroller and had it *faxed* to the vendor while she waited for confirmation that it arrived on time. Glenda then wrote a brief memorandum summarizing the situation and explaining what she did and attached a copy of the purchase order to it. She placed a copy of the memorandum on the desks of the dean, vice-president, and president. Then Glenda spent the weekend pacing the floor and stressing over what might happen when her superiors read the memorandum on Monday.

As she feared, first thing Monday morning, the dreaded call came. Glenda was summoned to the president's office. When she walked in, there sat the dean glaring daggers at her and the vice president sweating bullets. Only the president knew what he was going to do, but it was clear from the looks on their faces Glenda could expect no support from the dean or vice president. The president wasted no time. He said, "Everyone in this room knows how I feel about following procedures. If we allow people to ignore approved procedures, we will soon have chaos." Glenda sensed the axe was about to fall, and it was her head on the chopping block.

The president continued. "But, in this case, Glenda could not follow established procedures because the three of us decided to sneak out early Friday when she needed our help." In a flash, Glenda saw a glimmer of hope. Now it was the dean and vice president who were squirming uncomfortably in their chairs. "Glenda, I want to thank you for taking the initiative to get this purchase order processed in time to enjoy the discount and secure the additional equipment. That's good fiscal management. You are the leader of your department and a leader must know when to take the initiative. Knowing how I feel about following approved procedures, what you did took courage." The dean and vice president nearly fell out of their chairs, but their attitudes toward Glenda changed in the blink of an eye. Suddenly, both were all sweetness and smiles.

Only later did Glenda learn both the dean and vice president recommended she be removed as department chair. Fortunately, for her, the president of our college valued initiative, particularly when it stretched a dollar. He made it clear to Glenda, the dean, and the vice president the situation in question was an exception, not the rule. He still expected all employees to follow approved procedures, but he also expected administrators to take the initiative when necessary to get the job done.

A FINAL WORD ON SERVANT LEADERSHIP

Servant leadership is an approach that works. By developing and consistently applying the traits of the servant leader explained in this chapter, you can lead men and women in the workplace. Servant leadership works because people—men and women—want to be valued, listened to, appreciated, and treated with dignity and respect. There is no mystery to why servant leadership works well. Just ask

yourself the following questions about who you are most likely to follow in the workplace:

- Someone who is trustworthy or someone you do not trust?

- Someone who has a worthy vision and shares it or someone who says, "Don't ask questions, just do as I say"?

- Someone who listens to you and values your input or someone who brushes you off and ignores your ideas and suggestions?

- Someone who clearly cares about you as well as the work to be done or someone who cares only about herself?

- Someone who exercises situational awareness or someone who is constantly allowing the team to be blindsided?

- Someone who has the credibility to influence team members for good or someone who lacks credibility and influence?

- Someone who seeks your input before making decisions or someone who makes unilateral decisions and then expects you to carry them out?

- Someone who is sufficiently committed to the vision to make personal sacrifices or someone who expects you to do all the sacrificing?

- Someone who treats you fairly or someone who plays favorites and excludes you?

- Someone who has the courage of her convictions or someone who will throw you under the bus to protect herself?

- Someone who will set an example of persevering during difficult times or someone who gives up and quits when the going gets tough?

- Someone who maintains a positive attitude, regardless the circumstances, or someone who mopes, complains, and displays a defeatist attitude when the job becomes difficult?

185

- Someone who knows when and how to apply common sense or someone who hides behind the rule book?

- Someone who is patient as you learn or someone who expects you to do things you have not yet learned to do and, then, becomes angry when you can't?

- Someone who is a good steward or someone who looks out for number one, while ignoring the resources entrusted to her?

- Someone who takes the initiative in ambiguous situations or someone who is afraid to act?

Now, having made my point about servant leadership, I will close this chapter with a caveat. This is a message I always share with my leadership students on the last day of class. It is simply this. My experience over the past four decades suggests about 85 to 90 percent of the people you work with can be positively influenced by good leadership. Those who fall into this group will eventually respond to servant leadership; however, there are those who will not be led, even by the best leaders. This 10 to 15 percent is comprised of people who want a paycheck, not a career. They want a job but don't want to work. Their agenda is completely self-centered, a fact that will not change, regardless what you do.

If you have consistently applied what is explained in this chapter over a period of time and still have a few subordinates who refuse to respond appropriately, they probably fall into the group of people with self-serving agendas who will not respond positively, no matter what you do. I call people in this category "HR problems." By this, I mean, rather than wasting your time and energy trying to lead people who will not be led no matter what you do, it is better to enlist the help of HR professionals in terminating their employment. It is difficult enough to lead those who want to do well. Don't waste your time on those who don't.

PRAYER FOR LEADING IN THE WORKPLACE

Dear Lord,

You've called a lot of women into leadership roles in the workplace. Those of us who seek Your voice in the work we do recognize we're in a position of servant leadership. We genuinely serve the people we work for, and the ones we work with. At the same time, we strive to serve You as well.

It's not an easy task, but You've guided me and others to take our responsibilities to heart and lead in ways that honor each person who is part of our team. I pray You open my eyes today to recognize that, no matter what else my position in leadership might be about, it is, first and foremost, about relationships. As a leader, I pray for wisdom to guide my decisions, vision as I consider the goals set by my team, and faithfulness as I seek opportunities that will allow each person to shine.

I ask for patience and a willingness to listen to the men and women on my team, respecting their observations and their input, and skillfully managing their expectations and our predetermined processes and procedures. Let me be aware of any time I am moving too quickly or sacrificing quality performance. Let me cast a vision that strengthens my team each day as we move forward.

Lord, I don't always understand the bias that still remains between men and women in the workplace, but I pray to be all I'm meant to be, working in integrity and joy. Help me see the bright side of most situations and even laugh at myself over momentary craziness. Help me respect the thoughts and ideas of every man and woman I work with and support them with confidence and trust in my role as a servant leader.

In a world that does not always operate under standards of truth or fairness, let me be willing to take a stand in favor of mentoring, serving, and leading the people who are part of my team. Help me work with each person diligently and in ways that please You. Never let a gender bias influence the work we all do together. I pray I will stay steadfast and strong in the work I do, devoted to Your service in every choice I make. When moments come where someone questions my authority as a woman over the men who work for me, let me be gracious, but firm; kind, but deliberate in my response. Help me lead with Your authority, trusting You have given me the responsibility and the heart to do my job well. Continue to teach me Your ways so I honor Your name. Amen.

GROUP DISCUSSION CASE: "I don't know if I can lead this department"

Lucy was in a bind. She faced one of those good-news-bad-news situations. The good news was she was just promoted to a management position, the first woman to achieve this milestone in her male-dominated company. The bad news was, of the fifteen people in the department she would now lead, ten were men. Of these, not one ever reported to a woman, two expressed reservations about doing so, and several were openly critical of the decision to promote Lucy to a management position.

Lucy worried the way some of the male department heads in the company treated their team members would violate her Christian principles. She wondered if that kind of behavior was necessary to lead men. The vice president who recommended Lucy for the promotion told her she would face a real challenge in leading her department but expressed confidence she could do it. Lucy wished she shared his confidence.

Discussion Questions:

1. What obstacles do you think Lucy is going to face in trying to win the confidence and support of the men and women in her department?

2. How would you advise Lucy to proceed in this situation? How can she win the hearts and minds of her team members and do so without compromising her faith?

REVIEW QUESTIONS FOR INDIVIDUALS AND GROUPS

1. How would you respond to a fellow Christian who opposed women leading men in the workplace?

2. Describe the *act-like-a-man* syndrome some women face when they become managers.

3. What are some reasons men might resent being led by a woman in the workplace?

4. Should women expect other women to automatically be supportive when they are promoted to management positions? Explain your answer.

5. Describe a societal misperception woman sometimes face in seeking management positions.

6. What are some examples of bad advice women who become managers sometimes receive from well-intended people?

7. How can Christian women who become managers ensure their Christianity is not viewed as weakness in the workplace?

8. Define the concept of servant leadership.

9. List the personal traits of servant leaders.

10. Describe why servant leadership is such an effective approach for leading men and women in the workplace.

189

CHAPTER 8

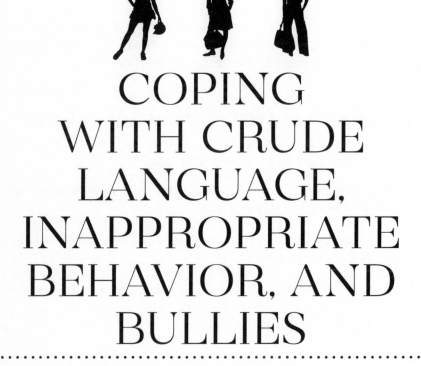

COPING WITH CRUDE LANGUAGE, INAPPROPRIATE BEHAVIOR, AND BULLIES

....

"But I say to you who hear, love your enemies, do good to those who hate you, bless those who curse you, pray for those who abuse you." Luke 6:27-28

Inappropriate behavior is not uncommon in the workplace. In fact, the workplace—with its pressures, deadlines, conflicting personalities, competing agendas, competition, and temptations—can be a breeding ground for bad behavior. Any Christian woman who works outside the home is going to be confronted by behavior

190

at odds with her faith. Expect to deal with behavior in the workplace ranging from marginally inappropriate to downright offensive. You will not excel in your career until you know how to deal with inappropriate behavior, behavior that has no place at work or anywhere else, for that matter.

Over the course of my lifetime, what is considered acceptable behavior in the company of others has changed, and not for the better. This claim is not just the conjecture of a grouchy old man dreaming of the good old days. More than 80 percent of employers today complain about the rudeness, profanity, and boorish behavior of their personnel. Some of the complaints are about intrusive and inconsiderate use of cellphones, inappropriate dress, a lack of respect for authority, and unprofessional behavior. But the most common complaints are about profanity, rudeness, lewd jokes, suggestive comments, and bullying.

Not surprisingly, the coarsening of language, manners, and comportment occurring in American society is showing up in the workplace. As a result, Christian women who work outside the home find themselves increasingly confronted by offensive behavior. Like Marnie, many of these women fear they cannot walk through a pig sty, day after day, without at least some of the mud sticking to them. This concern is why we are warned in Ephesians 5:4 to avoid foolish talk and crude jokes. These things have no place at work or anywhere else, for that matter.

The Bible makes clear we should reject the kinds of behaviors Marnie was concerned about. In addition to the Scriptural reasons for rejecting these behaviors, there is a practical reason. If you ignore rudeness, profanity, and boorish behavior, your silence may be interpreted as approval. This, in turn, will encourage more bad behavior. Never forget, when dealing with people, you get more of what you reward. To remain silent in the face of inappropriate behavior is to reward that behavior and, in turn, risk subjecting yourself and others to more of it.

An important question then is this: How should Christian women in the workplace deal with crude language, inappropriate behavior, and bullies? The key is to apply Matthew 10:16 when confronting inappropriate behavior so your actions reflect positively on you. This chapter provides specific, positive, pro-active methods you can use when forced to deal with profanity, rudeness, sexual harassment, and bullying. These specific behaviors were selected because they are the ones Christian women I counsel complain about most often. The strategies provided will work best if you have the support of higher management when it comes to dealing with inappropriate behavior at work. Consequently, before getting into specific strategies for dealing with specific behaviors, a few words about management support are in order.

MAKE SURE YOU HAVE THE SUPPORT OF HIGHER MANAGEMENT

In any organization, higher management sets the tone for how employees interact with each other. Therefore, it can be difficult to deal effectively with the inappropriate behavior of coworkers without the support of your organization's top executives. You can determine if your organization's executives are tuned into this issue by asking yourself the following questions:

1. Are there policies or written ground rules in place that set high expectations for how employees will behave toward each other, customers, suppliers, and the public?

2. Are supervisors aware of the role they are supposed to play in enforcing management's policies and promoting appropriate behavior?

3. Have supervisors been trained to play an effective role in enforcing management's expectations concerning professional behavior?

4. Are the expectations concerning employee behavior included in the job descriptions of all personnel?

5. Are the expectations concerning employee behavior evaluated as part of the performance appraisal process?

6. Is higher management receptive and supportive when the issue of inappropriate behavior is raised?

You should be able to answer "yes" to all of these questions about your organization. If you cannot, it might be necessary to recommend that higher management take the steps necessary to rectify the situation. It is not enough for an organization's top managers to claim they expect or reject certain behaviors. They must demonstrate their commitment by establishing a supportive infrastructure of policies, processes, and practices. Then they—the organization's executives—must set the tone by their examples.

DEALING WITH PROFANITY AT WORK

Living near a middle school gives me a window into the lives of the young people in our community. The language I hear coming from them can be shocking. Middle school students—boys and girls—regularly use language that would embarrass the saltiest Marine I ever served with. Profanity has become an all-pervasive fact of life in contemporary American society. You hear it on television, in movies, and even on the nightly news.

Just recently, I watched a U.S. Senator interviewed on one of the major television networks. When he didn't like the tone of the interviewer's questions, this member of America's most prestigious legislative body launched into a profanity-laced diatribe. Not one of his words was bleeped. It is as if Americans can no longer express themselves without using profanity. It should come as no surprise, then, this kind of language is being heard more and more in the workplace.

Most professional literature on this subject recommends three options for dealing with profanity on the job: 1) ignore it, 2) confront it, or 3) report it. Options two and three represent good advice, in my opinion, but option one does not. Ignoring inappropriate behavior can be interpreted as accepting it. To ignore profanity at work is to give tacit approval to it. For Christian women in the workplace, I recommend a slightly different set of options: 1) set an example of never using profanity yourself and walk away when others use it, 2) quietly confront it in private, and 3) take your complaint to the next higher level of authority. Let's look at each of these options.

Set the Example: Refuse to Use Profanity Yourself

As a Christian, you know what is written in Ephesians 4:29. This verse warns that we are to let no debasing or undignified talk come out of our mouths. Rather, our words should build up and encourage those who hear them. The absence of profanity in your speech will be noticed by others. Often, this is enough to minimize its use by coworkers, at least in your presence. But the opposite is also true. If you are heard using expletives, your coworkers will take it as permission to use profanity themselves. Don't give them permission and, when possible, walk away when others use profanity. Just walking away can send a powerful message.

Quietly Confront the Profane Person

People who watch a lot of television and movies can become so accustomed to foul language they don't even realize they are using it. Then there are those who see nothing wrong with profanity and use it as a matter of course. In either case, confronting the individual in question may be the only way to make a difference. But how you confront someone on this issue is important. No matter how offensive their language might be, don't publicly confront those who use profanity at work. Embarrassing a coworker in front of others is not likely to produce a positive result. Instead, ask to talk with the offending person in private.

Take Your Complaint to the Next Higher Level of Authority

Approaching coworkers privately about their use of profanity is a fitting and proper response but understand some people will remain stubbornly unmoved, no matter how you handle the situation. If you have approached a profane coworker in private and stated your case wisely, but that individual refuses to change, it is time to raise the issue at the next higher level of authority. If the supportive infrastructure mentioned earlier in this chapter is in place, your complaint should be well-received. You are simply calling attention to a policy being ignored and, therefore, violated; however, if the supportive infrastructure is not in place, this step becomes more difficult, and Matthew 10:16, once again, becomes your guiding principle.

When taking your concerns up the chain of command to supervisors or managers, the wise course of action is to state your case about profanity in terms that will interest them personally and professionally. Although the language in question is offensive to you personally, there are bigger issues involved, at least from a manager's perspective. One issue is the image of managers who, by allowing the profanity to persist, appear to accept, condone, or even approve of it. Another issue is the image of the overall organization. A final issue is how customers, suppliers, and the public might perceive the organization when they are subjected to profanity.

Employees who become accustomed to using profanity at work are apt to slip up and use it when serving customers, working with suppliers, or interacting with the general public. This is especially true in situations involving pressure, disagreement, and acrimony. For many people, the use of profanity becomes their normal mode of expression. Employees who regularly lace their conversations with off-color language can cause big problems for their employers. When customers, suppliers, or members of the general public find themselves on the receiving end of profanity, their negative impression is not limited to the offending employee. Rather, they generalize it to the entire organization, including its management team.

Remember this point when taking a complaint about profanity up the chain of command in an organization lacking the kind of policy infrastructure needed to discourage foul language. Your organization's executives may not care that profanity offends you, but they will care that it casts them in a bad light.

DEALING WITH RUDENESS AND INCIVILITY AT WORK

Teaching business etiquette has become a growth industry. Why? Because few people learn manners in the home anymore or, at least, those who do are exceptions. Rude, inconsiderate, thoughtless behavior has become ubiquitous in American society. Since what occurs in the general population eventually finds its way into the workplace, poor manners have become a problem there too. In meetings, people talk over each other, butt in, interrupt, fiddle with smartphones instead of listening, arrive late without apologizing, and even talk on cellphones without leaving the room.

Traditional terms of courtesy such as "please," "thank you," and "you're welcome" have become passé. Showing respectful deference to people in positions of authority, once common, is becoming a thing of the past. For example, every semester, without fail, I have college freshmen who want to call me by my first name instead of "professor" or "Dr. Goetsch." They have no sense of deferential courtesy. Think about this: How often do you hear the terms "yes, sir," "no, sir," "yes, ma'am," and "no, ma'am" used these days? How often does a clerk or fast-food worker respond to your "thank you" by saying "no problem" instead of "you're welcome"? It's as if they wouldn't wait on you if doing so was problematic, in spite of the fact waiting on problematic customers is what they are paid to do.

I sometimes wonder if rudeness represents the new normal in contemporary society. One could certainly make a case for this assertion but, even if this claim is true for the general population, it should not be true for Christians. We have a higher mandate. For Christians, manners and gentility are Scriptural principles. Romans 12:10 commands us to show brotherly affection and love to one another. Titus 3:2 encourages us to avoid speaking evil and quarreling. Correspondingly, it admonishes us to be courteous to all people. Consequently, you and I have no excuse for being rude, inconsiderate, or thoughtless to others. But our behavior is only half of the equation. What about the behavior of our coworkers, particularly those who are unbelievers? Do they get a pass when it comes to manners? They shouldn't. If manners were not important in the workplace, teaching business etiquette would not be the growth industry it has become for corporate trainers.

So how should you deal with coworkers who are rude, inconsiderate, or thoughtless? Should you just ignore their boorish behavior as some suggest? This is not a good idea, in my opinion. I counsel Christians to be careful of what they accept because what they accept can become who they are. While it is probably wise to simply ignore instances of rudeness from normally polite coworkers who are just having a bad day, ignoring habitual offenders is a bad idea. People who are regularly and even compulsively rude will just be encouraged by your silent acquiescence. What follows are several strategies I recommend to Christian women who are dealing with rude, inconsiderate, or thoughtless behavior in the workplace.

Set a Consistent Example of Good Manners in All Situations

Manners are like the flu. They can be contagious. If your coworkers are around you enough, they might catch your manners, good or bad. Consequently, it is important you set an example of good manners in all situations. In fact, if you want your coworkers to exhibit good manners, the worst mistake you can make is to respond in kind when they don't. Any lapse in manners on your part will just encourage bad manners on theirs. On the other hand, many people will treat you the same way you treat them. Often, your good manners will encourage good manners in others. Consequently, it is important for Christian women in the workplace to heed the admonition in Luke 6:31 to treat others the way you want them to treat you. When you

want to improve the manners of others, applying the Golden Rule is a good way to start.

Confront the Rude Person in Private

Unfortunately, there are those who will not improve their manners, no matter how well you treat them. Even in these cases, it is important to treat the individuals in question with courtesy and consideration. When confronting coworkers about their rudeness, you want to be able to approach them from a position of strength. You do not want to give them the ability to respond, "Who are you to complain about rudeness? You're worse than I am."

If you have set a consistent example of good manners in dealing with coworkers, you have every right to expect reciprocal behavior on their part. You also have every right—and I would argue a responsibility—to confront them about their poor manners. Philippians 4:5 admonishes us to let our reasonableness be known to others. It is certainly reasonable to expect people to be well-mannered, considerate, and thoughtful in the workplace, particularly since doing otherwise can undermine morale and, in turn, performance. This is the approach Machiko took when she confronted a coworker, Larry, about his rudeness.

Machiko was raised in a home where manners were a matter of both religion and culture. Her parents were Japanese Christians who taught their children manners based on Scripture and traditional Japanese culture. Consequently, when Larry was transferred to her shift, Machiko found his rudeness, lack of consideration, and thoughtlessness offensive. So did the other nurses on the shift. Larry was impatient with his coworkers and quick to make unkind comments about them. He would even interrupt a fellow nurse who was caring for a patient and criticize her methods in the presence of the patient. Larry missed meetings or arrived late, talked loudly and profanely on his cellphone, interrupted coworkers in mid-sentence, and was openly dismissive of every opinion but his own. He was one of those people who is often wrong but never in doubt.

Machiko was not Larry's supervisor, but she felt compelled to confront him when his rudeness began to undermine the morale and performance of the other nurses on their shift. Nobody on the shift wanted to work with Larry. Because of him, absenteeism was up and patient satisfaction down. When Machiko asked to meet with him in private, Larry made a suggestive comment full of sexual innuendo about her motives. His comment only increased her determination to confront Larry about his behavior.

When they met, Machiko was kind but frank. She told Larry his poor manners were hurting the performance of their nursing team. Larry responded, "That's their problem, not mine." Undeterred, Machiko asked Larry if he knew how the nurses on their shift were evaluated each year. New to the shift, he didn't. Machiko explained that their supervisor used the 360-degree method for conducting annual performance appraisals. This meant, before assessing the performance of a nurse, the supervisor collected feedback from all of the other nurses on the shift. She also collected patient feedback. Seeing the concern on his face, Machiko smiled and told Larry, "I thought you would want to know. Without a good evaluation, you can't get a raise. In fact, nurses with subpar evaluations don't receive the annual Christmas bonus, either."

Not surprisingly, in the following days and weeks, Larry's manners showed some improvement. The sad fact was he never learned good manners. Larry didn't know how to be thoughtful and considerate. Frankly, he seemed more comfortable with rudeness. When Larry asked Machiko for help, she recommended he enroll in a business etiquette seminar periodically offered by a local community college. He did the next time the seminar was offered and completed it. Larry took what he learned to heart, and his manners showed noticeable improvement. Over time, Larry became a thoughtful, courteous, and considerate team member. The performance appraisal covering his first year on the shift was not good, but those for subsequent years got better and better. In the years that followed Larry's conversation with Machiko, he never again missed out on a Christmas bonus because of a poor performance appraisal.

In applying Matthew 10:16, Machiko was both innocent and wise in how she approached Larry. She was innocent in her expectation of good manners accorded with Scripture. She was wise in explaining the situation to Larry in terms of his best interests rather than her aversion to poor manners. This is the approach I recommend to Christian women who, in these kinds of situations, are likely to be dealing with unbelievers. People like Larry may not understand your Biblical beliefs, but they do understand their own self-interest. Hence, their self-interest can be used to improve their manners.

Recommend Management Provide Business Etiquette Training

There was a time when youngsters learned good manners as a normal part of growing up. Training in this area occurred in the home and was reinforced in the schools. For example, my seventh grade English teacher used to make students whose comportment needed work copy pages from Emily Post's book on etiquette. By the time I finished seventh grade, I had copied that entire book at least twice and learned a lot in the process. That was then, and this is now.

I frequently tell corporate executives, if they want their personnel to have good manners, they should provide business etiquette training, and make it mandatory. I also tell them good manners are good business. The gears of human interaction run more smoothly when lubricated with good manners. Consequently, it is reasonable for employers to expect their personnel to practice good manners. What is unreasonable is to expect good manners from people who have never learned them, people like Larry in the previous example.

When reluctant executives say their employees should have learned good manners in the home, I agree. They should. Unfortunately, many don't, and those who don't can undermine an organization's morale and performance, not to mention its image with customers and the public. So, rather than complaining about the shortcomings of contemporary society, organizations are well-advised to provide business etiquette training themselves. This is one of those situations where executives must decide whether they want to solve a problem or just complain about it. In other words, they have to decide whether they want to make progress or just make noise. I recommend progress.

The reason I bring this issue up is that you may have to raise it with your boss. When poor manners prevail in an organization, there is a management problem. Management problems are solved by management action. In the case of widespread bad manners, the management solution is to take the bull by the horns and provide business etiquette training on a mandatory basis. The first participants should be the organization's top executives.

If only a few of your coworkers are rude, thoughtless, or inconsiderate, deal with them one-on-one in the way Machiko dealt with Larry. If rudeness is endemic in your organization, a broader and more comprehensive solution, such as business etiquette training, may be needed. I have seen this kind of training improve the morale and performance of individuals and entire organizations. When the personnel in an organization learn to practice what is taught in Luke 6:31—the Golden Rule—they benefit, their coworkers benefit, and the organization benefits.

DEALING WITH SEXUAL HARASSMENT AT WORK

Dealing with sexual harassment in the workplace is similar to dealing with other types of inappropriate behavior in that there are things you can do individually and things you might have to encourage the organization to do corporately. Sexual harassment is one of the worst forms of inappropriate behavior a Christian woman can experience on the job. Its effects on you can be devastating. They include emotional trauma, isolation, alienation from coworkers, a decline in job performance, feelings of shame, and destruction of your self-esteem. Ironically, some women who are subjected to sexual harassment actually come to blame themselves.

The term coworker is used frequently throughout this book and typically refers to your peers on the job; however, in this section the

term should be interpreted in the broader sense to include peers, subordinates, superiors, and even third-party contractors. There are many documented cases of sexual harassment perpetrated by people in all of these categories, mostly men but increasingly women, too.

The harm from sexual harassment is not limited to its primary victims: those who are targeted by unscrupulous coworkers. The employer is also hurt. Employers who do not act to prevent this kind of behavior or who do not respond quickly and decisively when it occurs will be plagued by a variety of problems. These problems include an increase in tardiness, absenteeism, and turnover; legal costs from lawsuits; a decline in productivity and quality as employees take sides and resentment grows in both camps; sharp downturns in morale; and the costs associated with replacing employees who leave.

Fortunately, you have a lot of help available when confronted by sexual harassment. Sexual harassment is a violation of Section 703 of Title VII of the Civil Rights Act. The Equal Employment Opportunity Commission (EEOC) publishes guidelines dealing specifically with sexual harassment. These guidelines are available at the following website:

https://www.eeoc.gov/laws/types/sexual_
harassment.cfm

You can also access the guidelines by searching on "Equal Employment Opportunity Commission Guidelines on Sexual Harassment." If you are being sexually harassed at work or if there is even a hint of this kind of behavior from coworkers, it is important to take appropriate action immediately. What follows are several strategies you can use for dealing with sexual harassment at work.

Understand What Sexual Harassment Is

Many women think sexual harassment involves only a boss demanding sexual favors in exchange for work-related benefits (e.g., raises, bonuses, promotions, better assignments, nicer offices, etc.). This kind of exchange can indeed constitute sexual harassment, a form

known as *quid pro quo* sexual harassment. But sexual harassment is a much broader concept than just this aspect of it. It also consists of unwelcome words, actions, or conduct of a sexual nature. Further, it is not limited to those in authority over you. You can be sexually harassed by superiors, peers, subordinates, third-party contractors, and even customers.

It is not necessary for there to be a blatant demand for sexual favors (quid pro quo) for inappropriate behavior to qualify as sexual harassment. Unwelcome words, actions, or conduct of a sexual nature that intimidate or create an offensive or hostile work environment can also constitute sexual harassment. This kind of sexual harassment is called *condition-of-work harassment.* Condition-of-work sexual harassment is the more common of the two types.

The EEOC uses three criteria for determining if an individual is being sexually harassed at work: 1) submission to the unwelcome words, actions, or conduct can be interpreted by the victim as a condition of employment, 2) acceptance or rejection by the victim of unwelcome words, actions, or conduct is used as the basis of making employment decisions, and 3) the unwelcome words, actions, or conduct affect the victim's job performance and/or create a hostile work environment. The majority of sexual harassment cases are based on this third criterion.

Understand Sexual Harassment Is, First and Foremost, a Violation of God's Law

Sexual harassment violates the law as stated in Section 703 of Title VII of the Civil Rights Act. But, more importantly, it violates God's law. When it comes to quid pro quo sexual harassment, Ephesians 5:3 warns that impurity of a sexual nature is to be strictly avoided. When it comes to condition-of-work harassment, Ephesians 5:4 warns that there is to be no indecent talk or joking. Scripture is clear, as believers, we are forbidden to practice sexual harassment. But the Word of God does not stop there. We are also to confront the perpetrators of sexual harassment.

1 Corinthians 15:33 makes clear keeping the wrong kind of company can ruin your morals. If we ignore coworkers who practice sexual harassment, we are keeping bad company and running the risk of ruining our good morals. Proverbs 13:20 warns against becoming the companion of a fool. To ignore unwelcome words, actions, or conduct of a sexual nature is to be a companion of the fools who practice this kind of behavior. The Bible and the EEOC are in accord in that both encourage you to act immediately if subjected to sexual harassment.

Talk to First-Time Offenders and Demand They Stop Their Inappropriate Behavior

Coworkers who practice sexual harassment often begin by testing the water to determine if their words, actions, or conduct will be welcomed, spurned, or just ignored. These probes should be dealt with immediately and decisively. The first step, unless the actions in question are blatant or threatening, is to have a private talk with the offending individual. Make it clear the individual's words, actions, or conduct are unwelcome and will not be tolerated. Then write a contemporaneous memorandum to yourself summarizing the situation, when it occurred, where it occurred, what was said, and how you responded. Keep that memorandum on file for future reference. If you ever have to take further action, it is important to be clear about the details.

Make the Situation Known to Management

If talking to the offending individual does no good, the next step is to make the situation known to management. Begin with your supervisor and the organization's HR director. Record what has transpired up to this point in writing, give the document to your supervisor with a copy to the HR director, and request a meeting. During this meeting, inform your supervisor and the HR director of what is taking place and the effect it is having on you (as well as on

others, if applicable). Request their assistance in putting a stop to the unwelcome advances or inappropriate behavior. If you get no help from your supervisor or the HR director, repeat the process with each successively higher level of management until you get help or it becomes clear you are not going to. If it becomes clear help is not forthcoming from within the organization, your remaining option is to file a formal complaint with the EEOC.

File a Formal Complaint with the EEOC

With all the attention and publicity generated over the past three decades by instances of sexual harassment at work, it is hard to imagine an organization that would refuse to intervene if an employee asked for help; however, this does still happen. When you have talked face-to-face with the offending person, discussed the situation with your supervisor and HR director, and made the situation known to higher management but still received no help, it is time to file a formal complaint with the EEOC. An organization is obligated to act on sexual harassment claims, unless, of course, they have good reason for believing a claim to be false or scurrilous. False claims do happen. A few words about that are in order.

Unfortunately, a policy intended as a tool for good can be turned into a weapon for revenge or other perverse motives by people with self-serving agendas. Consequently, not all sexual harassment claims are valid. This is why the EEOC evaluates claims with an objective eye. The EEOC considers all facts in a given case including the nature, circumstances, and context of the unwelcome behavior before making a ruling. This is where the EEOC applies the three criteria stated earlier.

To review, those criteria are: could submission to quid pro quo advances be interpreted by the victim as a condition of continued employment? Was rejection (or acceptance) of the unwelcome behavior used as a factor in making employment decisions affecting the targeted employee or any other employee? Did the unwelcome behavior adversely affect job performance or create a hostile work environment?

Before filing a complaint with the EEOC, ask yourself the kinds of questions the EEOC reviewer will ask about the complaint. Make sure you understand the EEOC's criteria and file your claim on the basis of one or more of these criteria. Claims should be filed promptly. In most cases—although there are exceptions to this rule—you will need to file your complaint within 180 days of the offensive behavior. This is why it is important to act immediately when a coworker is guilty of unwelcome behavior of a sexual nature toward you. If you think you need to file a sexual harassment complaint with the EEOC, begin by visiting the following website. You will find specific directions for filing a claim and other helpful information at this site:

http://www.eeoc.gov/employees/howtofile.cfm

DEALING WITH BULLIES AT WORK

In recent years, there has been an increase in the number of complaints I receive from counseling clients—particularly women—about workplace bullies. Some complain about face-to-face bullies while others complain about cyberbullies. Regardless of whether they confront you face-to-face or via the internet, workplace bullies are coworkers who repeatedly use intimidation, threats (subtle or blatant), yelling, humiliation, criticism, insults, gossip, lies, insinuation, and even sabotage to gain power over you. This is an important point to understand about bullies. Their goal is to gain power over you.

Bullying at work should not be taken lightly. Victims of workplace bullies complain about health problems such as headaches, trouble sleeping, increased blood pressure, and depression. Some even suffer from post-traumatic stress disorder (PTSD). These health issues, in turn, cause work-related problems such as increased absenteeism, loss of morale, declining motivation, and, inevitably, diminished performance. Workplace bullying can have a detrimental effect on your health, your performance, and the performance of your organization. It should not be ignored.

It's not just my counseling clients who complain about workplace bullies. We appear to be in the midst of a bullying epidemic. The statistics are staggering. More than fifty million people a year complain they have been bullied at work. Men are not the only perpetrators when it comes to bullying. Approximately 40 percent of workplace bullies are women and most of their victims are other women. Some women in the workplace target female coworkers for bullying as a way to advance their own agendas. Based on feedback from women I counsel, Christian women are sometimes viewed as *soft targets* by workplace bullies, male and female. It is not uncommon for workplace bullies to view Christian women as easy prey because of their propensity for turning the other cheek, treating coworkers with the kind of love described in 1 Corinthians 13, and forgiving their transgressors. Having faith viewed as weakness is a common problem among Christians in the workplace, particularly women.

It is clear from Scripture you are not expected to meekly accept the abuse of bullies. Doing so will only encourage their bad behavior, and not just toward you but toward others, too. This being the case, you have a responsibility to confront bullies. Proverbs 22:24 warns us to have nothing to do with an angry or wrathful person, an apt description for a bully. How we go about dealing with bullies is important. It can be tempting when you are bullied to lash out and give your tormentors a taste of their own medicine. As Christians, we want to avoid retaliating in kind or seeking revenge.

Remember the admonition in Proverbs 15:1 as you apply the strategies presented in the remainder of this section. This verse explains that responding to anger with kindness rather than harshness will bring better results. As with everything we do in the workplace, our response to bullying should reflect the image of Christ. That said, let me remind you the image of Christ is an image of strength, not weakness. When He willingly submitted to the abuse of those who crucified Him, Christ was not being weak. On the contrary, He demonstrated extraordinary strength in putting Himself through unspeakable agony, abuse, and abasement to carry out His Father's plan. There is no weakness in that.

The strategies explained in the remainder of this section apply to dealing with both face-to-face bullies and cyber bullies. Those that apply specifically to cyberbullies are explained last and noted as such. I always warn counseling clients dealing with bullies requires strength and courage. Confronting a bully is never easy; however, unlike the bully, you have Christ on your side. When you begin to apply the following strategies, be comforted by the words of Philippians 4:13 that state we can do anything when we have Christ to strengthen us.

Understand Why Bullies Need to Intimidate Others

When Christ was tempted by Satan in the wilderness (Matthew 4:1–11), our Savior knew precisely who He was dealing with. Armed with this knowledge, He knew exactly how to handle His adversary. When dealing with bullies in the workplace, emulate Christ: Know your adversary. Remember the warning in 1 Peter 5:8 to be on guard because the devil is always lurking in the shadows looking for a victim. Bullies are just Satan's minions who he uses for his purposes. Here are some things you should know about bullies that will help you understand how to deal with them more effectively:

- Bullies have poor self-images. They compensate for their own weakness and other shortcomings by seeking to exert power over other people.

- Bullies target people they view as weak or easily intimidated.

- Bullies in the workplace are insecure people who feel threatened by the success of others. Rather than work hard to succeed, they would rather undermine the success of coworkers who do work hard.

Keep these characteristics of bullies in mind as you apply the other strategies in this section. Also keep one additional profile

in mind. Some people who are not naturally bullies will stoop to intimidation, threats, and other methods associated with bullies when they get in over their heads at work, feel pressured to perform, and don't have the skills to get the job done right, on time, and within budget. Rather than admit their shortcomings, they turn into bullies who try to get others to do their work for them.

Confronting Bullies in the Workplace

One of the issues Christian women who seek my counsel struggle with is what it means to turn the other cheek in a workplace setting. The confusion arises out of how some interpret Matthew 5:38–42. Many Christians believe these verses require them to meekly submit to abuse. This is a mistake. In these verses, Christ is warning against retaliating in kind and being vengeful. He is not saying we should be doormats for abusive coworkers. Rather, He is telling us we should not retaliate or respond in kind to people who treat us poorly. It is a warning against becoming like those who abuse us, not a prohibition against standing up to them.

When you are the victim of abuse at work, it is important to act immediately and with confidence and strength. Let bullies get away with their bad behavior and you will be their victim forever. When dealing with people, you can count on getting more of what you accept and less of what you don't.

It is important to show bullies you aren't a soft target. There are two reasons for this. First, bullying will diminish your ability to do your job as well as you should. Since you are responsible for how well you do your job, allowing a circumstance to persist that inhibits your performance is unacceptable. Second, even if you are willing to passively endure bullying, your acquiescence will just encourage the bullies to add others to their target list. Hence, when you become the target of a bully at work, you must act. Having made this point, a caveat is in order.

How you act when confronting a bully is important. In Matthew 5:44, we are told to love our enemies, do good to those who mistreat

209

us, and pray for those who abuse us. This means that, even as you confront a bully, you are to be kind to that individual and treat him with Christian love. Do not respond in kind and do not respond out of anger or vengeance. Also, pray for bullies. Pray God will fill the void in their hearts that make them feel the need to compensate by intimidating and controlling others. If you will do these things in conjunction with the following strategies, your response will be both wise and innocent in the eyes of God:

- Confront the bully and describe exactly what he does you find offensive. Do not use vague terms or generalities. Be specific. Then tell him to stop. For example, you might say: "John, in meetings, you interrupt me, talk over what I am trying to say, and openly belittle my opinions. You also try to intimidate me by invading my personal space. I am telling you to stop." Do not discuss your assertions, get into a debate with the bully, or even answer questions. Just make it clear you expect the offensive behaviors to stop and then walk away. You don't confront a bully to open a dialogue about his behavior or to enter into a debate. You confront him to stop the behavior.

- Tell the bully her behavior is undermining the quality and quantity of your work. Explain you do not want to name her as the reason when the supervisor asks why your work is suffering, but you are prepared to do so. Then, tell the bully that, the next time this kind of discussion is necessary, it will take place in the presence of the supervisor and HR director.

- Document every instance of bullying. Keep careful contemporaneous notes with accurate dates, locations, and times as well as the names of any witnesses who were present. This will help if you have to take your complaint up the chain of command. Further, many organizations have procedures in place that allow employees to file grievances. These grievances are typically heard by a special ad hoc committee.

Normally, the person filing the grievance is allowed to select one member of the committee, the person being charged selects one, and a third member is selected by management or the HR department. Should you ever feel the need to file a grievance against a bully, it is important to have an accurate, comprehensive record so you can give specifics rather than easily denied generalities. For example, it would be difficult for a bully to deny a claim in which you say, "On March 15th at 9:45 a.m. in Conference Room B, he got right in my face within inches of touching me and yelled obscenities. The incident was witnessed by Mike Smith and Sally Meriman." On the other hand, a bully could easily deny a claim in which you say, "I don't remember exactly when, but he yelled at me like he always does." Specificity and accuracy are your best friends in grievance hearings.

- When cyberbullying is the problem, the strategies just explained still apply, but there are additional strategies. The following strategies apply specifically and additionally to cyberbullying: 1) If the cyberbullying is done on company technology such as your organization's local area network (LAN) or even on company time, report the abuse along with screen shots to your supervisor and the HR department. 2) Block the cyberbully online and through your cell phone (your providers can do this for you). 3) If all else fails, change your contact information so the bully has no way to get in touch with you. In addition to these specific strategies, there is one more to consider. Bullies often become emboldened when they carry out their disreputable deeds on social media and via the internet. They will say things online and through social media they would never say face-to-face. The supposed anonymity and distance provided by the internet sometimes emboldens cyberbullies to cross the line into making threats. If you receive a cyber threat, document the threat and take it to the police. At the same time, notify the management of your organization. Do not take cyber-threats lightly.

The strategies explained in this section may not reform a bully. This is too bad, but it is true. Because the need to intimidate, manipulate, and control grows out of deep-seated insecurities, bullies may not be reformed unless and until they seek the help of a minister or counselor or both; however, what the strategies explained in this section will do, in most cases, is remove you from the bully's target list. This is your primary goal. If a bully is moved by your Christ-like example and prayers to change for the better, be thankful. But your immediate goal is to show bullies you aren't a soft target.

The message a bully will get when you apply the strategies explained in this section is this: The price he will pay for trying to intimidate and control you is too high. Bullies target those they view as weak. Once they realize you will not meekly submit to their intimidation and manipulation, they will move on to someone else. When this happens, you will be able to give wise counsel to the next victims concerning how they should deal with bullies. They, in turn, will be able to help others and, before long, the bullies in your organization will run out of soft targets. If you struggle with confronting a bully in private, just remember Christ is by your side and, with Him, you can do anything. Bullies are cowards at heart, so proceed with confidence and know you are in the right.

As Christians, we are called to treat people with dignity, respect, and the kind of love described in 1 Corinthians 13. Consequently, some of my counseling clients are uncomfortable with the idea of confronting coworkers who engage in profanity, inappropriate behavior, and bullying tactics. I will end this chapter by telling you what I always tell them. You are called to stand firm against sinful behavior and reject it wherever and whenever it occurs. Think of Christ when He threw the moneychangers out of the Temple (Mathew 21:12). Then recall the admonition in 1 Corinthians 15:33, where we are warned about how keeping the wrong kind of company can ruin our morals.

We turn the other cheek in the workplace by refusing to retaliate and respond in kind to the inappropriate behavior of coworkers, but we do not ignore that behavior. To do so is to give it tacit approval

and, in turn, encourage more of it. As a Christian, you can be kind and respectful when confronting coworkers who use profanity, display poor manners, are thoughtless, engage in sexual harassment, or employ bullying tactics. Being kind and firm are not mutually exclusive concepts. In fact, I would argue the effectiveness of your efforts will be multiplied by your calmness, confidence, and quiet strength of character. Few things will take the wind out of the sails of those who behave inappropriately faster than someone who will stand up to them in the same way Christ stood up to Satan in the wilderness.

PRAYER FOR COPING WITH CRUDE LANGUAGE AND INAPPROPRIATE BEHAVIOR AT WORK

Dear Father in Heaven,

I'm not sure how many times You've warned us in Scripture to be aware of the words we say to others. You even remind us that, someday, we will be held accountable to You for the foolish words we've spoken, the moments we let off steam, or levied a thoughtless comment about someone. That idea strikes fear in my heart, Lord, even though I genuinely try to be aware of what I say to those around me. I know words have great power and they can either build up the body of Christ or they can tear it down; they can bring joy into our hearts or they can grieve our spirit for years to come.

Father, I'm sometimes appalled at the words tossed around in my work environment. I'm ashamed more care is not given to honor each person there and we sometimes speak unkindly and inappropriately about one another. I'm even surprised by women who indulge in language unbecoming to anyone. Why don't we care? Do we think men will respect us more if we act more like them, or in ways more comfortable to them? Of

course, I know You're aware of these things. How often must You hear someone take Your name in vain?

Please help me to be an example of strength and kind words. Help me maintain a high standard that refuses to do anything but respect each person I work with. Let me walk away from gossip or stand up to someone who bullies others. Help me set the bar that honors who I am as a woman in business, and who You are as my Lord and Savior. Let me catch a glimpse of Your Spirit in the hearts of those around me, so I become a force for good any place I might be.

I know a good word fitly spoken, appropriately communicated, and generously shared can do a lot to set a more positive atmosphere at work. Those words serve as a reminder of Your grace and mercy. Help me be wise in dealing with those who choose to offend me and strengthen my resolve to honor them, despite behavior that does not serve anyone at all.

Thank You, Lord, for opening my eyes to be aware of the importance of each word we speak, and how precious a kind word can be. Let me shine Your light through the words I speak each day. Amen.

GROUP DISCUSSION CASE: A Modern-Day Sodom and Gomorrah?

Helene had her hands full. Like her, Helene's three closest friends worked in banking, but for different banks. All three of her friends approached her recently for advice on how to handle inappropriate behavior they were encountering at work. Patty worked in an office where profanity was the norm unless her coworkers were serving customers. Even then, coarse language occasionally slipped out. Marcie worked for an overbearing boss who constantly made comments about her body and told off-color jokes full of sexual innuendo. Valerie was being bullied by a female coworker who seemed to view her as competition. Helene was older and more experienced than her friends and she worked in the human resources department of her bank. Because of this, they came to her for help. While contemplating what advice to give her friends, Helene said to herself, "Sometimes I think the workplace is just a modern-day version of Sodom and Gomorrah."

Discussion Questions:

1. Have you ever had to deal with profanity, rudeness, sexual harassment, or bullying in the workplace? If so, what were the circumstances and how did you handle the situation?

2. If you were in Helene's place, what would you advise Patty to do? Marci? Valerie?

REVIEW QUESTIONS FOR INDIVIDUALS AND GROUPS

1. How can you tell if higher management is likely to support employees who complain about profanity in the workplace?

2. List and explain three strategies for dealing with profanity in the workplace.

3. What are some examples of rude or thoughtless behavior you have observed at work?

4. How should you go about confronting coworkers about their rudeness?

5. How would you go about convincing higher management of an organization of the value of providing business etiquette training for all employees?

6. Define the concept of sexual harassment.

7. Where can you obtain guidelines for dealing with sexual harassment in the workplace?

8. Distinguish between *quid pro quo* and *condition-of-work* sexual harassment.

9. What are the three criteria the Equal Employment Opportunity Commission uses to determine if sexual harassment has occurred?

10. List and explain the strategies for dealing with sexual harassment at work.

11. What are some reasons why some people become bullies at work?

12. List and explain the strategies for dealing with bullies at work (include cyberbullies).

CHAPTER 9

STAYING CALM, FOCUSED, AND POSITIVE WHEN WORK IS STRESSFUL

·······································

*"Peace I leave with you; my peace I give to you.
Not as the world gives do I give to you. Let not your
hearts be troubled, neither let them be afraid."*
John 14:27

The workplace can be a virtual factory for producing anxiety and stress. More than 70 percent of working people claim stress is an ongoing problem for them. Looming deadlines, demanding customers, grumpy bosses, budget shortfalls, staffing shortages, uncooperative coworkers, business restructurings, corporate downsizings, personnel changes, work overload, mounting responsibilities, and role ambiguity all add up to one thing: stress. Then, on top of the stress you incur on the job, there is the added stress caused by adversity in your personal life. Health problems, relational difficulties, personal tragedies, and family strife just magnify the stress you bring home from work.

Prolonged stress can result in a crushed spirit and a crushed spirit can lead to physical, emotional, relational, and faith-related problems. This is why it is important for you to learn how to stay calm, focused, and positive when work is stressful. This chapter will help you develop emotional resilience while learning how to deal pro-actively, positively, and effectively with stress. Better yet, it will help you learn to do this in ways that reflect the image of Christ. As you read this chapter, keep the message from Psalm 34:18 in mind. In this verse, we are assured God is with His children who are brokenhearted, and He will save those who are crushed in spirit.

What is unique to Christian women in difficult workplace situations is not the stress. Most people in the workplace experience stress, regardless their worldviews. What makes stress a unique challenge for Christian women is God's expectations of how you and your sisters in Christ will deal with it. God reveals in Philippians 4:6–7 how His children are expected to deal with anxiety and stress. In these verses, we are warned against becoming anxious and stressed by the ongoing challenges of life. Instead, we are to place our anxieties at the feet of Christ through prayer. By doing this, we can gain the peace of Christ.

Setting an example for others of taking your burdens to Christ is the unique aspect of coping with stress for Christian women. Not only do you need to cope with stress in ways that protect your physical and emotional well-being, you need to do it in ways that conform to the teachings of Scripture. Christ expects His children to cope with stress in ways that set a positive and helpful example for others. Your unbelieving coworkers, on the other hand, are not subject to this expectation. They can be completely self-serving in how they respond to stress, and often are. For example, they might look for relief in drugs and alcohol. This is an unfortunate but all-too-common response to stress. Of course, this kind of response is one of those solutions that is worse than the problem.

To deal with stress in a manner that protects your physical and emotional well-being while also conforming to the teachings of Scripture, you need to be able to do at least four things: 1) cope with stress in the moment, as it occurs; 2) relieve stress after the fact so you don't let it build up; 3) adjust your attitude toward the things causing stress in your life; and 4) stay calm and focused in the midst of crisis situations. Regardless your level of susceptibility to stress, you can learn to do all four of these things and honor God in how you do them. This chapter explains how.

COPING WITH STRESS AS IT OCCURS

Most of the literature on stress recommends various after-the-fact strategies for relieving it at the end of the workday and on weekends. I cover some of these strategies later in this chapter. But, first, you need to know how to cope with stress in real time, as it occurs. Waiting until after work to relieve stress eating at you for hours is not wise. It's like having a headache and saying, "As soon as I get off work, I am going to take two aspirin." By waiting, you just make the headache worse.

It is wise to deal with stress in the moment, as it occurs, so it doesn't build up and affect your health and work. When you find yourself feeling stressed on the job, the best time to act is now. I recommend three strategies for dealing with stress as it occurs: 1) silent prayer, 2) Scripture reading, and 3) venting to a fellow believer. Each of these strategies is explained in the subsections that follow.

Coping with Stress through Silent Prayer

One of the reasons we become overly stressed at work is we allow the problems and personalities we are dealing with to divert our attention from God. When we focus solely on workplace issues, stress is inevitable. In a fallen world full of sinful people—ourselves

included—things don't always go the way we want them to or even the way they should. When work doesn't go well, you can become stressed. But, by stepping back and looking at the big picture, you can get a better perspective on things. Begin with silent prayer. Through communion with God, you can gain a better perspective, get out of the weeds, and refocus on the flowers in your life.

1 Thessalonians 5:17 encourages God's children to pray continually. Proverbs 3:5–6 tells you to trust in the Lord rather than leaning on your own understanding. The verses from Proverbs go on to say God will make your path straight if you acknowledge Him. When you feel stressed, take a deep breath, then reach out to God in prayer. He is always there for you. The prayer provided at the end of this chapter will help you employ this strategy.

Coping with Stress through Scripture Reading

I advise Christian women to keep a Bible in their desk drawer, purse, or briefcase at all times. As an alternative, have a Bible app on your smartphone. Having access to Scripture during times of stress can be a life saver. When you feel burdened by stress, step away from what you are doing for a few minutes and read your Bible. A good place to start is Jeremiah 29:11. This is one of the most reassuring verses in the Bible. In this verse, God tells of His plan for the exiled Jews. It is a plan for a better future, a plan that gives hope.

Just as He had a plan for His people in Biblical times, God has a plan for you today. Just as His plan for the exiled Jews promised them hope and a better future, His plan for you offers the same assurance. This being the case, you can approach with confidence the problems causing you stress because God has a plan for you, and His plan is bigger than your problems and the stress they cause. This is not to say the problems causing you stress are small or insignificant. They aren't. But comparing them with the majesty of God's plan will put your problems in a better perspective.

Psalm 119:105 states God's word is a lamp that will light the way for your feet. In the current context, this verse means God will guide you through the emotional wilderness stress can cause, if you ask Him. So, as you read His word, pause for a moment and do just that: ask Him. Go back to the previous step and pray again. Let God help you handle the challenges, problems, personalities, and other factors causing you stress. Also, let Him help you sort out specifically why you are feeling stressed. Sometimes we become stressed because we don't know how to handle the problems we face. At other times, we become stressed because we know exactly what we should do, but don't want to do it. In both cases, Psalm 119:105 applies. God will light your path when you don't know what to do, and He will help when you know what to do but don't want to do it.

Coping with Stress by Venting to a Fellow Believer

One of the best friends you can have is a fellow believer who will listen when you need to vent. Venting is an excellent way to relieve stress in the moment. When dealing with stress, remember this: You are like a teapot; if you don't vent, you might explode. If you have a coworker who is a fellow believer, take a break and talk things over with that individual. If you don't have a coworker who shares your faith, call a friend from church or another fellow believer you trust.

Tell this person you just need her to listen while you vent. You are not asking her to solve your problems. This does not mean you should ignore any wise counsel your venting partner might provide. Rather, it means your primary goal is to blow off steam to someone who understands. Any other benefits that come from the conversation are extra. If you work in a stressful environment, it is a good idea to establish a venting relationship with a trusted friend in advance, so your calls don't take this individual by surprise.

Having a venting partner is a strategy that comes directly from Galatians 6:2, where fellow believers are admonished to share each other's burdens. Your venting partner can help bear your burdens and you, in turn, can do the same for her, should it become necessary. Venting can be cathartic. At the very least, it will help relieve the pressure that builds up from stress. If your venting partner has wise counsel to offer, listen and apply anything that might be useful. But, remember, the point of this strategy is for you to release *emotional steam* so you can think more clearly about the situation you face and hear God more clearly when He speaks to you about it.

REGULARLY RELIEVING STRESS BEFORE IT BUILDS UP

Feelings of stress are a lot like unwanted calories. If not burned off regularly, they accumulate over time. Stored-up stress, like stored-up calories, can undermine your physical and emotional health. It can undermine your work performance as well. There are a number of practical things you can do to relief the stress that builds up over the workday. Those I recommend to counseling clients are explained in this section.

Physical Activities for Relieving Stress

One of the best ways to *burn off* stress quickly is through physical activity. Walking, running, bicycling, working out in the gym, dancing, kayaking, rock climbing, canoeing, hiking, yard work, home repairs, gardening, and other forms of exercise are all excellent stress relievers. The key is to find a physical activity you enjoy and will do on a regular basis once you start. For stress relief, regularity is more important than the level of exertion. I enjoy running and working out in the gym and do both regularly; however, I found to my surprise that square dancing is just as effective at relieving stress, at least for me. The key is to discover what works for you.

Once you find a physical activity that works for you, regularity is the next hurdle to confront. Stress that builds up today should be relieved today. It is especially important to work off stress before going to bed at night. You will not sleep well when burdened by pent-up stress, and a lack of sleep just multiplies the negative effects of stress. Experts have long debated the value of exercising before work versus after work. My view is: for stress relief, after work is best. If you wait until the next morning to exercise, you will have to contend with stress all night.

Relaxation Activities for Relieving Stress

Another way to effectively relieve stress is to engage in relaxation activities. Whereas physical activities burn off stress rapidly, relaxation activities let the stress slowly seep out of you. The most important thing relaxation activities do is take your mind off work and refocus you on pleasant, enjoyable, and fun things. To this end, engaging in relaxation activities is Scriptural. Philippians 4:8 tells us to fix our minds on things that are good, pure, lovely, and right. Stress does just the opposite. It focuses us on things that are worrisome and negative.

One of the ways to comply with Philippians 4:8 is to find relaxation activities that will help replace the stress you are feeling with thoughts that nourish your spirit rather than sapping it. Popular relaxation methods include deep breathing, biblical meditation, massages, hot showers, soaking in a deep tub, relaxing in a whirlpool, painting, going to a movie, shopping with a friend, dining out, and nature walks, to name just a few. As with physical exercise, the key is to find those activities that work for you and then do them regularly.

To illustrate how effective relaxation activities can be for relieving stress, consider that Winston Churchill attributed his longevity, in part, to painting. Churchill served for almost forty years in various government positions in Great Britain, including Prime Minister at the most crucial juncture in his country's long history: World War II. His life in politics and government was impossibly stressful. Consequently, when he began to feel overwhelmed by the incredible burden of responsibility he shouldered, Churchill slipped away to his country home for a few days to paint. In the process, he became quite the accomplished artist. More importantly, he was able to relieve the stress that might have clouded his judgment as he faced the momentous decisions he had to make to save his country from Nazi tyranny.

My wife is an artist in watercolors. She says it is almost impossible to stay focused on the problems causing you stress when you get absorbed in creating a painting. You become so focused on the painting the negative issues in your life fade into the background. By the time you finish painting, the stress has seeped out of you and a more positive perspective has replaced it. The same is true of most any relaxation activity you enjoy and will do regularly.

ADJUSTING YOUR ATTITUDE TOWARD THINGS THAT CAUSE YOU STRESS

Much of the stress we feel at work and in life is self-inflicted. This is to say it is brought on by unrealistic expectations of human nature. A common refrain heard from my counseling clients is this: "Why can't people just do what they are supposed to do?" While the question is certainly understandable, it is not realistic. In response to this question, I refer counseling clients to the book of Genesis and what occurred in Garden of Eden.

Since the Garden of Eden, we have lived in a fallen world. Consequently, people don't always do what they should do, and things don't always work out the way we would like them to. These hard truths are going to cause you no end of stress unless you learn to adjust your attitude about the inherent flaws in human nature and the intrinsic imperfections of organizations. This section explains how to adjust your attitude toward the human and organizational flaws you observe in the workplace.

Accept that Life Isn't Always Fair, but Don't Use This Fact as an Excuse

How many times have you heard someone proclaim in exasperation, "This isn't fair!" Frankly, they are probably right. Much in life is not fair. I suspect you already know this from experience. There is much in life that can seem unfair, but don't let this fact be a stress producer. Life has not been fair since that unfortunate event in

the Garden of Eden, and it is not likely to be fair this side of heaven. Understanding this reality is a necessary first step in preventing the unfairness you experience at work from becoming a major cause of stress in your life.

If you find yourself indulging in self-pity because of the unfairness of things at work, step back for a moment and think about the "unfairness" of Christ dying on the cross because of your sins and mine. Consider the unfairness of being made to carry the very cross on which you will be crucified. It would be bad enough to be crucified for one's own sins, but to be scourged, abased, taunted, ridiculed, and then led to an agonizing death for the sins of others gives new meaning to the concept of unfairness.

Don't let the seeming unfairness of situations at work increase the stress you feel. Expect life to be unfair from time to time and learn to deal with unfairness in positive, productive, and helpful ways. How does one do this? Here are a few strategies that will help:

- Ask yourself if you can solve the problem or change the situation you view as unfair. If you can, do so. If not, label it a fact of life and move on. Problems that cannot be solved are no longer problems; they are facts, like the weather. You may not like the weather, but you cannot change it, so why become stressed over it?

- Heed the warnings in Ecclesiastes 6:1–12 about vanity. Remind yourself to rejoice in life's blessing rather than stressing over life's unfairness.

- Refuse to view yourself as a victim. Victimhood just makes things worse by causing you feelings of helplessness.

- Refuse to fixate on and obsess about the problems that seem unfair to you. Stress is an emotional wound that cannot heal until you stop fixating on the unfairness of your situation.

Having made the point that life can be unfair, let me make another equally important point: Never use the fact that life can be unfair as an excuse for treating coworkers unfairly. Although life can be unfair, we are called to treat the people we work with as fairly as is possible in a fallen and inherently unfair world.

Do Not Create Emergencies in Your Own Mind

I once worked with a colleague who could turn any situation into an emergency. As a result, she was always stressed, harried, and out of sorts. Anything that failed to work out exactly as planned, any project that fell behind schedule, or even a missed phone call became an emergency in her mind. Don't do this. You will face enough emergencies in your life without creating them where they don't exist. In college, I had a roommate who thought something as inconsequential as running out of peanut butter constituted an emergency. He wasted a lot of time every day frantically rushing about with his hair on fire because of supposed emergencies.

An emergency is a serious, unexpected, and potentially dangerous situation that can have dire results. For example, a fire in the office is an emergency. Having to go to Plan B because Plan A didn't work out is not an emergency. In fact, having a Plan B is a way to prevent an emergency. When you find yourself dealing with what you consider an emergency, ask yourself the following questions:

- Is the situation really serious or just another one of those problems that crop up in the workplace every day?

- Is the situation really unexpected? In a fallen world, Christians learn to expect imperfect outcomes and plan for them. Doing this will relieve the stress caused by *unexpected* circumstances.

- Is the situation dangerous? Will there be dire consequences if the problem is not solved immediately? When answering this question, remember "dire" means more than just upsetting a grouchy boss or a demanding customer.

Proverbs 14:12 warns us the way that seems right can actually lead to death. This certainly applies to stress in the workplace. It may seem right to approach work-related problems in ways that result in stress, but constant, unrelieved stress can lead to health problems and even death. At the very least, it can be detrimental to your emotional well-being. Reduce your stress by reducing the number of emergencies you have to deal with. Reduce the number of emergencies you have to deal with by adjusting your attitude concerning what constitutes an emergency.

Choose Your Battles with Care and Purpose

The workplace can be a battleground of competing agendas and personalities. Turf wars, office politics, budgets battles, conflicting ideas, personalities quirks, differing perspectives, status-seeking, and competition for promotions, raises, and perquisites are just a few of the issues that can lead to conflict on the job. Sometimes the conflict is between departments, sometimes it is between groups, such as management and labor, and sometimes it is between individuals. In any case, the workplace offers plenty of opportunities for conflict, and conflict is a major source of stress.

One of the most effective ways to reduce work-related stress is to engage in fewer conflicts. To reduce the amount of conflict in your life, learn to choose your battles carefully and with purpose. Choosing your battles carefully means choosing to fight only those you really need to win. The battles you need to win can be determined by asking yourself a simple question: *Will winning this battle serve the mission of our organization better than losing it?* If you can answer this question with an unequivocal "yes" the battle is probably worth fighting. Fighting for the good of the mission is acceptable. But when the reason behind your fighting is ego, self-interest, or misguided ambition, it is time to step back from the fray. Battles fought for selfish reasons can undermine the morale of your team, the performance of your organization, and the trajectory of your career.

Choosing your battles with a valid purpose means engaging in battles only when you have a definite goal that cannot be accomplished without fighting for it, and the goal is not driven by selfish interest. For example, fighting for policies to ensure fair and honest dealings within the organization is appropriate. Fighting for a decision that is in the overall best interests of the organization is appropriate. But fighting to feather your nest, enhance your status, gain recognition, or boost your ego is not. These kinds of self-serving purposes do not serve the overall good of the organization.

Choose One Thing from Your To-Do List and Do It

One of the most common sources of stress in the workplace is overload. It happens to all of us. While we are putting out fires and dealing with problems that take longer than expected to resolve, work backs up and begins to stack up. When this happens, the sheer volume of work to be done can seem overwhelming. Few things are more stressful than feeling overwhelmed because you have too much work to do and too little time. People in these situations often come down with a case of what I call *overload paralysis*. There is so much to do they don't know where to start. As a result, they become mentally paralyzed. While in this state, their work continues to pile up and, as a result, their stress level continues to go up.

When you feel overwhelmed because the stack of work demanding your attention weighs more than you do, think about what is written in Matthew 6:25–27. These verses tell us not to worry or fret because, if God provides for even the birds of the air, He will certainly provide for us. God has provided for you. He has prepared you to handle this very situation, so don't despair. He has given you the intelligence, skills, knowledge, and experience needed to attack the stack overwhelming you.

When being overloaded tempts you to throw up your hands in frustration and give up, recall what is written in 1 Corinthians 10:13. This verse assures us God will not let us be tempted beyond what we can handle. When overwhelmed by a mountain of work, all you have to do is wisely apply the intelligence, skills, knowledge, and experience God has given you. I recommend a three-step approach for conquering overload paralysis and trimming down your stack of unfinished work.

First, go through your work stack and make a list of everything in it. Leave nothing out. Second, circle the three most critical and time-sensitive items on your list. Finally, choose one of these three items and go to work on it. While working on the first item, give no thought to the other two or any other items on the list. Pick them off one at a time. The progress you make by choosing one item and completing it will encourage you to keep going. Before long, the momentum will begin to shift in your favor. Soon, you will find your list is not as formidable as you thought. In fact, once you get past the feeling of being overwhelmed, you will be pleasantly surprised at how fast you can whittle down the list. You may also find a few items on the list that are not so important after all. These can be scratched off the list, put aside until later, or even delegated.

Get Comfortable with Change: Be Flexible and Adaptable

Few things in the workplace cause more stress than change. If you are like most people, your tendency is to get comfortable with the status quo and cling to it. This means your stress level will increase anytime there is a change, which, of course, is most of the time. Characterizing change as a major workplace stressor is not just supposition on my part. My counseling clients often complain about the stress change causes them. Consequently, it is important for you to learn to be flexible and adaptable in coping with change. Begin by understanding why, as a rule, change makes people uncomfortable.

Several factors account for human resistance to change, but, in my experience, three stand out. First, there is the issue of familiarity. We are comfortable with the familiar because it represents the known. Change raises the specter of the unknown. Even when we don't particularly like the situation that currently exists, we know how things are and how they affect us. When change is coming, we don't know how it will affect us or, at least, we aren't sure.

Second, people in the workplace often feel like change is something done to them rather than for them or with them. Someone higher in the organization decides to make a change. Often, this individual fails to consult with those who will be affected by the change or who will have to carry it out. Employees are expected to accept and implement the change, whether they like it or not. When making decisions about a change, failing to consult with those who have to implement it is a common management mistake. This mistake is one of the main reasons more than half of major organizational changes fail to live up to expectations.

Finally, there is the issue of unintended consequences. Decision-makers in organizations often make changes without considering the possibility of unintended consequences and there are always unintended consequences. This is why it is important that, before making final decisions about changes, managers ask employees to help identify any possible unintended consequences.

Unintended consequences can derail even the most desirable organizational changes. At the very least, disruptions caused by unintended consequences will be resented by the personnel they affect. The unintended consequences of a poorly planned change can create sufficient resentment, frustration, and resistance among employees to undermine the change, causing it to fail. Higher management can require the personnel in an organization to make a change, but they cannot require them to like it or accept it. Not surprisingly, if they don't like a change, employees won't put their whole hearts into making it succeed.

Yet, in spite of the fact change is often mishandled in organizations, it remains a constant. Perhaps the only thing that does not change in the workplace is the certainty of change. It is going to happen, and you are going to be affected by it—count on it. The effect change has on you might be good or bad, depending on circumstances coupled with your attitude toward change. But one thing is certain: To excel in today's rapidly changing workplace, you must get comfortable with change and learn how to deal with it in positive, productive, and helpful ways. In other words, to prevent change from being a major stressor in you work life, you need to be flexible and adaptable.

To help my counseling clients deal with change, I remind them they have one constant in their lives, it never changes, and never will change: the love of God. Hebrews 13:8 assures us Jesus is the same in the past, present, and future. Knowing you have an unchanging, constant, and reliable Savior can provide a secure anchorage when you are tossed about on a sea of change. The constancy of Christ can also cast workplace change in a different and better perspective. With Christ as your anchor, you can adopt a better attitude toward change, an attitude characterized by flexibility and adaptability. You have an unchanging Christ to cling to in all situations. Let Him be your anchor when change makes you feel as if you are cast adrift on sea of uncertainty. The rope that tethers you to Christ will never break.

Clear Your Mind Several Times a Day

I am supposed to be the counselor, but it was a counseling client who taught me an effective method for dealing with stress. That method is to clear your mind several times a day. Edwina has one of the most stressful positions there is: customer complaint specialist. All day, every day, she deals with unhappy and even irate people. Her job is to make them happy. Edwina works for a local resort located on Florida's beautiful Emerald Coast. It is one of the most popular tourist destinations in Northwest Florida, and one of the most expensive. Its customers pay high prices to stay there. They expect a lot in return. When things don't work out as planned, the unhappy tourists end up in Edwina's office. She one told me unhappy tourists will actually complain to her about the weather, as if she created it and can change it.

To cope with the stress of dealing with unhappy people who are accustomed to getting anything they want, when they want it

and how they want it, Edwina has developed an interesting strategy. Three times during the workday—mid-morning, noon, and mid-afternoon—Edwina closes her office door and takes about ten minutes to clear her mind of the stress that has built up. She begins by closing her eyes and taking several deep breaths. When her heart rate settles down, she reads a few pre-selected Bible verses.

Her favorite verse for clearing her mind of stress is Psalm 120:1. The author of this Psalm says, when in distress, He calls to the Lord and the Lord answers. Edwina calls to the Lord when she is stressed. She prays God will clear her mind and help her maintain a pleasant, positive, and helpful attitude toward customers. The final part of her strategy comes at the end of the day.

Because her office is housed in a resort located on the sugar white beaches of Florida's Emerald Coast, Edwina ends each day by taking a short walk along the beach, barefoot. Surrounded by the beauty of God's creation, Edwina lets the emerald green water, refreshing sea breeze, and soft sand wash away the stress she is feeling. Because she applies this strategy regularly and without fail, the stress of her job never builds up for long. Better yet, she never takes it home with her. By using Scripture, prayer, and the beauty of God's creation to clear her mind, Edwina is able to excel in a highly stressful position.

You can replicate the first part of Edwina's strategy in almost any job, but the last part may not be so easy. If you don't have a place nearby to surround yourself in the splendor of God's creation, buy a DVD of the world's most beautiful locations and watch it at the end of the day. Variations on this theme are listening to calming music, pondering God's kingdom, puttering in a garden, or doing anything else that helps clear your mind of stressful thoughts at the end of the work day. The key is to follow Edwina's example of regularity and consistency. This will prevent stress from building up over the course of the day, robbing you of sleep at night, and carrying over to the next day.

Don't Be So Serious. Laugh a Little

Gracie had an unorthodox but effective way of relieving workplace stress: laughter. Her commute home from work took thirty minutes or longer, depending on traffic. Gracie put that time to good use. Every day, without fail, she spent her driving-home time listening to comedy routines she downloaded. Alone in her car, Gracie could let go and laugh uproariously without fear of embarrassment, although she did occasionally get inquisitive looks at stoplights.

When I asked her how she came to use this innovative technique for relieving stress, Gracie's answer surprised me. The idea came not from extensive research or baring her soul to a counselor. Rather, she just stumbled onto it. After one particularly stressful day at the office, Gracie remembered she was supposed to go to a movie with a friend that night. Overwrought from work, going to a movie was the last thing she wanted to do. In fact, she considered cancelling the date but didn't, which turned out to be a fortuitous decision. The movie was a comedy. Twenty laugh-filled minutes into the film, Gracie noticed the stress she was feeling was gone. In fact, it was replaced with a pleasant feeling of relaxation, comfort, and peace of mind.

Gracie's discovery of the stress-relieving power of laughter was a serendipitous accident. The benefits of laughter were news to her, but they are not news to medical and mental-health professionals. Laughing will take your mind off the problems causing you stress, but this is just the beginning of the good things that laughter will do for you. Laughter has long been known to stimulate circulation, decrease blood pressure, soothe tension, increase oxygen intake, and promote the release of endorphins from the brain. Laughing even burns calories and, if that is not enough, laughing is Scriptural. Proverbs 17:22 says that feelings of joy are medicinal.

Don't Borrow Other People's Problems

A counseling client once told me: when dealing with coworkers, she sometimes feels like a carpenter with a new hammer. To her, every problem raised by a coworker looks like a nail. Consequently,

233

one of the biggest stressors in Huong's life was taking on the problems of others. As a committed Christian, Huong wanted to help others bear their burdens. She took the message in Galatians 6:2 seriously. But where she got off track was in defining what it means to help others bear their burdens.

To Huong, bearing her coworkers' burdens meant adopting their problems and making them her own. Any time a coworker asked for advice with a problem, she quickly inserted herself into the situation, taking over. I told Huong her desire to help coworkers who were struggling was commendable, but helping a coworker solve a problem is not the same thing as adopting the problem and making it your own. Her approach was like a teacher who, instead of helping a student with a difficult assignment, does the assignment for her.

That often-quoted Chinese maxim about teaching a man to fish instead of just giving him a fish applies in this case (yes, this is a Chinese adage, not a Bible verse as many believe). Her part in bearing the burdens of coworkers should consist of listening empathetically when they need to talk, offering wise counsel, steering them away from foolish responses, and making helpful referrals. It should not be adopting their problems and trying to solve the problems for them.

I told Huong she would have enough problems of her own to deal with without adopting the problems of coworkers, and, if she really wanted to help them, she should teach coworkers how to solve their own problems. Every time she solved a problem for a coworker, she just made that individual more dependent on her. She was like a softball coach who, instead of showing a player how to hit the ball, just took the bat from her and hit it himself. Every time that player comes up to bat, she will need the coach to hit the ball for her, which, of course, is not possible. Gain a reputation for adopting the problems of other people, and you will soon be inundated with problems, most of which you cannot solve. This is too much of a burden for any person to bear.

Once Huong gained a better perspective on helping people solve their problems, as opposed to adopting those problems as her own, she became adept at providing wise counsel and making helpful referrals. The coworkers she helped, in turn, became more adept at solving their own problems. Huong now lives out the admonition in Galatians 6:2, but without accumulating a disabling level of stress. Hers is a good example to follow when coworkers approach you with their problems.

Understand the Work is Never Done

When my counseling clients say they are stressed out over what seems like a perpetual stack of unfinished work, I explain my *dishes-and-laundry principle* to them. The D & L principle posits that, as soon as you finish washing the dishes or doing a load of laundry, there will just be more, so why get stressed about it? Your work is sometimes like this. As soon as your inbox is empty, it starts to fill up again, and often before you can even breathe a sigh of relief. This is the nature of the workplace, especially in organizations that are doing well.

There will be times when your work will get backed up and seem never-ending. It happens. In fact, this is not so much a problem as it is a fact of life. The distinction is important to understand. You do not solve facts, you learn to cope with them. Stressing over periodic backlogs of work is like stressing over the weather. What is the point, when you cannot change it? Learn to distinguish between problems and facts. This alone will decrease your level of stress.

Next time you find yourself facing a mountain of unfinished work, rather than stressing over it, do what you do when the weather doesn't cooperate: adapt. If it's raining, you wear a raincoat or use an umbrella. If it is cold, you wear an overcoat and gloves. If your work gets backed up, adjust your schedule for a few days and get caught up. While coming in a little early or staying a little late to get caught up, look to Scripture for solace.

A good place to start is Psalm 61:2 where the author cries out to God when he feels overwhelmed. Rather than stressing over a stack of work that just seems to have no bottom to it or a to-do list that seems to never end, cry out to God and ask him to lead you to that rock taller than your work stack and anything else in life. When stressed out because you think you will never get caught up, consider the message in Isaiah 40:28, where we are reminded the Lord never grows weary. Lean on God when you feel overwhelmed by your workload. He doesn't grow weary. Get the strength you need to persevere from Him. Then do the next task on your to-do list, and the next, and the next, and just keep going. I have always found the work stack gets whittled down faster than I anticipated when I use this approach.

Do Not Be Surprised When Plans Go Awry

Expecting plans to work out perfectly in an imperfect world is just inviting stress into your life. Think of the message in Isaiah 53:6, where we are reminded all of us have gone astray. This, in turn, is why our plans are imperfect: They are developed and carried out by imperfect people. Mimi had expectations of perfection, and these expectations were a major cause of stress for her.

Mimi was a conference planner. She spent every workday planning the details of meetings for business and professional organizations. Mimi had to concern herself with schedules, facilities, meals, audio-visual equipment, accommodations, speakers, and a host of other factors, most of which were moving targets. No matter how well she planned, it seemed something always went wrong, or adjustments had to be made at the last minute. Mimi hated this.

Once she had a plan, she expected everything to go according to the plan and became upset when it didn't. Mimi had one of those personalities that could make caffeine nervous. Conference planning is a stressful job for anyone, but, for a perfectionist like Mimi, it is a nervous breakdown waiting to happen. To avoid a breakdown, Mimi had to learn to be flexible, adaptable, and comfortable with change. Fortunately, she did learn these things and is now a well-respected, much-sought-after professional in her field.

When it comes to planning your day, work, events, career, or life, get comfortable with imperfection. The only perfect plan that ever existed or ever will is God's plan. Jeremiah 29:11 gives us the assurance that God has plans for His children and those plans provide for our welfare and future. His is the only plan that needs to work out perfectly and you can take comfort in knowing it will. Not only that, but you are included in God's plan.

This does not mean you should be satisfied with poor planning or sloppy execution. You shouldn't. Sloppiness and poor planning will not help you excel at work. Rather, it means you should plan for perfection but adjust and adapt to imperfection. It also means you should refuse to get stressed over changes to plans, even last-minute changes, especially when they are caused by factors over which you have no control. The ability to maintain a flexible, adaptable attitude when plans go awry will make you an asset to your organization and, in turn, help you excel in your work.

MAINTAINING YOUR COMPOSURE IN HIGH-STRESS SITUATIONS

Have you ever had to deal with a crisis or any other kind of high-stress situation at work? If you haven't, you probably will at some point. Here are just a few of the high-stress situations I have had to deal with over the course of my career: a coworker having a heart attack in his office, a hungry bear inviting himself into a lunch meeting at my college, a student being raped in a restroom on campus, an alligator joining the students in line during registration for classes, a brutal murder at one of our branch campuses, a multimillion-dollar federal grant that had to be postmarked no later than 5:00 p.m. handed to me incomplete at 4:45 p.m., an outdoor ribbon-cutting ceremony for the opening of a new campus disrupted by a sudden thunder storm, a convicted felon on probation with a car full of automatic rifles and other fire arms hanging around campus, and an elderly woman needing the Heimlich maneuver during an awards banquet, right at the moment the U.S. Secretary of Education was making the presentation to our college.

Crises at work run the gamut from minor to serious. At one end of the spectrum is the ubiquitous looming deadline and the fire-breathing boss demanding you meet it or the indispensable team member who quits or becomes ill in the middle of an important project. At the other end of the spectrum are more serious events, such as fires, natural disasters, injured workers, or active shooters on the premises. Regardless of the nature of the situation, sudden, unexpected events at work can cause your stress level to go through the ceiling. For this reason, it is important to learn to maintain your composure in high-stress situations. What follows are several strategies to help you stay calm, unstressed, and focused in a crisis:

Remember the Outcome is in God's Hands

Since it is certain you will face high-stress situations from time to time, before they ever happen, get it settled in your heart and mind the outcome is in God's hands, not yours. Implant Isaiah 41:10 firmly in your heart and lean on the message in this verse when a crisis erupts. Isaiah 41:10 says we shouldn't fear because God is with us. He will strengthen, help, and uphold us in all situations. Once you accept this truth from Scripture, no crisis is too big for you to handle. But let me be clear, in a crisis, you do not just sit back and hope God will make things turn out well, while doing nothing yourself. Rather, you stay calm and focused knowing the outcome is in God's hands and He may use you as His instrument in determining the outcome. Do all you can and trust the rest to God.

Close Your Eyes, Take a Few Deep Breaths, and Pray

A crisis, by definition, is a serious and unexpected event, an emergency situation that can cause your stress level to elevate quickly. The serious and unexpected nature of the event coupled with uncertainty concerning what to do about it can drive your stress level through the roof. People are sometimes so stricken by a crisis they become paralyzed by shock, fear, and awe. Other people respond by

panicking. They run around with their hair on fire, adding to the pandemonium and confusion that typically accompany a crisis. Neither response is helpful.

When a crisis erupts, the first thing to do is to get a grip on your emotions, hold them in check, and settle your nerves. An effective way to do this is to take a few deep breaths to let the shock pass. Then, calm yourself by saying a prayer. Ask God to help you stay calm, focused, and in control. Ask Him to strengthen you for what must be done to eliminate or, at least, mitigate the crisis. With this done, you are ready to respond in positive, productive, and helpful ways.

Be Deliberate and Intentional, but Not Hectic

One of the reasons people panic during a crisis is they shift into high gear, become hyper-stressed, and start rushing around without thinking clearly. The tone of their voices changes and the volume increases. Rushing about and shouting orders can make you feel like you are doing something, but this approach isn't really helpful. Agitation just makes things worse. Hyperactivity and volume can increase stress levels and cause people to panic.

Prompt, deliberate, intentional action calmly taken is the best approach. Hectic activity will just cause foggy thinking, increased stress, and fear. In a crisis, acting deliberately, intentionally, and with purpose will reduce stress levels and contribute to a better result. Keeping your voice calm will help others keep their emotions in check. When you tell others to do something that needs to be done, look them in the eyes, talk directly to them, and hold down the volume. Be specific about what you want them to do. For example, never yell, "Someone call 911!" Instead, look directly at a specific individual and tell her to make the call. Then observe to make sure she does it.

Focus on Solutions, Not Problems

When you find yourself in a crisis, focus on what needs to be done to solve the problem, not the problem itself. People who focus on the problem instead of the solution are like the tennis player who focuses on the scoreboard instead of the ball. She is bound to lose. Instead, pick one task that needs to be done—no matter how small—and do it. Then do the next thing and the next and so on. Your calm, deliberate action will often snap others out of their shocked and stunned state and get them started doing other things that need to be done. Further, the act of doing something positive will reduce your stress level.

Give People Something to Do, No Matter How Small or Inconsequential

This strategy is an extension of the previous one. In a crisis, most people want to help, but often don't know what to do. The crisis situation may be so unfamiliar to them and the shock so extreme they have to be told what to do. When people in a high-stress situation don't have something helpful to do, they are more likely to panic or get in the way of those who are trying to respond. The solution to this phenomenon is to give them something to do.

There is an instructive scene in the movie based on Jane Austen's book, *Sense and Sensibility,* where Marianne has fallen seriously ill. The outlook is grim. While she is being treated, Colonel Brandon, who is in love with Marianne, paces outside her room, wringing his hands in a fit of helplessness. He wants to help, but there doesn't seem to be anything constructive he can do. Marianne's sister, Elinor, observing Brandon's obvious discomfort, tries to console the Colonel, but nothing she says helps.

It is then Brandon tells Elinor to give him something to do or he will go mad. Seeing an opportunity, she sends him to fetch their mother, which he does. The mother's arrival is a balm to all involved, including Marianne. The patient eventually recovers, and the mother, Elinor, and, most importantly, Marianne, are all grateful to Colonel

240

Brandon for his help. You probably know the rest of the story. After all, it is Jane Austen. If not, you will just have to watch the movie. The point is that giving Brandon something to do got him out of the way before his pacing increased everyone else's stress levels.

Remove Panicking, Out-of-Control Coworkers from the Scene

Panic is a common reaction in high-stress situations. This is unfortunate because panic can be contagious. When trying to focus on what needs to be done in a crisis, it is important to keep on-lookers from panicking. Giving agitated coworkers something to do, as recommended in the previous step, will often be enough to ward off panic. But, when that strategy does not work, it is important to remove panicking coworkers from the scene. Few things will raise your stress level so quickly as being around people who are panicking. Consequently, for the good of all, it is best to remove them from the scene.

One way to remove a panicking individual is to ask a coworker to escort her to a nearby office and sit with her. Another way is to send the panicking individual on a simple and easy errand. For example, in the case of the coworker who had a heart attack, it was necessary to remove the panicked individual who first found him stricken in his office. To do this, I asked him to go to the supply room and get two gallons of spring water. We didn't really need the water, we just needed him out of the way. By the time he returned, the ambulance was well on the way to the hospital with our coworker who, thanks be to God, eventually recovered and was able to return to work. We used the water in our office coffee machine.

PRAYER FOR MAINTAINING YOUR COMPOSURE IN HIGH-STRESS SITUATIONS

Dear Father of Peace,

Lord, I come to You today with just one request. Help me absorb Your peace in a way that will allow me to function well at work. Lately, I find myself exhausted as each day ends, stressed by my work environment, some of the issues going on there, and even some of the people who make the work we're trying to accomplish a challenge.

Help me start with You the moment I feel job pressures building up and threatening my focus. Help me to simply stop everything and take my eyes off the obstacles and put them back on You. Nudge me to pray, right where I am, and remind me that nothing happening is a surprise to You. Give me the courage to do what I can and trust in You for those things I cannot do by myself. Show me how to be a calming influence in the midst of stressful situations.

I thank You that, when I allow the work issues or personal issues to push me into stress overload, I am blessed to have some place to turn. I am grateful I can always come to You and we can work things out together to find the best solutions and possibilities.

In the heat of a challenging moment or the schedule that overloads my heart and mind, I can forget to seek Your face, Your light, and Your wisdom. Lord, I ask as Your daughter, remind me I can put every moment of stress at Your feet and You will help me carry each burden. Cause me to be aware of anything I might be doing to add to the pressures I'm feeling and help me to deal with those things quickly.

I ask that You bring to me and to each person with whom I work the blessing of Your Spirit of cooperation, kindness, and peace. We all need Your mercy and grace. Thank You for calming my soul and strengthening my spirit today. Amen.

GROUP DISCUSSION CASE: "I don't know if I can handle this much stress"

Iliana didn't know it would be like this. She recently returned to work after staying home until her daughter, Chloe, was in first grade. During the six years she was out of the workforce, much had changed. The company she returned to was sold during the interim and the new owner was a brusque, profane, and demanding task master. Most of her old colleagues were gone, and there were new company rules against any form of religious expression in the office (i.e., no Scripture verses on office walls, no Bibles on desks, and no prayer breakfasts in the break room before work). Iliana's workdays were now filled with stress.

To make matters worse, because of the new owner's perpetual dissatisfaction with everyone and everything, even minor problems were viewed as major disasters. Nobody wanted to incur the wrath of the owner. As a result, the slightest glitch, snag, or complication would send Iliana's coworkers into paroxysms of panic. Iliana had never felt so stressed in her life. Compared to her new job, childbirth was a breeze. After enduring the situation for several weeks, Iliana finally admitted to herself, "I don't know if I can handle this much stress."

Discussion Questions:

1. What can Iliana do—other than find another job—to cope with the stress her job is causing?

2. Since every problem is viewed as a crisis in her office, how should Iliana deal with crises?

REVIEW QUESTIONS FOR INDIVIDUALS AND GROUPS

1. List as many factors as you can that might make the workplace a stressful environment.

2. What are the four things you must learn how to do if you are going to cope effectively with stress in ways that will protect your physical and emotional well-being, while also conforming to Scripture?

3. List and explain several strategies for coping with stress in the moment, as it occurs.

4. Explain how to regularly relieve stress before it builds up and carries over from day to day.

5. Explain how to adjust your attitude toward the things causing you stress.

6. List and explain several strategies for staying calm and focused in the midst of a crisis.

CHAPTER 10

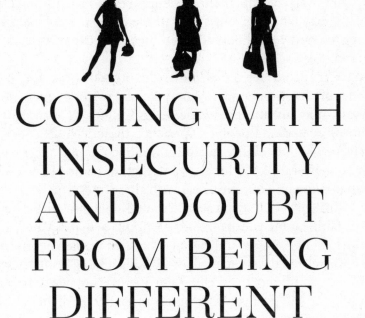

COPING WITH INSECURITY AND DOUBT FROM BEING DIFFERENT

....

*"Do not be anxious about anything, but
in everything by prayer and supplication with
thanksgiving let your requests be known to God."*
Philippians 4:6

Being different from those you work with can be hard. I begin with this fact because, as a Christian woman, you are different from your unbelieving coworkers and in important ways. But you are like your coworkers in one way: You were created as a social being. As a social being, it is only natural to want to fit in. This is not a criticism; it's how God made you. Most of His children are social by nature. Relatively few people are hermits. Consequently, wanting to fit in at work is only natural. As we try to fit in with our coworkers, comparing ourselves to them is tempting. In fact, the practice is probably inevitable. As Christians, these comparisons often reveal differences, and your differences can breed insecurity. Insecurity, in turn, can breed self-doubt.

With that said, let me acknowledge insecurity is not the sole province of Christian women. Many people who work—men, women, believers, and unbelievers—experience feelings of insecurity and doubt. Most working people experience these feelings concerning such factors as their ability, qualifications, income, advancement, job security, appearance, clothing, and weight, to name just a few. As a Christian woman, you must deal with these and other insecurities your coworkers feel, but you also face additional insecurities relating to your faith. Living your faith in the workplace makes you different. If those I counsel are any indication, Christian women often struggle with faith-related differences when working among unbelievers.

Your commitment to excelling at work does not necessarily make you different. Many of your coworkers probably share this ambition. Doing so without compromising your faith does make you different, and this fact can breed insecurity. As a result, a lot of Christian women struggle with inner doubt as they compare themselves, sometimes unfavorably, with coworkers. Christian women who approach me for counseling often voice feelings of insecurity and doubt relating to their work. Invariably, their insecurities grow out of self-comparisons to coworkers who do not share their faith. Here are just a few examples of the kinds of concerns Christian women have shared with me:

- I dress professionally, but modestly. Some of my coworkers, on the other hand, dress suggestively, as if going to a cocktail party. I don't want to dress like them but have to admit I feel frumpy and unattractive around them. Compared to my coworkers, I feel like a plain Jane.

- Most of my colleagues went to prestigious public and private universities. I went to a small Christian college. I don't know if I am as well prepared for this job as they are. Sometimes I feel like a minor league player who snuck into the big leagues and doesn't belong there.

- I am the only member of my work team who does not use profanity. My moderate language makes me stand out like a sore thumb. I'm afraid my coworkers think I'm a prude.

- Even my married colleagues like to get together for happy hour at a local tavern before going home at night, and without their spouses. Because I don't join them, I feel like an outcast. I worry about missing out on important work-related discussions and relationships by skipping these outings.

- My coworkers seem to put their jobs ahead of their families. They work late and on weekends. Then they take work home every night. I don't know when they see their families. I try to keep my work and family obligations in balance but am afraid some of my coworkers question my dedication to the job.

- For my coworkers, Sunday is just another day. Most of them come into the office on Sundays to catch up on work or get a head start on the new week. Because I try to reserve Sundays for church and family, they think I am a slacker.

- When just chatting in the office, my coworkers talk about television programs and movies I don't watch and wouldn't. As a result, I never seem to have anything to talk about on breaks or at lunch.

Living and working in ways consistent with your faith will make you different than your unbelieving coworkers, and the differences will be noticeable. These differences can lead to comparisons between you and coworkers who do not share your faith. Such comparisons can, in turn, plant seeds of doubt that eventually sprout into full-fledged insecurities. Consequently, it is important for you to understand insecurity as a concept and why it is important to face up to your insecurities. You also need to understand there is only one true source of security. It's not money, talent, insurance, alarm systems, or connections. It's Jesus Christ.

WHAT IS INSECURITY?

The kind of insecurity dealt with in this chapter consists of feelings of inadequacy and inferiority based on the rejection or disapproval of coworkers or just unflattering comparisons to coworkers you make yourself. It is difficult to cope with rejection and disapproval of any kind but, when your faith is the basis for the rejection and disapproval, the level of difficulty increases. Unfavorable self-comparisons are no fun either, particularly when you think living your faith causes you to suffer by comparison. In a setting where people are ambivalent about your faith or even reject it, your differences will be noticed.

LOOKING FOR SECURITY IN ALL THE WRONG PLACES

Years ago, there was a popular song about looking for love in all the wrong places. Christians who struggle with insecurity are often guilty of the same mistake: looking for security in all the wrong places. We look for security in money, relationships, physical appearance, retirement accounts, insurance, jobs, clothing, promotions, safe neighborhoods, new cars, health care, alarm systems, and—worst of all—the approval of others.

I have counseled a lot of people who thought they would be more secure if they could just put some money aside for a rainy day, get better insurance, earn a promotion, close a big deal, lose twenty pounds, find the right spouse, and so on and so on. What these people had in common was they were looking for security in all the wrong places. Until we learn to find the security, we seek not in the things of the world, but in the arms of Christ, our search will be in vain. This is the message in Philippians 4:6–9. These verses tell us to

avoid being anxious by going to God in prayer and with a thankful heart. If we do this, the peace of Christ can be ours to enjoy.

Think about the people who laughed at Noah as he built the Ark (Genesis, Chapters 6–9). They felt secure in their work, relationships, neighborhoods, homes, and other things of the world. They scorned Noah's supposed foolishness in building an Ark. Unfortunately for them, the security they found in things of the world turned out to be false security. You know how that story ended. People in the workplace who look for security in the approval of their coworkers or anywhere else but the arms of Christ are like those who scoffed at Noah. They are looking in all the wrong places.

OVERCOMING INSECURITY AND DOUBT

Have you ever heard someone make this comment about another person: "She is comfortable in her own skin"? The observation is typically intended as a compliment. This kind of comment about a person indicates she radiates quiet self-confidence and does not stress over the opinions others may have of her. People who are comfortable in their own skin appear centered and grounded. They don't invite insecurity into their lives by comparing themselves unfavorably with their peers. Such people are easy to admire, but be careful when making these kinds of observations. Appearances can be deceiving. What is important is why they are comfortable in their own skin.

Some people who are comfortable in their own skin are *self-confident,* a state of mind we find appealing but, in reality, can be a one-way street to heartache. Self-confidence is an inherently weak foundation on which to build a sense of security. When the source of your security is self, meaning such things as talent, appearance, rank, financial assets, and health, your security will last only as long as these assets last. The obvious problem here is these kinds of assets seldom last forever.

The key to permanently overcoming self-doubt is to stop looking for security in the wrong places and start looking in the only place it

249

really exists. John warned of this in his Epistle, 1 John. In 1 John 2:15, the Apostle warns against loving the things of the world. He makes clear God is not in those who do this. The only true, real, and lasting source of security you will ever have is God. This is also the message contained in 1 Timothy 6:17. In this verse, Paul warns against being arrogant or putting one's faith in wealth. He goes on to proclaim that God is the only true source of hope. As long as you look to others for validation, you will always be vulnerable. If your confidence is self-confidence, it will always be precarious and fleeting. But, when your security comes from knowing Jesus Christ as your Lord and Savior, it will be solid and permanent.

God created you as a unique individual. He made you who you are and loves you just as you are. Therefore, comparisons to your peers—unfavorable or favorable—are irrelevant. Judgments from coworkers and other people are just feedback to keep in its proper perspective. The opinion that truly matters is God's opinion. If you are living a life pleasing to God, worldly anxiety, fear, doubt, and insecurity are just gnats to be swatted away with prayer. When you feel doubt and insecurity bubbling up inside you, remember who you are. Stop what you are doing long enough to say a prayer. Ask God to help you refocus on what and who really matters. The prayer provided at the end of this chapter will help in these situations.

Do not misread my message here. I am not saying you, a Christian woman, are free to ignore your appearance, preparation, performance, or other factors that can help you excel at work. When it comes to all of these things, God expects you to do the best you can with what you've got. Further, your job is a gift from God and He expects you to do it well.

The take-away from this chapter is you are a child of God, and this fact makes you infinitely valuable. By this fact, you are validated beyond anything worldly comparisons can provide. On your worst bad hair day, God thinks you are beautiful. In your most ill-fitting outfit, God thinks you are lovely. Remember what the Lord said to Samuel on this subject. In 1 Samuel 16:7, He tells Samuel people make the mistake of looking at outward appearance, but He looks at the heart. There is nothing wrong with desiring a sense of security. Just make sure you look for it in the right place. Look to God for your security, and you will find the real, true, and eternal kind.

PRAYER FOR OVERCOMING INSECURITY AND SELF-DOUBT

Heavenly Father,

It's funny how we struggle with our insecurities and even a sense that we are different from the people we work with who don't yet know You. It's funny because the answer is so obvious! We are different! We're different because You are busy remolding us and reshaping our hearts, so we can live in this world, but not be drawn into those things that simply don't serve You or us very well.

When I consider this, I think perhaps a part of me still reacts as a little girl, a wallflower, the one who felt left out of the circles popular girls enjoyed. My imagination runs wild as I wonder about the ways I might be judged or measured at work. After all, I am not the best dresser, or the most intent people-pleaser. I say prayers over my lunch and I look for Your help with big decisions I have to make through the day.

I suspect there are a few people who scoff at me a bit because I don't join into the office gossip or raise my voice with angry words when things go wrong. It's just not my style. Help me to be confident in Your grace and mercy. Strengthen my resolve to be Your example, no matter how strange I may seem to others. Lord, help me to get over my little insecurities and give me a sense of humor about them. I pray, if I stand out for being different in some way, I stand strong and I honor You with my words and actions all the time.

I know, with You, I cannot afford to have wallflower faith. I don't have to please anyone but You, and so I thank You for creating me just as I am. Help me peel away those layers of doubt and insecurity that may linger in my heart and mind and clothe me in the armor of Your strength and grace. Let me be a mirror of Your love and reflect Your goodness in all I do at work, or anywhere I happen to be. Amen.

DISCUSSION CASE: "I just wish I could have some peace of mind"

Ellen couldn't help comparing herself to the other members of her team, and the comparisons weren't favorable. She worked with a group of high-achieving teammates who were proud of their status as the best-performing team in the company. The team's sales figures were almost double those of the next team behind them, and there was a lot of peer pressure within the team to maintain that status.

Ellen was also a high achiever. But, unlike her coworkers, she tried to maintain a healthy balance between work and life outside work, a life including family and faith. Her coworkers stayed late, worked weekends, and plied potential customers with lavish gifts. In fact, some of their sales methods bordered on the unethical. Ellen, on the other hand, maintained a more balanced work schedule and used only the strengths of the company's products to sell those products. As a Christian woman, she refused to engage in questionable business practices to attract new customers.

Ellen's sales numbers were as good as anyone else on her team, but she was still racked with insecurity and self-doubt. Every hour she spent with her family or in church, Ellen worried her teammates were using that time to get ahead of her. She couldn't get over feeling insecure and that, one day, she would lose her job or be transferred to a lesser team. Ellen told a friend and confidante in her church, "I just wish I could have some peace of mind."

Discussion Questions:

1. Have you ever struggled with work-related insecurities that came from comparing yourself to coworkers or any other source? What were the circumstances?

2. If you were Ellen's friend and confidante from church, what advice would you give her about finding the security and peace of mind she seeks?

REVIEW QUESTIONS FOR INDIVIDUALS AND GROUPS

1. Why can it be so difficult to be different than the crowd?

2. Define the concept of insecurity within the context of the workplace.

3. What are some common sources of insecurity?

4. Give an example of looking for security in all the wrong places.

5. What is the fundamental problem with self-confidence?

6. Explain how you can find a true, real, and lasting sense of security in your life.

POSTSCRIPT

Christian women on the job face a number of challenges, and even obstacles, to success that are either unique in nature or unique in how Christian women are called to overcome them. In this book, we focused on ten of these challenges. Our intention in writing this book was to equip you biblically to excel at work, in spite of the challenges you face and without compromising your faith. We have provided specific strategies that will help you apply Scripture in dealing with the job-related dilemmas, confrontations, problems, and discouragement that can sometimes seem overwhelming.

An overarching goal of this book is to help you be both innocent and wise (Matthew 10:16) in confronting the realities of working in a secular environment where your Christian beliefs may not be the dominant worldview. Another goal is to help you deal with resistance from within the church or from brothers and sisters in Christ who question women working outside of the home. In our fallen world, there will always be obstacles to your success. But never forget you have an ally who is bigger and stronger than anyone or anything that might stand in your way at work. With Christ at your side, you can do anything. Consequently, we have attempted to demonstrate, in practical terms, how to approach your career with Christ at your side. Do this, and the problems, challenges, and dilemmas you face from time to time will be just bumps in the road.

One final word of encouragement we want to leave you with is this: In the long run, the most effective way to excel at work is to apply biblical principles, remain faithful to your beliefs, and seek help when you need it from the best source of help there is—the Word of God. Do these things, and not only will you excel on the job, you will excel in ways that honor God. Then, when you reach the end of your career, you will have the satisfaction of being able to look back on it and know you excelled the right way—God's way. Even more importantly, one day in the future, you will hear these words: "Well done my good and faithful servant." That is when you will know your career and your life have truly been successful.

ABOUT THE AUTHORS

David Goetsch is a Biblical counselor, professor of business, and widely-published author whose ministry focuses on helping Christians translate Scripture into action as they face faith-related challenges at work and in other aspects of their lives.

Karen Moore is the bestselling author of over one hundred inspirational and devotional books. She often speaks at women's retreats and conferences. Karen is married and lives in Savannah, GA.